»Faith in the World«

Rafael Zawisza, Dr. phil., obtained his PhD with distinction at the Faculty of Artes Liberales at the University of Warsaw. *Ludger Hagedorn,* Dr. phil., is a Permanent Fellow at the Institute for Human Sciences (IWM) in Vienna.

Rafael Zawisza, Ludger Hagedorn (eds.)

»Faith in the World«

Post-Secular Readings of Hannah Arendt

Campus Verlag
Frankfurt/New York

Institut für die Wissenschaften vom Menschen
Institute for Human Sciences

Fritz Thyssen Stiftung
für Wissenschaftsförderung

ISBN 978-3-593-51488-8 Print
ISBN 978-3-593-44901-2 E-Book (PDF)
ISBN 978-3-593-45092-6 E-Book (EPUB)

Cover design: Campus Verlag GmbH, Frankfurt am Main.
Typesetting: le-tex transpect-typesetter, Leipzig
Typeset from Alegreya
Printed in the United States of America

www.campus.de
www.press.uchicago.edu

Contents

Part III: Final Destination: Secularity

Part IV: Politics Without the Absolute

Acknowledgments

As editors, we would firstly like to thank the contributors to this volume, who have upheld their dedication to writing over the pandemic. We are grateful to all of them for trusting us to find the best publishing opportunity for a non-mainstream topic dedicated to the iconic thinker and political theoretician Hannah Arendt; we're delighted that the book has found a quality intellectual environment with Campus Verlag and The University of Chicago Press.

We would like to express our sincere thanks to Judith Wilke-Primavesi, Head of Program Management at Campus, who immediately took an interest in this publication and was very supportive in making its realization possible. Special thanks as well go to Catharina Heppner from the editorial office at Campus, who was extremely helpful in so many regards and patient enough to answer all our formatting questions.

We would also like to express our gratitude to all those who helped realize this project: the Institute for Human Sciences (IWM) for organizing and hosting the conference on »The Cryptotheological Legacy of Hannah Arendt,« which took place at the IWM, Vienna, 17–19 October 2018; the former Rector of the IWM, Professor Shalini Randeria, whose advice and constant encouragement was indispensable for the initiation and finalization of this book; Ivan Vejvoda, who largely contributed to the realization of the conference; and the institute's staff who helped immensely in the facilitation of all matters practical, especially Luise Wascher for her engagement in organizing the conference and creating a friendly and inspiring environment.

The conference could not have happened if it wasn't for the generous support of the Fritz Thyssen Stiftung. It is a great privilege and sign of trust that the foundation decided to sponsor our project.

We are greatly indebted to the conference's participants, whose full presence, acute awareness and brilliant contributions turned the meetings into three intense days of intellectual work on Hannah Arendt's place in post-secular studies. We would like to express our gratitude for their excellent collaboration during the editing process and their patience with unpredicted pandemic-related delays.

We would also like to thank those who agreed to spend days with us in Vienna and act as hosts during the sessions: Samuel Abraham, Jason W. Alvis and Sandra Lehmann.

Very special thanks go to Mark Farrier, who proofread this book. Our extensive collaboration extended into minute editorial deliberations, inspiring discussions about the essays and Hannah Arendt's philosophy. Thanks also go to Manuela Kölke for her invaluable consultation on the translation of certain citations from German into English and to Elad Lapidot, who assisted with transliterations from Hebrew.

Thanks to the generous agreement of The Hannah Arendt Bluecher Literary Trust, we were able to reproduce some archival material. We would very much like to thank Jerome Kohn from the Trust and Valerie Borchardt from the Georges Borchardt agency for this. Diana Edkins, Cora Markowitz and Michael Slade facilitated the process. Thanks also go to Dana Kresel and Michelle Margolis Chesner (Institute for Israel and Jewish Studies, Columbia University) as well as Christopher Matson (Cecil H. Green Library, Stanford University) for helping research Salo W. Baron's papers. We are also grateful for the assistance of Dr. Riccardo Bernardini (Eranos Foundation), and Dr. Brigitte Parakenings and Dr. Daniel Wilhelm (Archiv der Universität Konstanz), who guided us in our questions about the Gershom Scholem and Hans Jonas archives.

Rafael Zawisza would like to individually thank Christine Harckensee-Roth for her exceptional hospitality and professional academic collaboration during his research stay in spring and early summer 2018 at the Hannah Arendt Archive, Oldenburg, Germany. The stay was possible thanks to the generous invitation of Professor Matthias Bormuth (Karl Jaspers-Gesellschaft) to spend a few months in the Karl Jaspers-Haus.

Generosity is a precious gift. We are grateful for having experienced it on so many occasions.

Ludger Hagedorn and Rafael Zawisza, Berlin/Vienna, August 2021

Editorial Note

All the biblical quotations come from the standard version of the King James Bible.

Italicized non-foreign words in quotations signify original emphasis.

Faith in the World or: The Philosophical Contraband of a Hidden Spiritual Tradition

An Introduction by Rafael Zawisza and Ludger Hagedorn

On the 7th day of Tevet, 5687, Gershom Scholem wrote, from Jerusalem, a letter addressed to Franz Rosenzweig, who at that time was already unable to speak. It was at the invitation of Martin Buber and Ernst Simon that Scholem composed this text, one among forty prepared by Rosenzweig's friends. In Germany, it was the 26th of December, 1926, just one day after Christmas. Characteristically, Scholem wrote this letter about the »renaissance« of the Hebrew language... in German. It is a unique document that captures an extraordinary moment, when new inhabitants of Palestine—themselves speaking all the languages of the world, including Yiddish, Polish, Russian and German—prepared the first generation of young people who, not having any other common tongue, would speak only Hebrew, this reborn language in which they would have to live and love, laugh and swear. Scholem is aware of the cruelty inscribed in the fate of those newcomers: »a generation of transition,« doomed to »live within that language above an abyss.« He repeatedly writes to Rosenzweig about »our children,« although he never had any of his own—it is clearly the kind of voice that comes from a father of a nation, a patriarch who awaits his progeny with a gaze full of passion, hope and, above all, fear. Scholem noticed that the Hebrew spoken in the streets was often a »ghostly language« (*gespenstische Sprache*) that created an »expressionless linguistic space« (*ausdruckslose Sprachwelt*), a space he saw as arising from a secularization that he fiercely rejected: »the secularization of the language is no more than a *manner of speaking*, a ready-made expression. It is impossible to empty the words so bursting with meaning, unless one sacrifices the language itself.«

It was due to a justified fear for that crucial generation—who would have to live without tradition in an »abyss« (*Abgrund*) and »emptiness« (*Leere*)—that Scholem, in his letter, made such a powerful proclamation of faith in the autonomous life of *names*, stored in the holy language, always ready to erupt with revolutionary force. Scholem wanted to believe that when this hidden »force« of sacred language is evoked daily, even if unconsciously, that it does have unforeseeable consequences »[b]ecause at the heart of such a language, in which we ceaselessly evoke God in a thousand ways, thus calling Him back into the reality of our life, He cannot keep silent.«[1]

Just four years later, in 1930, Hannah Arendt co-authored with her then husband, Günther Stern, an essay dedicated to Rilke's *Duino Elegies*, which also touched upon the topic of secularization. The authors observed that since Jewish and Christian religions were of an acoustic character—one has to listen to God—modernity brings a specific crisis whose final result is not a logical passage to atheism but rather a »religious ambiguity« (Arendt and Stern 2007, 3). The fact that God is no longer audible can be interpreted as God's hiddenness *or* God's non-existence. Our time is characterized by »the absence of an echo« (ibid., 1). In stark contrast to Scholem, who expected God to speak again through Hebrew, the twenty-four-year-old Arendt dismissed the idea that God could ever speak again. Secularization doesn't lead to one particular destination that can be known in advance but, at the same time, it is a process that cannot be undone once it has happened. »The absence of an echo,« with its double negation, is the most salient metaphor for a God who has evaporated, or better yet, a God whom the various sonars of the Enlightenment revealed as »residing« beyond the boundaries of Creation. It is as if there was a very thick wall, impenetrable to any sound coming from outside the world.

Although she rarely recorded strictly personal views in her *Denktagebuch* (›thought journal‹), Arendt made the following entry in May of 1965:

> Since I was seven years old, I have always thought *of* God [*an* Gott gedacht], but I have never really thought *about* God [*über* Gott]. I have often wished that I no longer had to go on living, but I have never posed the question of the meaning of life (Arendt 2016, II, 641).[2]

The enigmatic nature of these words notwithstanding, Arendt expresses here a characteristically *Jewish* response to a *post-Christian* modern nihilism, one which culminates in the thought that without God life has no meaning and that everything is permissible. From this point of view, nihilism and tradi-

1 Quoted from the translation by Ora Wiskind (Scholem 1990). The letter was found in March 1985 in Scholem's papers by Stéphane Mosès and the same year published for the first time by him in French. For the German original, see Brocke 1986.

2 It seems that Hannah Arendt was a speculative thinker since the age of seven, which is not surprising. We know that around that time she honestly said to rabbi Hermann Vogelstein, a family friend, that she did not believe in God. The wise rabbi responded: »And who asked you?« (Young-Bruehl 2004, 10). All the biographical information we provide comes from Young-Bruehl's biography of Arendt.

tionalism are nothing but two sides of the same coin. Arendt's question is not how to rebuild a religious worldview or how to restore the vision of nature (*physis*) as sacred—something which was exactly the goal of Leo Strauss' philosophy. Instead, Arendt poses the question in this way: After the demise of metaphysics (closely connected to the Western concept of religious transcendence), must humanity necessarily conform to an absolutely secularized immanence? Hence, the central difficulty lies not in the disappearance of God but in a human *nostalgia for the absolute*. Hannah Arendt's response to that was to rescue the world even while God seemed completely irretrievable.

Historical Panorama

Born in 1906, Hannah Arendt grew up into a Jewish secular family from Königsberg. Although her parents were non-religious, they allowed young Hannah to attend synagogue in the company of her maternal grandparents, who belonged to Reform Judaism (*liberales Judentum*). She mainly learned about Christianity at school and was impressed by stories about Jesus. Later, when she was a teenager, Arendt became a dedicated reader of Søren Kierkegaard, which can be seen as the initial signs of her interest in theology. In 1924, in Berlin, she attended the lectures of Romano Guardini, a Catholic theologian who only reinforced her passion for Kierkegaard. Arendt then studied philosophy and theology with Martin Heidegger and Rudolf Bultmann until she left Marburg for Freiburg in the spring of 1926 to study with Edmund Husserl. In Freiburg she met Karl Jaspers who would become the supervisor of her doctoral dissertation, which was defended in the autumn of 1928 and published in Berlin in 1929 under the title *Der Liebesbegriff bei Augustin: Versuch einer philosophischen Interpretation*. Many themes from the dissertation migrated into her post-war oeuvre in different theoretical languages. In a 1964 televised interview, she told Günter Gaus that studying theology and philosophy »fit together in such a way that for me they both belonged together. I had some misgivings only as to how one deals with this if one is Jewish... how one proceeds. I had no idea, you know. I had difficult problems that were then resolved by themselves« (Arendt 2013, 15).

Although secularization wasn't Arendt's central topic in the 1930s, almost all of her writings from that period revolve around the concept of a *godless world*. In 1930, on the fifteen hundredth anniversary of Augustine's death, she wrote a short article entitled »Augustin und der Protestantismus« in which she complained that the Protestant world was not adequately celebrating this important figure, unlike the Catholics, who, »[i]n calling him *Saint* Augustine, [...] [have] confiscated him as their own« (Arendt 1994a, 24). Arendt called Catholicism »a distortion of original Christianity« (ibid., 27); by contrast, she saw Protestantism (similarly to Max Weber) as the vehicle through which Augustine's most crucial anthropological »discovery«—inwardness—came to our times in the form of a deeply introspective and psychological type of Western man (Goethe, autobiographies, novels). This religious achievement, in the last stage of its metamorphosis, became »autonomous self-development« (ibid., 27).

In the same year, in her long review of Karl Mannheim's *Ideologie und Utopie* (published in 1929 and entitled »Philosophie und Soziologie«), Arendt criticized the author's Marxist approach and defended philosophy as irreducible to any particular socio-economical »position,« insisting instead that »philosophy's transcendence« (Arendt 1994b, 30) is another name for human freedom. Defending this freedom, Arendt, just like in *Der Liebesbegriff*, disassociated the concept of the absolute from that of transcendence, which might be an echo of her vision of a non-absolute God. What is more, she referred to the example of early Christianity, chiliastic movements and Franciscan tradition in order to demonstrate that the experience of human »homelessness« in the world began with apocalypticism and, thus, is older than capitalist alienation.

Another highly significant example of Arendt's early interventions is her 1932 article entitled »Adam Müller-Renaissance?« Studying German Romanticism at the time, she wrote the article to register a protest against the growing tendency of academics to search for precursors of Nazi ideology in Romanticism. Insisting that the thought of the Catholic thinker, Adam Müller (1779—1829), cannot be adopted into fascism, Arendt wrote a piece of theological critique borrowed from Erich Przywara (1889—1972), an anti-Nazi Jesuit theologian of Polish-German descent. Przywara was invoked by Arendt because, although she could not herself embrace a theological point of view (especially not a Christian one), she wanted to direct an appeal to Christians, particularly Catholics, to oppose Nazism.

In 1932, she published two articles dealing with Jewish and Christian roads to secularization; the first one was entitled »Aufklärung und Judenfrage« and the second »Søren Kierkegaard.« Then, in 1935, Arendt published »A Guide for Youth: Martin Buber,« where, in an untypical manner, she praised Buber as the one who gave Jewish tradition a new life (not for her but for the youth). The idea of an unofficial tradition being clandestinely transmitted was first presented in her 1944 essay »The Jew as Pariah: A Hidden Tradition.« We can only speculate what happened during the war, but as we have seen, Arendt was both already detached from religion years before the Shoah and attempting to create a hidden tradition for secularity. This was surely inspired by her exchange with Gershom Scholem, which culminated in 1948 with Arendt's enthusiastic review of *Major Trends in Jewish Mysticism* entitled »Jewish History, Revised,« in which the author expressed her admiration for the Jewish heterodox movement initiated by Sabbatai Tsevi.

The secularizing passage from religion to culture in Arendt's writings was first thematized by Martine Leibovici (Leibovici 2003), who pointed at the 1947 essay »Creating Cultural Atmosphere« as the programmatic manifesto of Arendtian secularism. In it, Arendt called for a reinvigoration of Jewish secular culture by Yiddish literature. The essay includes a general explanation of the secularization process: »Culture, as we understand it today, made its appearance rather recently and grew out of the secularization of religion and the dissolution of traditional values« (Arendt 2007a, 298). That is why »[c]ulture is by definition secular. It requires a kind of broadmindedness of which no religion will ever be capable« (ibid., 299); it is impartial, tolerant and »hospitable.«

It is irrelevant whether one believes in God or not; what counts is that »secularization transformed religious concepts and the result of religious speculation in such a way that they received new meaning and new relevance independent of faith« (ibid., 298). This transformation can occur when academic research inspires great literature. Arendt observed in the discoveries of »our present historical and philological sciences« that they grew out of »the fear of being robbed of the specifically human background of a past, of becoming an abstract ghost like the man without a shadow« (ibid., 298). It is only through the collaboration of both scholars and talented individuals that culture—this domain newly inhabited by the spirit—can flourish, not being reduced only to antiquarian »preservation« or »dry scholarship« (ibid., 299). In a strategic fragment of the essay, Hannah Arendt reveals what is really at stake:

> There is first of all that great religious and metaphysical postbiblical tradition which we will have to win back from the theologians and scholars—to both of whom we owe, however, a large debt of gratitude for having preserved it at all. But we shall have to discover and

deal with this tradition anew in our own terms, for the sake of people to whom it no longer constitutes a holy past or an untouchable heritage (ibid., 300).

This means that all the traditions of the past belong to everyone. Culture as a new zone of independence thus annihilates the validity of the label »heresy« since culture as such is driven by a »heterodoxical imperative.«[3] Hence, the shift from religion to culture presented by Leibovici can be interpreted polymorphically, for example, as atheism, but Julia Kristeva calls Arendt's stance a »subtle atheism« (Kristeva 2001, 97).[4] This a-theism does not signify that God does not exist or never existed but that worldliness and mortality are the absolute horizon of humanity. If this is the case, what happens when religious traditions get locked within the »iron cage« of historical immanence? Without the horizon of redemption, they can die out and be buried; however, Arendt reminds us that there is also a »hidden tradition,« namely something forgotten, skipped, repressed. She describes it as »a dimension which had not been handed down by tradition—neither by the traditions of customs and institutions nor by the great tradition of Western thought and concept« (Arendt 1990, 197). And here the mission of culture begins. Paradoxically, it is only thanks to secularity that this hidden dimension of the past can reappear »with unexpected freshness and tell us things no one has yet had ears to hear« (Arendt 1961b, 94).[5] This dimension must be won back from the theologians and adapted according to modern »taste.«[6]

Secularity is not always and not only a revolt against the past. In line with Vivian Liska's conception of Arendt and her German-Jewish contemporaries, one can even risk saying that their main concern was the »afterlife« of *all* our legacies. It can also be observed in the Jewish tradition of *zakhor* (Yerushalmi 1982), in which the afterlife is safeguarded by the generations of those who

3 This term is a slightly revised version of Peter Berger's »heretical imperative«; see Berger 1979.

4 In fact, it seems that it was rather a peculiar trust in God, so discreet that it is all but invisible even for the most insightful readers of her oeuvre. For more on this topic, see Jim Josefson's essay in this book. Be that as it may, the point here is that we are not discussing Arendt's intimate beliefs, but the faith in the world.

5 It is significant that these words appear in the essay »What is Authority?« where she celebrates the creative possibilities brought about by the fact that all traditions—political and religious alike—lost authority.

6 If we say this about Arendt's cultivated theological taste, it is because in the essay on Rilke, which she wrote with Stern, they very firmly disassociate themselves from »today's literary production, which either dismisses God as a matter of course, without misgivings, or exploits religious property in a non-obligatory manner, or, finally, satisfies our so-called ›religious needs‹ with surrogates« (Arendt and Stern 2007, 22). Our choice of terminology here refers to Jim Josefson's work in which he underlines the importance of »taste« for Arendt (Josefson 2020).

remember. But what makes this modern reinvention of *zakhor* dramatically incomparable to its predecessors is a suspicion that what has been inherited does not include everything that should have been rescued. The dead ones return and oblige us to search for what has been lost. This Derridean »archive fever« is the salvific drive of culture which recollects forgotten remnants hidden in a no man's land, just like it is in the Lurianic Kabbalah where the lost sparks of divinity call for salvation. In a similar vein, one could understand Rosenzweig's *neues Denken*, which encapsulates an apprehension that together with the demise of the divine, something deeply human could fade away—and that this, not God, has to be rescued. What Scholem saw in Jerusalem—the ghastly state of culture and language—unquestionably belongs to the modern Jewish experience; however, since generational inheritance has been interrupted in modernized societies, every generation becomes »a generation of transition.«

Faith in the World

With Hannah Arendt we have the fascinating example of a secular Jew who preserved a clandestine relation to *deus otiosus*. This does not necessarily mean that one can »decipher« a certain »hidden« yet well-defined theology of Hannah Arendt—all she left behind are confusing traces, mystifying allusions, and cryptic references. One of those traces, which gave the title to this collection, can be found in *The Human Condition*, at the very end of the chapter entitled »Action« where Arendt is musing over the difference between the Greek and Judeo-Christian traditions. According to her, the ancient Greeks did not cherish faith and hope:

> It is this *faith in and hope for the world* that found perhaps its most glorious and most succinct expression in the few words with which the Gospels announced their »glad tidings«: »A child has been born unto us« (Arendt 1958, 247; our emphasis).

Hannah Arendt does not give any explanation of this mysterious phrase: faith in the world. The »world« occupies a prominent place in her thinking—hence her concise formula: *amor mundi*—but »faith« seems to be non-intuitive. Why does one need to have faith in the world? That problem can be traced back to her doctoral dissertation where she asked: »Why should we make a desert out of this world?« (Arendt 1996, 19).[7] The essays collected in the current book engage with these riddles.

Faith in the world cannot be based on faith in God. Arendt reminds us that the modern notion of natural law maintains the stability of the world despite the fact of whether or not one believes in God: »The point was not to deny the existence of God but to discover in the secular realm an independent, immanent meaning which even God could not alter« (Arendt 1961a, 70). In her essay in this book, Agata Bielik-Robson refers to »the Marrano lovers of the worldly,« as they were described by Yirmiyahu Yovel. Marranos there stand for worldliness as the only thing worthy of spiritual investment after the disillusionment with traditional creeds. Are they not identical with the *dilectores mundi* (lovers of the world) from Arendt's dissertation, where she defended them against Christian calumnies? For Augustine, what proved the fallen nature of human beings was their attachment to the world, an attachment that Arendt called »earthliness« and years later described as »the very quintessence of the human condition« (Arendt 1958, 2). This forms a significant bridge between *Der Liebesbegriff bei Augustin* and *The Human Condition*. It is evidenced in her statement from a letter to Jaspers, where Arendt describes that secularity not only has to stabilize the world but also deal with our explorations of the cosmos: »we're trying for the first time and in all seriousness to turn the universum into the mundus, if I may go back to old Augustine once again« (Arendt and Jaspers 1992, 50).[8] The indispensability of the faith in the world comes to the fore in the context of a new Gnosticism, one which can return as a double alienation, that is, as an alienation from both the world and the cosmos: »It is as though we no longer needed theology to tell us that man is not, cannot possibly be, of this world even though he spends his life here« (Arendt 1958, 270). Already in the late 1920s, on the brink of an unprecedented historical catastrophe, Arendt was thinking about a remedy for the deep confusion infiltrating the Occident. Her proposal is hidden in two words: *verwurzelt*, which means »rooted« and *vertraut* which refers to familiarity, intimacy and closeness. Humans should live a rooted life, but the ultimate ground for such existence is not in »blood and soil,« as the fascist would have it. What

7 The question sounds different in the original German text: »In der caritas lebend wird die Welt zur Wüste, statt zur Heimat, sie ist leer und fremd dem, was der Mensch sucht. Warum aber ist die Welt für das Suchen des Menschen die Wüste?« (Arendt 1929, 13). In Mark Farrier's translation: »Living in caritas, the world becomes a desert instead of a home, it is empty and foreign to what human beings seek. Why is it that the world is a desert when it comes to human being's seeking?«

8 Arendt to Jaspers, July 9th, 1946.

accompanies rootedness and overcomes it is the act of *vertrauen*, trust, which has its orienting point in the world, encompassing all creatures. Their lives all share the same origin but only faith in that fact can become the obliging precondition for building the common world.

By extracting a secular core from theology, Arendt chose her own way to secure the migration in the profane (to paraphrase Theodor Adorno's words describing Walter Benjamin's method) as the most radical test for any religious legacy: if anything sacred can pass through the wall of fire and survive the destruction, it can be preserved; the rest will simply perish. This complicated operation is responsible for what Susan Neiman identifies in Arendt's writings as »the tension between a clear, but nearly private inclination to think in sacred categories and a healthy suspicion of the transcendent« (Neiman 2001, 70). Rodrigo Chacón portrayed the tension by locating Arendt between belief and unbelief (Chacón 2012, 93, 105). However, since she herself was not concerned with this binary, one needs to be very precise here: in Arendt's case, religion was not an existential, personal dilemma. Rather, in her philosophy she made a move away from inwardness and toward a worldly in-between that provides the *locus* for speculative thinking in a secularized world.

Even when Arendt's reflections head towards atheism, God remains a *pretext for thinking*. On April 14th, 1951, Arendt made the following entry in her *Denktagebuch*: »God as the Creator of the world: only when we insist on asking for causes [*Ursachen*] in the first place. That we do this at all is because we ourselves are always the cause [*wir selbst immer Ursache sind*]« (Arendt 2016, I, 65). One could say that human beings create God out of their lack of self-sufficiency. To put it differently, human beings are so afraid of their own capacity to create new beginnings that they prefer to abdicate this terrifying power. Seen from this angle, theology is what Peter Sloterdijk calls *Theopoesie*, a discourse that reveals more about mortals than about God (Sloterdijk 2020).

While it is true that »Arendt's writings are charged with theological language« (Neiman 2001, 69), Arendt never actually created any kind of theology. Instead, following Franz Rosenzweig, she created a hybrid discourse that blurs the boundaries between philosophy and theology and confronts both. Because of that, we have to be prepared to face what Susan Neiman brilliantly referred to as Arendt's »consequent ability to live with *creative confusion*« (ibid., 71; original emphasis). The tendency for Arendt's writings to be confusing was very well understood by Margaret Canovan who noticed that even her basis for human rights can be seen as cryptotheological:

> Plurality in itself does not entail equal rights: so is Arendt smuggling in from outside politics a moral absolute about the equal worth of all human beings? In all probability Arendt's own conviction of human equality did indeed have its base outside politics, in religion. But this is not to say that she smuggled a religiously based moral absolute into her political thinking. The point is that Arendt [...] was at one and the same time sure of her own convictions *and* sure that no one's personal convictions can be authoritative for politics (Canovan 1992, 198—199).

How exactly did she smuggle in her enigmatic message?

A Life Spent on *Schmuggel*

Schmuggel or *Schmuggelware* are the German terms for »contraband« (*Schmuggel* is less specific and closer to the English »smuggling«). However bizarre this »intellectual contraband« may sound, it carries the original etymological meaning—roughly, against the ban—which came to English via the French *contrebande* from Italian *contrabbando*, where *bando* signifies »announcement,« »notice« but also »ban« or »banishment.« Contraband in all those languages refers to cross-border, illegal transportation of goods—a clandestine commerce whose aim is to ignore the borders and to avoid paying taxes. It sometimes also refers to smuggling persons from war areas or even trafficking legally banned products, like drugs or weapons. The intellectual *Schmuggel* became the fate for Hannah Arendt and many of her contemporaries. Her long way from Berlin (via Prague) to Paris in 1933, and from Marseille (via Spain and Lisbon) to New York City in 1941 epitomizes the conditions of her »bio-graphy,« that is, of a life spent on writing. Between the borders of continents and languages, Hannah Arendt smuggled a lot and did not respect »the authorities« guarding the traditions. What interests us here particularly is what was contrabanded, that is to say: What was transmitted despite the Kantian »ban« on theology in modern philosophy?

Hannah Arendt's reflections on God, religion, and secularization are scattered throughout her writings. Julia Reinhard Lupton rightly points out the cryptic character of Arendtian reflections on religious themes: »In Arendt's writing, sexuality and religion are most revealing not when they

Hannah Arendt, passport photo, 1933, probably taken already in France.
Courtesy of the Hannah Arendt Bluecher Literary Trust / Art Resource, NY.

receive explicit thematization, but when they operate as psychotheology, opalescently reflected through figure, citation, and footnote« (Reinhard Lupton 2006, 10). This makes it tempting to explore unknown facets of the oeuvre and excavate hidden meanings by rallying a »speculative courage« (Arendt 1958, 259) praised by Arendt herself, a courage that gives the freedom to either fill in »lacunas« or expand on her thinking.

The development of Hannah Arendt's intellectual odyssey reflects the dramatic events of her life as a Jewish woman exiled from Germany. Very telling is the gap between the publication dates of her first two books: *Der Liebesbegriff bei Augustin* in 1929 and then, nineteen years later, *Sechs Essays* in 1948. Also, there is the abyss between her last German academic publications of 1933 and her first American essay in 1942. In between those years Arendt's writings are scarce: a few essays published in French during her Parisian years, one in Yiddish, with the rest being short newspaper articles, mostly related to Zionist politics. Recounting the period just after the war, she wrote to Jaspers: »for twelve years the peace necessary to do intellectual work has been something I've known only from hearsay« (Arendt and Jaspers 1992, 23).[9] The first step back to proper writing was Arendt's employment at Schocken Books. Although her work there primarily involved the editing of other writer's books, she still had enough time—thanks to Schocken's leniency—to write her first book in English, *The Origins of Totalitarianism* (1951).[10] It is worth mentioning that Arendt treated work at Schocken with the utmost seriousness and, according to Marie Luise Knott, fancied that being on the editorial staff for the publications of the works of Kafka, Scholem and Benjamin was like being present for the creation of a new Jewish, theological canon (Knott 2013, 35, 42). It was only after the success of *The Origins* that Arendt became an author in her own right. She received a Guggenheim Foundation research grant to write about the totalitarian aspects of Marxism and although she never finished a book on this topic, the years she spent on it were not in vain. We can see this in the fact that half of her *Denktagebuch* is composed of entries made between 1950 and 1954.[11] Arendt contrabanded much of what she collected at that time into her later publications: *The Human Condition* (1958), *Between Past and Future* (1961), and *On Revolution* (1963). Moreover, one can find in those works the traces of her speculations about God in her *Denktagebuch* entries, distilled and reformulated into secular, philosophical language.[12]

9 Arendt to Jaspers, November 18th, 1945.

10 Although that does not mean she wasn't busy working as an important editor at Schocken Books. She wrote a letter to Scholem on April 4th, 1948: »Thank God I've had some lower back pain and couldn't go to the office. This has allowed me to rest a bit, and to work« (Arendt and Scholem 2017, 88).

11 She wrote to Scholem on the 9th of April, 1953: »I want to make use of a couple years of rest and normality, but any longer than that I won't be able to handle« (Arendt and Scholem 2017, 176).

12 A hint of that »translation« from a religious to a secular register of language can be found in the opening pages of *The Human Condition*, where Arendt writes that human life is »a free gift from nowhere (secularly speaking)« that modern man »wishes to exchange, as it were, for something he has made himself« (Arendt 1958, 2—3).

Smuggling became Arendt's *modus operandi*. It started early on, at the time of her escape from Germany. Knowing that the books of Jewish authors were being burned in the Third Reich, Arendt must have assumed that the remaining copies of *Der Liebesbegriff* that she smuggled abroad were to become the only ones in existence.[13] Even still, she managed to smuggle another treasure that Walter Benjamin entrusted to her, namely, his *Theses on the Philosophy of History* (*Über den Begriff der Geschichte*), which in 1941 safely travelled with Hannah Arendt to the United States of America. When she was still in Southern France, fleeing the Gestapo, she wrote down her reflections on French anti-Semitism in a notebook; a year later, from those notes, she was able to compose her first above-mentioned essay in English: »From the Dreyfus Affair to France Today.«

The most seminal contrabanding occurred, though, between Arendt's earliest work on Augustine and her postwar writings. In a letter to Mary McCarthy in October 20th, 1965, she commented on her reworking of Ernst Basch Ashton's translation of *Der Liebesbegriff*:

> It is kind of a traumatic experience. I am re-writing the whole darned business, trying not to do anything new, but only to explain in English (and not in Latin) what I thought when I was twenty. It is probably not worth it [...] but by now I am strangely fascinated in this rencontre (Arendt and McCarthy 1995, 190).

Nevertheless, as her *Denktagebuch* from the early 1950s certainly shows, Arendt's dissertation was used, negatively, for the creation of a philosophical anthropology. Shortly after the completion of the manuscript of *The Origins of Totalitarianism* (finished in 1949), she decided to reinvent her intuitions about human birth from *Der Liebesbegriff* and placed them at the center of her philosophical thought. The point is not only that she reformulated her earliest ideas and translated them from German to English, but that she found a passage between *Der Liebesbegriff* and her later works: a chiasmus between a *nearly* theological dispute with Augustine and a *nearly* secular philosophy.

Nevertheless, Hannah Arendt was not an Augustinian; in fact, her readings of any author always involved deep revisions. She also defied the giant of Jewish thought, Gershom Scholem, who wanted her to come to Israel, learn Hebrew, and become a professor at the Hebrew University of Jerusalem.

13 On March 31st, 1945, she wrote to Scholem that she couldn't send him a copy »because, sadly, I just have one (stolen) copy; otherwise, it's nowhere to be found. This I heard from some university librarians who've been looking for a copy for years« (Arendt and Scholem 2017, 29).

Scholem expected that she would become a translator of his works into English, as if she was to remain a literary agent of others and not an author in her own right. In a letter from 1947, Scholem wrote in a strong tone of self-praise:

> Why don't you be so kind and learn Hebrew one of these days? Then I could send you this and that or the other, and besides, you could then enter heaven. My essay on the bankruptcy of the Science of Judaism, for instance, is an exceptional piece of writing, [...] composed in the best literary style. Impressive! (Arendt and Scholem 2017, 77).

Scholem characterized Arendt's work as »spiritual exercises in political thinking« (ibid., 200).[14] For her part, Hannah Arendt continued to intertwine a hidden spiritual tradition with philosophy, but it was apparently not enough for Scholem. When he sent her a copy of his 1963 essay, »Tradition und Kommentar als religiöse Kategorien in Judentum,« he left on it a handwritten note: »A bit of Jewish theology, recommended to Hannah from Gerhard« (ibid., see figure 12.). In any case, whether it concerned Zionism or Jewish theology, Hannah Arendt remained faithful to herself and warned Scholem that he should not wait for her »return«: »You have no choice but to look at me with consternation, for in my case repentance can hardly be expected« (ibid., 50).[15] She might have been impressed by Sabbatianism, but it didn't lead her to study the Kabbalah. To understand what Arendt might have taken from Scholem, one would do well to keep in mind a self-identification she formulated in a letter to Scholem on January 14th, 1945: »Ich bin (...) ein Epikaeures« (Arendt and Scholem 2010, 57). She was referring to her position in the Jewish community. The English translation renders it as »an epicurean,« which is only one of its many possible translations (Arendt and Scholem 2017, 26). The word *epikoros* (or *apikores*) was used among the Jews to denote a Jewish sceptic, an apostate or even a heretic; later it also referred to the adherents of Haskalah—the Jewish Enlightenment—or socialism. Writing to Scholem so openly and ironically was, no doubt, Arendt's way of indicating her detachment. Yet, she never rejected her Jewishness. Being an *apikores* was her chosen fate. That ambivalent neither-nor stance gave Hannah Arendt enormous freedom to shape her idiosyncratic response to the challenges of godless modernity. By definition confusing and cryptic, her thought evades any final interpretation. The hybrid, intentionally inconclusive discourse of *apikorsim* opens a space for

14 This is how he referred to Arendt's *Between Past and Future*, see Scholem to Arendt, April 13th, 1962.
15 Arendt to Scholem, April 21st, 1946.

speculation. It remains intriguing to contemplate why Hannah Arendt chose the roundabout method of speaking about messianic shards migrating into the profane. It might have been her reformed post-Hegelian sensitivity, shared with Walter Benjamin, that informed the recognition of secularity as the final destination of religion. This perspective determines for her the tasks enunciated on the first page of *The Human Condition*, namely, how to imagine the reconciliation with finitude and how to affirm earthliness. Such an intuition of a happy life appears in Arendt's defense of Heinrich Heine from the essay »The Jew as Pariah: A Hidden Tradition«:

> [T]he pariah, excluded from formal society and with no desire to be embraced within it, turns naturally to that which entertains and delights the common people. [...] He turns, in fact, from the world of men and the fashion thereof to the open and unrestricted bounty of the earth. And this is precisely what Heine did. Stupid and undiscerning critics have called it materialism or atheism, but the truth is that there is only so much of the heathen in it that it seems irreconcilable with certain interpretations of the Christian doctrine of original sin and its consequent sense of perpetual guilt. It is, indeed, no more than that simple joie de vivre which one finds everywhere in children and in the common people—that passion which makes them revel in tales and romances, which finds its supreme literary expression in the ballad and which gives to the short love-song its essentially popular character (Arendt 2007b, 72—73).

After all, it is not clear whether the passage into the profane is a simple abandonment of theology, that is, just completely forgetting all about it, or rather, that it is a new promised Epicureanism requiring an overcoming of the theological legacy together with its anthropological pessimism. Could it be that without this dialectical odyssey, the ephemeral *joie de vivre* cannot be transformed into a self-conscious philosophy of life? Only such a philosophy, discovered by Arendt through her deconstruction of theology, could save happiness and freedom and make them inseparable; yet, without »the speculative conditions for a philosophy of freedom« (Arendt 1981, 145—146), Epicureanism would not have been able to become a modern political theology. Is this *the* secret of Hannah Arendt's secularity?

Literature on the Topic

The early reaction to Arendt's cryptotheological work is characteristic of the whole reception of her thought. In their reviews, theologians criticized her doctoral dissertation for what they saw as its historical inaccuracies, freewheeling interpretative method, and disrespect of the boundaries of theological discourse.[16] On the other hand, sociologists like David Riesman wrote that *The Origins* book contains mystical insights into human nature (see Riesman 1952, 245). The British edition's title of *The Origins—Burden of Our Time*—conjures up religious connotations, which were detected by Philip Rieff:

> [I]t is precisely Miss Arendt's covert theology that has made her attractive to an antitheological intelligentsia. And this is what theologians must notice in a great deal of the most important contemporary social thought. Much of the best writing in contemporary social science is covertly religious-ethical writing. It takes it [sic] peculiar charm from its refusal to admit it (Rieff 1952, 120).

These different characterizations of Arendt's position only confirm that there was something unsettling about her writings, a certain undertone or hybrid language visible in discreetly transmitted phrases. That is why commentators coined numerous terms like »negative theology« (ibid., 119), »inverted theodicy« (King 1984, 248), »secular theology« (Vecchiarelli Scott 1988, 412), and »critical political theology« (Magun 2012, 567).

On the other hand, we have authors who try to disassociate Hannah Arendt from a theological legacy. Peter Eli Gordon states that »what Strauss termed the ›theological-political predicament‹ appears to have left virtually no imprint upon Arendt's thinking« (Gordon 2007, 857). Gordon sees Arendt's dialogue with her Jewish-German contemporaries as a »consistent rejection« and »reversal« (ibid., 872, 874). According to this line, Samuel Moyn, in his impressive defense of Arendt's secularity, divides her oeuvre into her early »youthful flirtation with theology« and her late »mature« thought directed towards the secular (Moyn 2008, 71; Moyn 2005, 77—87).

Another critical camp employs a very predictable religious and theological reading of Hannah Arendt. The authors belonging to this position either accuse Arendt of not being religious enough or they attempt to »convert« her thought into a religious one. The best example of this kind of scholarship is work by Stephan Kampowski (Kampowski 2008). Two further positions are worth mentioning. The first one can be detected in a collected volume of essays edited by James W. Bernauer entitled *Amor Mundi: Explorations in the Faith and Thought of Hannah Arendt* (Bernauer 1987); this was the first attempt to understand Arendt within a theological horizon. Although the Christian

16 For information about these reviews, see Vecchiarelli Scott and Stark 1996, xv—xvii.

perspective of the authors sometimes results in a distortion of the meaning of Arendt's religious sensitivity, or what could more accurately be called her theological »taste,« there are some essays, especially those by Patrick Boyle and Robert Burns, that initiated a discussion that we want to re-examine in the post-secular paradigm. Finally, there is a recent book by John Kiess entitled *Hannah Arendt and Theology* (Kiess 2016) that aptly criticizes the theological misinterpretations of Arendt's thought mentioned above. However, the very title of Kiess' book, particularly the word »and,« indicates that his intention, all in all, is to imagine and open new roads *for* theology *through* the Arendtian legacy.

Arendt is noticeably absent among the important contributions to post-secular studies. A huge collection of essays edited by Hent de Vries and Lawrence E. Sullivan mentions her incidentally, and then, only as a political theorist (de Vries and Sullivan 2006). Benjamin Lazier's great study on the intellectual history of the Weimar era (Lazier 2008) does not include Arendt. Finally, even though Arendt left behind a very insightful work on neighborly love, the authors of the book *The Neighbor* did not find it necessary to confront her views; there is only mention of her by Kenneth Reinhard in a footnote (see Žižek et al. 2005).

Nevertheless, there are some studies that have opened up a post-secular perspective on Hannah Arendt. Susan Neiman demonstrated how Arendt's intellectual confrontation with evil invoked the themes of theodicy, Creation, and Gnosticism (Neiman 2001). The first comprehensive study was Martine Leibovici's book locating Arendtian secularism within contemporary Jewish thought (Leibovici 2003). Christian Wiese's study on Arendt and Jonas shed light on a very intriguing exchange between both friends, although Wiese is skeptical about making Arendt's vitalism and Jonas' cryptotheology complementary (Wiese 2007). Véronique Albanel presented the first thorough investigation of Arendt's readings of Christianity (Albanel 2010). Rodrigo Chacón made another advancement by situating Arendt's thinking within a Weimar milieu and observing the »neglect of the theological sources of her thought« (Chacón 2012, 73). Finally, a possible »inconspicuous« messianism of Arendt was analyzed by both Susannah Young-ah Gottlieb (Young-ah Gottlieb 2003) and Daniel Brandes (Brandes 2010).

There are a few interpretations that could be called paradigmatic. Sigrid Weigel's elaboration of Arendt's bilingualism combined with the poetic and figurative character of Arendtian prose sets up a paradigm for future research that can take into account peculiarities of style and rhetoric (Weigel 2012). Agata Bielik-Robson reinterprets Arendtian anthropology as having a strong theological background, one which, nonetheless, only strengthens secular philosophy; she discovers this in the contemporary revival of Lurianic Kabbalah among German-Jewish authors (Bielik-Robson 2019). The influence of Gershom Scholem on Arendt is magnificently explored by Vivian Liska, whose essay on the relationship between the two authors establishes a new standard for future studies on the topic (Liska 2017). Although Liska's essay does not definitively determine what exactly was »transmitted,« we know for sure from Liska that Arendt understood Scholem in an idiosyncratic way.

Summary

The current collection of essays begins with two on the topic of love. Sigrid Weigel, through a detailed reading of Arendt's *Denktagebuch*, discovers a completely unknown project, one never realized by Arendt. This is the project that could elucidate her tripartite description of the human condition as well as her often criticized division between private and public spheres of life. The Arendtian loving subject can be read as endowed with an existential dimension that resists any subsumption by metaphysics, and which remains in accord with Arendt's critique of »ordered love« in *Der Liebesbegriff bei Augustin*.

Agata Bielik-Robson elucidates the substitution of *amor Dei* by *amor mundi* in Arendt as the proper expression of her Marranic cryptotheology. In order to do so, Bielik-Robson explores less known interconnections, like the influence of Franz Rosenzweig and Gershom Scholem on Arendt. The originality of Arendtian cryptotheology cannot be reduced, however, to external inspirations: it consists in the way Arendt revised certain ideas of Christian thinkers (especially Augustine and Duns Scotus) and created her own idiosyncratic discourse in which the worldly and the messianic cannot be distinguished.

The essay of Rafael Zawisza sheds light on the moment when this procosmic shift took place, namely, in Arendt's doctoral dissertation. Zawisza's analysis of the third part of *Der Liebesbegriff* demonstrates that Arendt's secularism was preceded by her deconstruction of theology, which was specifically directed against the doctrine of original sin. This seemingly apolitical deconstruction possessed a strong critical capacity in the context of Weimar era politics.

Another early encounter with theology is presented by Jim Josefson, who reflects upon the impact of German Lutheran and dialectical theologian Rudolf Bultmann. Although Arendt wrote to Karl Jaspers that she was indebted to Bultmann, that debt is far from obvious when one looks at her writings where there appears almost no reference to his works. Hence, Josefson attempts to reconstruct Bultmann's influence by connecting hints in the Jaspers letter and Arendt's scattered theological reflections with Bultmann's writings from around 1925, when Arendt attended Bultmann's seminar on the anthropology of St. Paul. By unpacking Arendt's conclusion that »faith communicates itself, wants to be understood and so understands itself,« Josefson claims that the basics of her cryptotheology can be traced to Christian sources, making her an exemplary philosophical Marrano.

The next two essays focus on Hannah Arendt's secularity. The underlying thesis of both authors is that even in her closest proximity to religious or biblical subject matter, Arendt remained a secular thinker, who interpreted the Judeo-Christian heritage liberally, that is, in the interest of culture and politics. Martine Leibovici brings together Hannah Arendt's and Michael Walzer's reflections on revolution, the Biblical Exodus, and the question of liberation. Both authors engage with those topics differently, although they share a mistrust of political messianism. Yet, Leibovici demonstrates that it is not just a negation of Biblical tradition that guides Arendt and Walzer; it is rather a deep conviction that although certain religious motives can remain an inspiration for secular culture, the secularization of those motives or figures is not a direct transposition. This careful examination of the distance between religious and secular perspectives results in a rich reflection on the various modes of »living-in-time« and the basis of law.

Christina Schües undertakes a question that is very crucial to a post-secular reading of Arendt, namely, to what extent the concept of natality can be regarded as a remnant of religion, as its afterlife. Schües resolves this dilemma by showing how Arendt extracts from religion only that which remains »within the reach of man« (Arendt 1958, 247). It is not justified to say that Arendt simply appropriates what was invented or stored in religious literature because, in metaphysics, the trust in the world and the promise inherent in birth—two main phenomena analyzed by Schües—are tethered to the afterlife, which changes their significance. Hence, Arendt's post-metaphysical thought is not a secularization but rather a reconfiguration of the meaning given to human finitude.

The last, political part of the collection is dedicated to the consequences of secularization for politics. Roger Berkowitz reconstructs Arendt's discussion of immortality as the basis for a meaningful life. In contrast to Christianity, which linked immortality with salvation in the extraterrestrial domain, Arendt invokes earthly immortality which in antiquity was given to great, memorable deeds. Berkowitz claims that the concept of »immanent transcendence« is necessary for the prospect of regaining this neglected dimension of public life, because politics must transcend actuality in order to reinforce the durability of the world.

Milan Hanyš's essay deals with the problem of evil in Arendt, who overcomes the traditional theological dualism of good and evil by reflecting on absolute goodness and radical evil; in fact, both extremes turn out to be equally destructive for the world. Here a religious point of view is not disqualified but rather bypassed through her secular concerns. Arendt's hesitation about whether to name the evil of totalitarian regimes »radical« or »banal« reflects her attempt to confront the Western theological legacy.

Aishwary Kumar offers an archaeology of political cruelty in India, the world's most populous democracy, and the consequences of its specifically subcontinental character for the place of public religion in global democratic life at large. Kumar analyzes in parallel the writings of Bhimrao Ramji Ambedkar and Hannah Arendt and expands the scope of Arendt's theories by elaborating a new category: »a jurisprudence of neglect« which is a systemic organization of a political structure that prepares people to accept and enable the complete abandonment of the minorities, among them Muslims and outcastes. Kumar's reflection on politics is accompanied by the question of whether this cruel logic has a theological bedrock; it therefore could be characterized as a psycho-theological analysis of politics.

Vivian Liska's epilogue to the book constitutes both a summary and an opening. On the one hand, Liska reads the figure of Abraham in Kafka and Arendt to demonstrate that a transition from religious to secular language is possible and accomplished (yet not politically valid) in the doctrine of human rights. On the other hand, Liska's reading of the Biblical scriptures as an example of »great literature« is a gesture of validation, that is, it suggests that literary works, whether theopoetic or not, can invent, test, and codify new ways of living together.

Works Cited

Albanel, Véronique (2010). *Amour du monde: Christianisme et politique chez Hannah Arendt*. Paris: Les Éditions du Cerf.

Arendt, Hannah (1929). *Der Liebesbegriff bei Augustin: Versuch einer philosophischen Interpretation*. Berlin: Julius Springer.

Arendt, Hannah (1958). *The Human Condition*. Chicago/London: University of Chicago Press.

Arendt, Hannah (1961a). The Concept of History: Ancient and Modern. In Hannah Arendt. *Between Past and Future: Six Exercises in Political Thought*. New York: The Viking Press.

Arendt, Hannah (1961b). What Is Authority?. In Hannah Arendt. *Between Past and Future: Six Exercises in Political Thought*. New York: The Viking Press.

Arendt, Hannah (1981). *Willing*. In Hannah Arendt. *The Life of the Mind*. Ed. Mary McCarthy. San Diego/New York/London: Harcourt Brace Jovanovich.

Arendt, Hannah (1990). *On Revolution*. London/New York: Penguin Books.

Arendt, Hannah, and Karl Jaspers (1992). *Correspondence, 1926—1969*. Ed. Lotte Kohler and Hans Saner. Transl. Robert and Rita Kimber. New York: Harcourt Brace Jovanovich.

Arendt, Hannah (1994a). Augustine and Protestantism. In Hannah Arendt. *Essays in Understanding, 1930—1954*. Ed. by Jerome Kohn. New York: Harcourt, Brace & Co.

Arendt, Hannah (1994b). Philosophy and Sociology. In Hannah Arendt. *Essays in Understanding, 1930—1954*. Edited by Jerome Kohn. New York: Harcourt, Brace & Co.

Arendt, Hannah, and Mary McCarthy (1995). *Between Friends: The Correspondence of Hannah Arendt and Mary McCarthy, 1949—1975*. Ed. and introduction Carol Brightman. New York: Harcourt Brace.

Arendt, Hannah (1996). *Love and Saint Augustine*. Ed. and interpretive essay Joanna Vecchiarelli Scott and Judith Chelius Stark. Chicago: University of Chicago Press.

Arendt, Hannah (2007a). Creating a Cultural Atmosphere. In Hannah Arendt. *The Jewish Writings*. Ed. Jerome Kohn and Ron H. Feldman. New York: Schocken Books.

Arendt, Hannah (2007b). The Jew as Pariah: A Hidden Tradition. In Hannah Arendt. *Reflections on Literature and Culture*. Ed. and introduction Susannah Young-ah Gottlieb. Stanford: Stanford University Press.

Arendt, Hannah, and Günther Stern (2007). Rilke's *Duino Elegies*. In Hannah Arendt. *Reflections on Literature and Culture*. Ed. and introduction Susannah Young-ah Gottlieb. Stanford: Stanford University Press.

Arendt, Hannah, and Gershom Scholem (2010). *Der Briefwechsel*. Hrsg. von Marie Luise Knott, unter Mitarbeit von David Heredia. Berlin: Jüdischer Verlag.

Arendt, Hannah (2013). »What Remains? The Language Remains«: A Conversation With Günter Gaus. Zur Person, ZDF TV, Germany, October 28, 1964. Transl. Joan Stambaugh. In Hannah Arendt. *Hannah Arendt: The Last Interview and Other Conversations*. Brooklyn: Melville House.

Arendt, Hannah (2016). *Denktagebuch 1950—1973*. Zwei Bände. Ed. Ursula Ludz and Ingeborg Nordmann. München: Piper Verlag.

Arendt, Hannah, and Gershom Scholem (2017). *The Correspondence of Hannah Arendt and Gershom Scholem*. Ed. Marie Luise Knott. Transl. Anthony David. Chicago: The University of Chicago Press.

Berger, Peter L. (1979). *Heretical Imperative: Contemporary Possibilities of Religious Affirmation*. Garden City, N.Y.: Anchor Press.

Bernauer, James W. (ed.) (1987). *Amor Mundi: Explorations in the Faith and Thought of Hannah Arendt*. Boston/Dordrecht/Lancaster: Martinus Nijhoff Publishers.

Bielik-Robson, Agata (2019). Being-Towards-Birth: Arendt and the Finitude of Origins. In Agata Bielik-Robson. *Another Finitude: Messianic Vitalism and Philosophy*. London: Bloomsbury.

Brandes, Daniel (2010). On Messianic Strains in Arendt's Theory of Political Action. *Tikvah: University of Toronto Journal for Jewish Thought* 1, 1—23.

Brocke, Michael (1986). Franz Rosenzweig und Gerhard Gershom Scholem. In Walter Grab (hrsg.). *Juden in der Weimarer Republik*, 127—152. Stuttgart: Burg-Verlag.

Canovan, Margaret (1992). *Hannah Arendt: A Reinterpretation of Her Political Thought*. Cambridge/New York: Cambridge University Press.

Chacón, Rodrigo (2012). Hannah Arendt in Weimar: Beyond the Theological-Political Predicament?. In Leonard V. Kaplan and Rudy Koshar (ed.). *The Weimar Moment: Liberalism, Political Theology, and Law*. Lanham: Lexington Books.

Gordon, Peter Eli (2007). The Concept of the Apolitical: German Jewish Thought and Weimar Political Theology. *Social Research* 74(3), 855—878.

Josefson, Jim (2020). *Hannah Arendt's Aesthetic Politics: Freedom and the Beautiful*. New York: Palgrave.

Kampowski, Stephan (2008). *Arendt, Augustine, and the New Beginning: The Action Theory and Moral Thought of Hannah Arendt in the Light of Her Dissertation on St. Augustine*. Grand Rapids/Cambridge: William B. Eerdmans Pub. Co.

Kiess, John (2016). *Hannah Arendt and Theology*. London/New York: Bloomsbury T&T Clark.

King, Richard H. (1984). Endings and Beginnings: Politics in Arendt's Early Thought. *Political Theory* 12(2), 235—251.

Knott, Marie Luise (2013). *Unlearning With Hannah Arendt*. Transl. David Dollenmayer. New York: Other Press.

Kristeva, Julia (2001). *Hannah Arendt*. Transl. Ross Guberman. New York: Columbia University Press.

Lazier, Benjamin (2008). *God Interrupted: Heresy and the European Imagination Between the World Wars*. Princeton: Princeton University Press.

Leibovici, Martine (2003). *Hannah Arendt et la tradition juive: le judaïsme à l'épreuve de la sécularisation*. Lausanne: Labor et Fides.

Liska, Vivian (2017). Tradition and the Hidden: Arendt Reading Scholem. In Vivian Liska. *German-Jewish Thought and Its Afterlife: A Tenuous Legacy*. Bloomington: Indiana University Press.

Magun, Artemy (2012). Karl Marx and Hannah Arendt on the Jewish Question: Political Theology as a Critique. *Continental Philosophy Review* 45(4), 545—568.

Moyn, Samuel (2005). *Origins of the Other: Emmanuel Levinas Between Revelation and Ethics*. Ithaca, N.Y.: Cornell University Press.

Moyn, Samuel (2008). Hannah Arendt on the Secular. *New German Critique*, 35(3), 71—96.

Neiman, Susan (2001). Theodicy in Jerusalem. In Steven E. Aschheim (ed.). *Hannah Arendt in Jerusalem*. Berkeley: University of California Press.

Rieff, Philip (1952). The Theology of Politics: Reflections on Totalitarianism as the Burden of Our Time. *The Journal of Religion* 32(2), 119—126.

Riesman, David (1952). A Grammar of Soviet Motives. *Partisan Review*, 19(2), 242—245.

Scholem, Gershom (1990). On Our Language: A Confession. Transl. Ora Wiskind. *History and Memory*, 2(2), 97—99.

Sloterdijk, Peter (2020). *Den Himmel zum Sprechen bringen: Über Theopoesie*. Berlin: Suhrkamp.

Vecchiarelli Scott, Joanna (1988). »A Detour Through Pietism«: Hannah Arendt's on St. Augustine's Philosophy of Freedom. *Polity* 20(3), 394—425.

Vecchiarelli Scott, Joanna, and Judith Chelius Stark (1996). Preface. In Hannah Arendt. *Love and Saint Augustine*. Chicago: University of Chicago Press.

de Vries, Hent, and Lawrence E. Sullivan (ed.) (2006). *Political Theologies: Public Religions in a Post-Secular World*. New York: Fordham University Press.

Weigel, Sigrid (2012). Sounding Through—Poetic Difference—Self-Translation: Hannah Arendt's Thoughts and Writings Between Different Languages, Cultures, and Fields. In Eckart Goebel and Sigrid Weigel (ed.). *»Escape to Life«: German Intellectuals in New York: A Compendium on Exile After 1933*. Berlin/Boston: De Gruyter

Wiese, Christian (2007). *The Life and Thought of Hans Jonas: Jewish Dimensions*. Transl. Jeffrey Grossman and Christian Wiese. Waltham/Hanover: Brandeis University Press/University Press of New England.

Yerushalmi, Yosef Hayim (1982). *Zakhor: Jewish History and Jewish Memory*. Seattle: University of Washington Press.

Young-ah Gottlieb, Susannah (2003). *Regions of Sorrow: Anxiety and Messianism in Hannah Arendt and W.H. Auden*. Stanford: Stanford University Press.

Young-Bruehl, Elisabeth (2004). *Hannah Arendt: For Love of the World*. 2nd edition. New Haven/London: Yale University Press.

Žižek, Slavoj, Santner, Eric L., and Kenneth Reinhard (2005). *Neighbor: Three Inquiries in Political Theology*. Chicago: University of Chicago Press.

Part I: Two Faces of Earthly Love

Traces and Transitions to Hannah Arendt's Unwritten Book on Love

Sigrid Weigel

In this article I want to come back to an argument that I made long ago about Arendt's unwritten book on love, which I suggested[1] exists virtually, in a latent state, concealed within the entries of her *Denktagebuch* (Arendt 2002). Even though Arendt's oeuvre commenced in 1929 with the publication of her dissertation *Der Liebesbegriff bei Augustin*—on his *concepts* of love, not on love, a fact that the English title *Love and Saint Augustine* (Arendt 1996) obscures—and even though Arendt's entire work has, since Elisabeth Young-Bruehl's seminal biography *For Love of the World* (Young-Bruehl 1982), has often been summarized under the title of *amor mundi* (e.g. Bernauer 1987; Borren 2010) or »love for the world,« Arendt never wrote a book on love, or at least no book on love that examines its different states, including passion and the intimate or affected relationship of lovers. As a consequence, the understanding of love in Arendt's thoughts is dominated by either her relationship to Heidegger or her book on Augustine and the specific modes of love discussed therein (the triad of *amor/cupiditas*, *caritas*, and *dilectio*) that lead to the role of the neighbor in *vita socialis*. As a consequence, even her later reflections on different expressions of love often get retranslated into Augustinian concepts.[2] And yet, the web of scattered passages concealed in her writings that form a potential book on love has to date hardly been acknowledged.

---

1 See Weigel 2005 and for the English version: Weigel 2009. Since then, the topic of love in the *Denktagebuch* has been discussed in some articles and a monograph: Hahn 2005, 51 ff.; Thomä 2007; Tömmel 2013; Tömmel 2017.

2 Even Rachel Paine, one of few scholars who acknowledge Arendt's emphasis of the contradictory relation between intimate love and love of the world in *The Human Condition*, translates the respective passage from the 1958 book back into the concepts of *cupiditas* and *caritas* from Arendt's dissertation (Paine 2013).

1. The Place of Thinking and Love

In speaking about an unwritten book, I am referring to something different than »the work that was not written,« as Ronald Beiner describes the third part of Arendt's project on *The Life of the Mind*, with which Arendt was occupied during the last years of her life. Composed as a three-part project consisting of *Thinking*, *Willing*, and *Judging*, this book remained incomplete because of the heart attack that caused Arendt's death in 1975. Beiner's phrase—»the work that was not written«—comes from his preface to the volume he composed, which was intended to replace the missing book with manuscripts of lectures that Arendt probably would have used as material for the book's production. Arendt did not live long enough to write *Judging*, Beiner argues, »[y]et students of her thought would have ample justification for believing that, had it been written, it would have been her crowning achievement« (Beiner 1992, vii). As Beiner explains, he thus compiled »the main available texts by Arendt on this important topic« but, in the end, found himself forced to admit that »these texts can be no substitute for the work that was not written« (ibid., vii). Yet, the German edition—entitled *Das Urteilen* (Arendt 1985)—does in fact present the volume as exactly such a substitute. In calling this never-written book on judging Arendt's »crowning achievement,« Beiner obviously considers *The Life of the Mind* to be her ultimate work, and in this way, he forecloses any possibility that Arendt would have made further outstanding contributions as an author if life had given her more time to write.

In this respect I disagree. In my view there are several clues as to why it makes sense to speculate that Arendt might have turned her attention to an issue that she touched on in several of her publications, and on which she reflected repeatedly, without ever making it into the primary theme of a book. Throughout her published writings, the mode and state of love as passion seems to form the other side of the role of love for the *vita socialis*, the social life. Or, to put it more precisely: in Arendt's theory, intimate love forms the other side of the *vita socialis*, even though it is at the same time the precondition for the *vita socialis* while also being excluded from social life and the public realm. Its state of concealment (*Verborgenheit*) in privacy might well be the reason why this kind of love marks a blind spot in Arendt's oeuvre. In any case, her unwritten book on love is nothing like a substitute or replacement. Instead, it raises a number of questions—up to what point and how advanced Arendt's thinking on love developed, and where and in what mode did its components surface? How close did the repeatedly discussed topic of love, in its various modes and appearances, come to being a book on love or a theory of love? And what place would the intimate or passionate relationship between two persons have in that book? Instead of searching for a substitute, I will therefore examine the respective traces in Arendt's writings. This way of approaching the issue requires a focus on the moments where the question of love appears and where it begins to fade away.

The reason for my assumption that Arendt might well have turned to writing a book on love after having finished *The Life of the Mind* is the fact that both thinking and loving occupy similar positions within Arendt's theory; what they share is that both are counterparts to the activities of *vita activa*. In an entry of the *Denktagebuch*, for example, Arendt states that they belong to each other in a »negative aspect,« because both flee the world.

> Just as the lover flees with the beloved from the world of daily affairs to engage in the dialogue of love, the philosopher flees with himself (with the Self discovered in θαυμάζειν [amazement]) to engage in the dialogue of thinking.
>
> (So wie der Liebende mit dem Geliebten aus der Welt der täglichen Angelegenheit flieht, um den Dialog der Liebe führen zu können, so flieht der Philosoph mit sich selbst (mit dem im θαυμάζειν [Staunen] entdeckten Selbst), um den Dialog des Denkens führen zu können) (Arendt 2002, XIX/25, 464).[3]

But as we will see, this negative aspect simultaneously implies a creative potential because thinking and loving remain in a dialectical relation to the *vita activa*, although each does so in a different manner.

More than a decade after the publication of *The Human Condition* (1958), in her last project *The Life of the Mind*, which evolved out of lectures and seminars on thinking from the early 1970s, Arendt returned to the core of her anthropological political theory elaborated therein. The central argument of this challenging conceptualization of »the political« is her fundamental understanding of human beings as »conditioned beings.« As is well known, in *The Human Condition*, she analyzed the human activities that modify these conditions »because everything they [human beings] come in contact with turns immediately into a condition of their existence« (Arendt 1998, 9); she concentrated on the three activities of *Arbeit* (labor for the reproduction of life), *Herstellen* (work in the sense of fabrication), and *Handeln* (acting between human beings) as indispensable modes of the *vita activa*. More than a decade later,

3 In what follows the *Denktagebuch* is cited by indicating the number of the notebook, the number of the entry and the page.

she shifted her attention to the other side of the human condition, the *vita contemplativa*, to pose the question, in the first part of *The Life of the Mind* on thinking, of the way in which thinking concerns the character of man as conditioned being. Echoing her book on Eichmann, in which she characterized him as being entirely thoughtless, she now develops the question of whether thinking may be »among the conditions that make men abstain from evil-doing or even actually ›condition‹ them against it?« (Arendt 1981a, 5). Given this discussion of thinking as a kind of supplement to Arendt's theory of the human condition, the absence of love in her work is all the more striking.

2. From the Trace of Love in the *Denktagebuch* to *The Human Condition*

The way in which Arendt elaborated the place of love and thinking in relation to the *vita activa* can be studied in a series of entries from the *Denktagebuch* that are obviously conceptual reflections for an emerging book. Here, Arendt worked up the composition and theoretical structure of her arguments—a structure that Tatjana Noemi Tömmel has rightly called a »topology of the *conditio humana*« (Tömmel 2013, 283). These entries belong to the period in which Arendt developed the ideas for *The Human Condition* after her book on totalitarianism was published. The first half of the 1950s (the years after her first journey to Europe from the US-American exile and the beginning of an academic career in this country) can be considered the decisive formative phase of her anthropologically grounded theory of the political, before she started to transform it into the manuscript of *The Human Condition*. Of the twenty-eight handwritten notebooks, comprising entries spanning twenty-three years, from June 1950 to June 1973, published posthumously as the *Denktagebuch*, the major part, namely twenty notebooks, were written during the first four years. During these first years of her *Denktagebuch*, Arendt filled five to six notebooks a year, thereafter just one notebook a year, and later even only one notebook every two years.

The initial, crucial idea of *The Human Condition* appears in October 1950, four months after Arendt started the *Denktagebuch*, in an entry on the concept of plurality where she discusses the various modes of mutual interdependence (*Aufeinanderangewiesensein*). The entry starts by making a fundamental distinction between (1) the facts of plurality and inequality, which determine politics and laws; and (2) the fact that »›love needs love,‹ that is, that no human being can exist alone« which she finds expressed in the existence of different sexes. Arendt then continues with an interesting distinction between the »Second« (singular) and the »Others« (plural) in order to characterize the different kinds of human relations in these two realms:

Here [in love], the One seeks (or needs) the Second (and a Third arises); in the case of plurality, conversely, the One always already has to reckon with and is dependent on—not a Second—but *Others*.

(Hier [in der Liebe] sucht (oder bedarf) der Eine des Zweiten (und es entspringt der Dritte); im Falle der Vielheit, umgekehrt, hat der Eine immer schon zu rechnen mit und ist angewiesen auf—nicht einen Zweiten—, sondern *Andere*) (II/8, 37).

Yet it does not follow from this fundamental distinction between different types of human relations that the two are entirely separated. Love cannot be excluded from Arendt's approach to politics, the epistemology of which she explicitly distinguishes from philosophy and from what she calls the »old Kantian questions« in order to develop, instead, her anthropological political theory. The way her work transgresses the path of philosophy in the strict sense[4] is brought up in an entry from January 1953 (this time written in English):

In this realm of plurality which is the *political* realm, one has to ask all the old questions—what is love, what is friendship, what is solitude, what is acting, thinking, etc., but not the one question of philosophy: Who is Man, nor the *Was kann ich wissen, was darf ich hoffen, was soll ich tun?* (XIII/2, 295).

This attests that the discussion of love occupies a central place within Arendt's move from philosophy to political theory.

A number of entries in the *Denktagebuch* on the elementary activities of human beings and the elementary relations between them return again and again to the question of how love is related to the *vita activa*, reflecting both how love is connected to and how it differs from the three activities of *Arbeit, Herstellen*, and *Handeln*. The first of this series appears in April 1952, in an entry in which Arendt argues that »the elementary relations between human beings« are based not on necessity (*Notwendigkeit*) but on need (*Bedürfen*):

---

4 Therefore, it leads to a quite limited understanding of Arendt's work when her thoughts get repeatedly interpreted in respect to the influence of her academic teachers Heidegger and Jaspers, even though she practiced a constant explicit or implicit argument with both of them, albeit in quite different ways.

Human beings find each other as persons because they need each other (love), and they live together as »citizens« because they must master *ἀναγκαῖα* [necessity].

(Menschen finden zueinander als Personen, weil sie einander bedürfen (Liebe), und leben zusammen als »citizens,« weil sie der *ἀναγκαῖα* [Notwendigkeit] Herr werden und bleiben müssen) (IX/3, 203).

In this context, Arendt emphasizes the »genuine reciprocity« of love. In several entries that follow, she examines the question by slightly shifting her viewpoint in each entry, in this way illuminating the respective activities successively from different angles and at each time varying the number of concepts involved in the argument. In this way love occupies one position within a constellation of three, four, or five concepts. In December of the same year, and three notebooks later, we find a short entry on »the political indications of the elementary activities, the active modes of being alive [*Lebendigsein*] as it were,« that lists the same four activities (*Arbeit, Herstellen, Handeln, Liebe*) by referring to the concepts of Greek philosophy: *pathein* (suffering, associated with the singular »relationship« of love), *prattein* (acting, ascribed to friendship), *poiein* (manufacturing, the world of objects, *homo faber*), *ergazesthai* (laboring for the purpose of reproduction) (XII/26, 289 f.). Nearly one year and seven notebooks later, in October 1953, another entry addresses these »elementary activities« from a different angle, namely as »modifications of plurality« and, from this viewpoint, extends the list to five concepts by adding thinking. Here, Arendt shapes her crucial ideas on thinking and love by characterizing thinking as two-in-one and love, by contrast, as being connected with worldlessness (*Weltlosigkeit*):

Thinking—solitude—two-in-one = conscience—the Others in the likeness of myself; humankind.

Loving—togetherness—worldlessness in nature—life—emergence of the world.

(Denken—Einsamkeit—Zwei-in-Eins = Gewissen—die Andern im Ebenbilde meiner selbst; Menschheit.

Lieben—Zweisamkeit—Weltlosigkeit in Natur—Leben—Entstehen der Welt) (XIX/17, 459).

Four months later, in February 1954, Arendt shifts the viewpoint again and takes the perspective of »*vita contemplativa*,« from where »all forms of nonthinking activities become essentially identical« and, in this way, shape the tripartite unity *Arbeit, Herstellen, Handeln*, which eventually would form the *vita activa* (XIX/41, 471). This triad is confirmed as a conceptual structure in an entry from May 1954 that first mentions the idea of a book (XX/9, 482—483). In August 1954, a longer entry shifts the viewpoint again by addressing the question of efforts that lack any outcome (*Resultatlosigkeit*). This entry argues that the effort of thinking and the labor to maintain life share the fact that both are without outcomes, since »as life itself, they are the human modes of being alive.« That means that life itself can't be summarized and considered as a kind of outcome. In the last part of this entry, love comes into play and Arendt writes:

Laboring—thinking—loving are the three modes of mere life, from which a world can never arise and which are therefore actually anti-world, *anti*-political.

(Arbeiten—Denken—Lieben sind die drei Modi des schieren Lebens, aus denen nie eine Welt erstehen kann und die daher eigentlich welt-feindlich, *anti*-politisch sind) (XX/28, 493).

At first glance this statement that »a world can never arise« out of love seems to contradict the entry from four months earlier, where love was associated with the »emergence of the world.« However, a closer look, which considers the shifting perspective, makes it clear that the seemingly contradictory relations of love to the world concern exactly the position of love at the threshold between two different realms: between love as a mode of being alive that produces no outcome on the one hand and the potential of love for the plurality of mankind on the other. In *The Human Condition*, Arendt will find a beautiful way to describe this threshold-position as a dialectical dynamic inherent in the many-faceted states of love, which is far from the conventional binary private-public relation.

Two entries in 1955, finally, conclude the conceptual carousel that appears as a fascinating trace of love in Arendt's notebooks. In the first one, dating from May 1955, she begins by drawing a distinction between *privacy* and *intimacy* (the intimacy characterized by concealment: *Verborgenheit*); she then locates both of them within a list of four concepts, in which these two modes of being are differentiated from the *public sphere* and from *society*. In this constellation, the necessity of labor (for the sake of maintaining life) is ascribed to *privacy*, whereas *intimacy* is considered as the realm of love and friendship. The *public sphere*, in contrast, is defined as the site in which one may appear and present oneself in liberty, whereas *society* is the realm of being together as depending-on-each other in need (*Bedürfnis*) (XXI/38, 529 f.). This dense description of four modes of the human condition shows Arendt's insisting on the relation between privacy and the public in a much more differentiated way than is acknowledged by her critics.

In July 1955, another entry entitled *Amor Mundi* reformulates the meaning of »world« as *in-between*, namely as »a space of time that emerges as soon as men exist in plurality,« and as the realm where we appear as persons:

> We are recognizable only in the in-between of the world, the name sticks to us in the in-between. Within the pure inside, there are no names; only I and you, which are interchangeable.
>
> (Kenntlich sind wir nur im Zwischen der Welt, der Name haftet uns im Zwischen an. Im reinen Innen gibt es keine Namen; nur ich und du, die verwechselbar sind) (XXI/55, 540).

With this entry, the conceptual framework for the book *The Human Condition*, which appeared three years later in 1958, seems complete: The first part, which elaborates the distinction between the private and the public realm, locates intimacy and love in the former, with the famous statement: »love, in distinction from friendship, is killed, or rather extinguished, the moment it is displayed in public« (Arendt 1998, 51), and it discusses the historical alterations of the public realm that is the site where we hear and see others and are seen and heard by others. The main part of the book shifts the viewpoint and concentrates on the analysis of human activities. In the prologue, Arendt explains that her book deals with »the most elementary articulations of the human condition« and adds that »the highest and perhaps purest activity of which men are capable, the activity of thinking, is left out of these present considerations« (ibid., 5), with the consequence that the human condition is systematically limited to labor, work and acting. The underlying theoretical reason for this exclusion is obvious. Since the in-between—as the site where persons appear and engage in exchange, where human beings interact and communicate, and where the political originates—forms the site of action in the public realm, therefore thinking—the mode of solitude—has no systematic place in the *vita activa*. In a later supplement to this book, namely, the first part of *The Life of the Mind*, Arendt will argue that thinking nevertheless plays a crucial role for the human condition. But what about love?

3. Love as a Transitional Concept in *The Human Condition*

In *The Human Condition*, love is discussed in several places, but it does not have a single, systematic place within the »elementary relations between human beings.« Love does not appear in just one guise but alters its shape, character, and mode in different constellations; it is subject to manifold transformations. Although it is not a central theme of *The Human Condition*, the book includes some dense reflections that illuminate love as a transitional concept, which mediates between intimacy and the realm of human affairs, all while undergoing certain metamorphoses of its own. It's not true that Arendt neglects the relevance of love and the private realm, nor is it the case that her approach to intimate love means that love falls into eternal worldlessness, as claims one of several misleading commonplaces in the reception of Arendt's theory. On the contrary, love is so essential for human life that it has to be protected. In the first part of *The Human Condition*, in the passage where Arendt talks about the »twilight« of our private and intimate lives when appearing in the light of the public realm, she explicitly stresses that this »does not mean that private concerns are generally irrelevant; on the contrary, we shall see that there are very relevant matters which can survive only in the realm of the private« (ibid., 51). That means that love can only survive when it is not »used for political purposes such as the change or salvation of the world« (ibid., 52). Consequently, Arendt in fact characterizes intimate love as unworldly and anti-political. This does not mean that love does not contribute to human affairs or the political. But this contribution follows an intricate movement rather than taking a direct path. This movement can be described as a complex dramaturgy in several steps; it runs from (1) a withdrawal from the world within the constellation of intimate togetherness of the two lovers via (2) the appearance of the third, who prepares the reentry into the in-betweenness of plurality, and (3) the return to the world of interaction.

The widespread critical rejection of Arendt's protection of intimate love against the light of the public sphere within feminist and post-colonial theory arises at most from an interpretation, which identifies love with privacy and reduces the way Arendt describes the complex dialectic constellation of different manifestations of human relations to a dualistic privacy-politics opposition. The critique emerges from the conviction that »the private is political,« as a famous slogan of the feminist movement puts it. Claiming the political character of privacy, this slogan from the 1970s[5] called for a radical change of the prevalent misogynous and often violent gender relations within sexual and social family structures; within Arendt's theory, this claim

5 As for example in Kate Millett (Millett 1970).

concerns the realm of *labor* for maintaining life in the first place. The private, however, is not political as such, rather politics has to take care that the society develops and provides conditions of the private sphere that make intimacy and love freed from power relations, violence, and normative gender-concepts. The realm in which to develop these conditions is *action*, that takes place in the in-betweenness of humans from which the political emerges. When Arendt insists on the *anti*-political—yet not un-political—character of intimate love, she cautions against any political instrumentalization of love,[6] namely the usage of love as a means for a certain end. Only if it is differentiated and protected from the public realm, can intimate love evolve as the precondition of natality and thus of an ever-possible new beginning. Love is a precondition of acting and thus of a kind of politics that is worthy of the name, but love is not a means for a »better« or »more humanist« politics. Therefore, the short-cut argument of the political character of privacy and the idea of a »politics of love«[7] are just two sides of the same coin.

The dialectic constellation of Arendt's theory of the human condition concerns the threshold between the *duality* of intimacy and the *triad* emerging from the appearance of the third, which creates the condition of possibility of plurality as well as the need to interact societally. In this way, Arendt reflects upon the same threshold that psychoanalysis—taking the developmental perspective of the infant—describes as the transition from the mother-infant dyad to a triadic constellation, the latter regarded as the entry into the social or into language and the symbolic, as Jacques Lacan (Lacan 2001) would put it. Arendt's dialectical view of the transitional character of love is developed in a slightly concealed but still very beautiful passage that appears in the section entitled »Unpredictability and the Power of Promise« in *The Human Condition*. Here, one finds a dense theory of love, conceptualized as the dialectic of intimacy and human affairs. Following a

6 An analogous danger of instrumentalization concerns pity; see Arendt's analysis from *On Revolution* of the way that the invention of pity as a means of revolution by Robespierre supported the transformation of the French revolution into a system of terror.

7 As, for example, represented in Shin Chiba (Chiba 1995). The article that seeks for a politics of friendship and draws this back to Arendt's reference to *amor mundi* includes a series of misunderstandings concerning her reflections on the different guises of love. It misinterprets Arendt's theory as a theory of »political identity« (ibid., 509) and ascribes to her a »political aversion to the notion of love« (ibid., 507). These misunderstandings are apparently based on the most fundamental one: the reduction of Arendt's description of three basic human activities in *The Human Condition* to a binary opposition of a »naturalistic« and »artificial dimension of life,« connecting the latter to political life. In contrast, for Arendt, the »artificial world of things« is the product of work (*Herstellen*), but political life takes place in the inter-subjective realm of action (*Handeln*).

discussion of the conviction that only love has the power to forgive, Arendt writes:

> Love, by reason of its passion, destroys the in-between which relates us to and separates us from others. As long as its spell lasts, the only in-between which can insert itself between two lovers is the child, love's own product. The child, this in-between to which the lovers now are related and which they hold in common, is representative of the world in that it also separates them; it is an indication that they will insert a new world into the existing world. Through the child, it is as though the lovers return to the world from which their love had expelled them. But this new worldliness, the possible result and the only possibly happy ending of a love affair, is, in a sense, the end of love, which must either overcome the partners anew or be transformed into another mode of belonging together (Arendt 1998, 242).

The way in which Arendt describes love as the interplay and counterplay between withdrawing from the world into intimacy and living in worldliness explains why love can have no unambiguous or stable systematic place in human relations and activities. Rather, it occupies a position at the transition between two areas and modes of life. It is not only elementary for mediating between these areas. It also changes its character according to the realm and mode in which it takes shape.

There are good reasons for the fact that these different forms of expressing love are denominated by the same word. As Sigmund Freud has observed, »the negligence of language in applying the word ›love‹ [...] is justified genetically« (*[dass] die Nachlässigkeit der Sprache in der Anwendung des Wortes »Liebe« [...] eine genetische Berechtigung [findet]*) (Freud 1999, 462). As Freud shows in *Civilization and Its Discontents* (*Das Unbehagen in der Kultur*, 1930), this justification lies in the connection of the different variants of love that emerge out of each other to shape distinct areas of life (sexuality, family, culture)—ultimately leading, for Freud, to an opposition between love and culture. Love may appear in a different light for Freud than it does for Arendt. But in their views of the place of love in relation to social life, they are not so far from each other[8]—despite Arendt's reservations against psychoanalysis. Actually, Arendt never really studied Sigmund Freud, yet, when observing her lack of interest in studying psychoanalysis and her critical view of »modern psychology«[9] (Arendt 2005, 201), one has to take

8 On this point, see Alphandary 2015.

9 The epilogue is »the conclusion of a lecture course titled ›The History of Political Theory‹ which Arendt gave at the University of California-Berkeley in the spring of 1955« (Arendt 2005, 204), as the editor explains.

into consideration the situation of the field at that time, namely the predominance of ego-psychology that was the prevailing school and practice in the United States during the 1950s.

But the passage cited from *The Human Condition* also makes clear that it is short-sighted to assume a dualistic concept of love in Arendt: here, the worldliness of the *amor mundi*, and there, the worldlessness of love as passion. It makes just as little sense to translate the metamorphosis of the different expressions of love into a system of different types, because this runs the risk of losing sight of how, for Arendt, the fundamental significance of love for the human condition lies precisely in its *threshold position* and its *transitional changing character*. Such a *systematic* distinction of different concepts of love in Arendt's work was attempted most recently, for example, with the distinction of »three or even four different concepts of love in the *Denktagebuch*,« namely love first as »worldless passion«; second, as eros; third, as *amor mundi*, i.e., love for the world; and fourth as »unconditional affirmation« in accordance with the Heideggerian reference to the Augustinian phrase *volo ut sis*, »I will that you be« (Tömmel 2017, 109).[10] And the entries on love in the *Denktagebuch* are in no way evidence of an »indecisiveness« (*Unschlüssigkeit*) in Arendt's conception of love, as, for example, Dieter Thomä argues in reading these entries as a »detour via passion« that »appears to have left hardly any traces in the final version of the *vita activa*« (Thomä 2007, 627). The changing meanings of love are rather the effect of its illumination from various perspectives in its relation to the *vita activa*. It is true that the passages about intimate love in *The Human Condition* are not particularly extensive. But they are enormously dense, lucid, and concise, which makes them all the more important. For, as a precondition for the fact that lovers »will insert a new world into the existing world,« which is the first step to the »return to the world,« love makes possible the world of being together and interacting—even if it remains excluded, as intimate love, from that world. Above all, these deliberations on love are the foundation for Arendt's concept of natality—a guiding notion in *The Human Condition*.

10 The consequence of this systematic approach is that Tömmel ascribes love to *vita passiva* as being an »independent mode of life,« although her approach that is the first intense and serious analysis of love in Arendt acknowledges that Arendt conceptualizes »the relation between love and the world« as a dialectic relation (Tömmel 2013, 109, 119).

4. *Denktagebuch*: The Space of Transition From Experience to Theory

The thematization of love in the *Denktagebuch* is much more extensive than the arguments later presented in *The Human Condition*. Above all, several longer entries (nearly essays in scope) justify discussing an unwritten book about love: the entries in question are like building blocks for a latent book. And these reflections differ from the more conceptual passages discussed above inasmuch as a different gesture of writing comes into play: a certain mode of writing, which the *Denktagebuch* first made possible; for, in beginning this diary in June 1950, Arendt opened up a new, unique space of thought.

The twenty-eight notebooks providing the archival source material for the brilliant edition of the *Denktagebuch* by Ursula Ludz and Ingeborg Nordmann are just one part of many additional notebooks that Arendt filled with writing during her whole lifetime, beginning in 1923 as a seventeen-year-old student at *Gymnasium*. It is true that the entries of the *Denktagebuch* differ significantly from her earlier notebooks. Yet neither of them has anything in common with a usual private diary. Although the title *Denktagebuch* does not originate from the notebooks that Arendt left behind after her death, we have the testimony of Lotte Köhler, Arendt's close friend and the executor of her literary estate, that this was the way Arendt phrased her entries. This title perfectly characterizes the entries according to Arendt's understanding of thinking. In *The Life of the Mind* for example, where she characterizes thinking especially in contrast to science and knowing, the state of thinking is identified with being »fully alive« and described as an activity »concerned with such concepts as justice, happiness, virtue, offered us by language itself as expressing the meaning of whatever happens in life and occurs to us while we are alive« (Arendt 1981a, 178). The entries in Arendt's *Denktagebuch* actually provide a space for reflecting upon what occurred to her, what she encountered in her life—and to discuss it in the framework of fundamental concepts of human affairs. In the sentence I just cited, what »occurs to us« reads as a literal translation of the meaning of *pathein*, a crucial Greek concept that in the recent theoretical discourse in German has been translated as *Widerfahrnis*—an experience akin to an encounter—in order to overcome the long-standing misreading of *pathein* as something merely passive, translated and interpreted as suffering. When Arendt refers in the notebooks to *pathein*, it is usually in the double sense of suffering and loving.

The beginning of the *Denktagebuch* marks a clear caesura in how Hannah Arendt dealt with what she experienced in her life—what occurred to her, in the sense of *widerfahren*. The texts of the earlier notebooks, which clearly refer to experiences that are articulated in poems and prose texts rich with metaphors, are strictly separated from the work of the philosopher: here, the person, there, the author. In contrast to this separated coexistence of personal entries written in poetic language and the published work consisting of philosophical texts and political articles, the entries in the *Denktagebuch* create an *intermediary, transitional space* connecting Arendt's experiences of her own life and contemporary history to her work in developing concepts and a genuine political theory. This turning point is located within a significant constellation of Arendt's personal life history and the history of her work: in 1950, she had already spent almost a decade in American exile and was soon to become a naturalized US citizen; her first book in English, the extensive study *The Origins of Totalitarianism*, had been completed and was in press; and Arendt had returned from her first trip to Europe after the war, which had lasted several months. On this journey, taken at the behest of Jewish Cultural Reconstruction, Inc., she not only returned to Germany for the first time since her emigration in 1933. She also met Martin Heidegger again for the first time after more than two decades. In this first post-war travel to Germany, Arendt returned to the sites of her former life as a different person; she had virtually settled in the United States, had managed to achieve a place in the Anglo-American public as an author of political theory, and—from this position—was able to look back at the past as well as into the future.

The caesura that indicates a new beginning in her mode of writing is visible in her notebooks; it is embodied by a little number that marks a significant positing and creates a great distance from the previous notebooks. In the middle of a notebook with entries that begin in 1942, the year after her arrival in the United States, Arendt places »1« in the upper right corner of the right page and, beneath the date June 1950, writes a longer discourse, without a title, on injustice, guilt, forgiveness, and reconciliation. The entries that are placed before this break and written usually only on the right page of the notebook, record impressions and mental states of a life in exile. They thematize the uncertain place of exile by using familiar metaphors of being, *Daseinsmetaphern* as Hans Blumenberg (Blumenberg 1997) calls them, such as a bridge, a door, and the shore. After the break, signified by the little »1« that expresses the will for something new and different, the pages are consecutively written on and numbered, while both shorter and longer en-

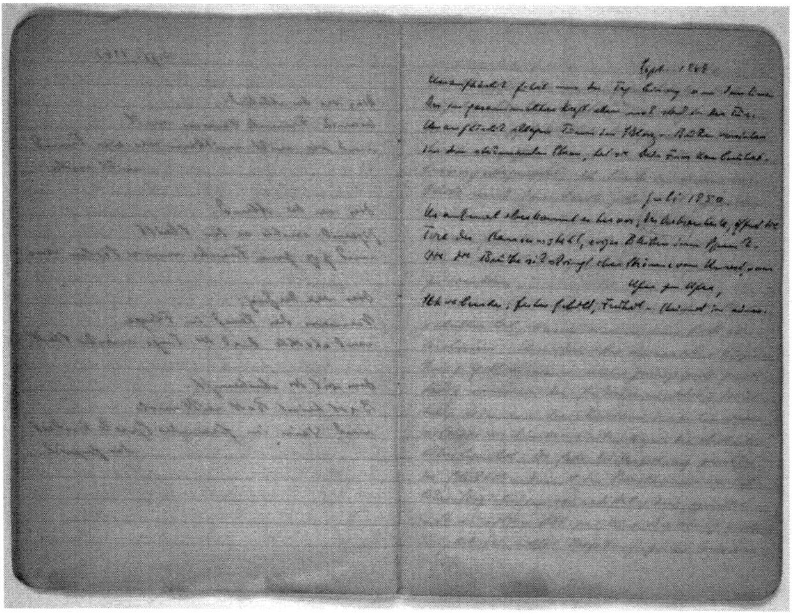

From Arendt's notebooks: the last pages before the beginning of what later becomes the »Denktagebuch«.
Courtesy of the Hannah Arendt Bluecher Literary Trust.

tries are often categorized by a topic or keyword, such as »On law« (*Ad Gesetz*), »power-omnipotence« (*Macht-Allmacht*), or »God-Gods« (*Gott-Götter*). These entries form a working journal, which provides for us the possibility to read and observe how theoretical questions and work projects emerge and develop out of Arendt's experience of the history of her day. Reading the three different parts of Arendt's writings in parallel to each other, i.e. her work, her correspondence with friends, and the *Denktagebuch*, makes it partly possible to reconstruct these historical and biographical contexts of experience. In the *Denktagebuch* itself, however, the distance from a personal diary is made most clear by the fact that her entries record neither names nor occasions. One exception is death, for the names of familiar or beloved individuals only appear if there is to be a report of their death—in accordance with Arendt's conviction that people only become a part of history after they have died. As long as they live, they are part of life but not history.

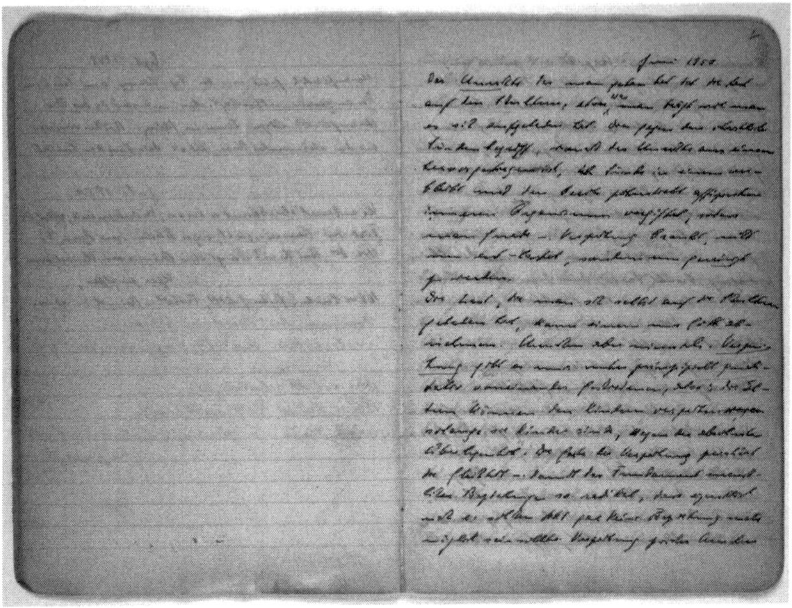

From Arendt's notebooks: the first page of the »Denktagebuch«.
Courtesy of the Hannah Arendt Bluecher Literary Trust.

5. Fragments of Arendt's Book on Love

In opening up a new space for reflection, the *Denktagebuch* also opens the door to a new scene of experience. One could call this the interior space of relations of love and marriage. The separation of philosophy and poetic reflections on personal experiences in Arendt's early work is especially characteristic of the topic of love. For example, many of Arendt's poems from the time of her studies bear clear traces of her relationship with Martin Heidegger during the years 1923 to 1926, and of the abrupt way she ended it (Arendt and Heidegger 1998). Her dissertation on Augustine, which, by contrast, discusses the significance of neighborly love for the *vita socialis*, represents an aloof and nearly unapproachable engagement with Augustine's terminology (see Weigel 2015). In the *Denktagebuch*, the drawing of a line between philosophy and experience is softened and partly leveled in a certain sense, and the boundary of purely theoretical reflection is breached. This is the case, above all, for the open ending of the passage from *The Human Condition* I cited above, which conceives of love as a transitional concept in the dialectic of intimacy and the world of coexistence. This open end is expressed as an either-or: »the end of love, which must *either* overcome the partners anew *or* be transformed into another mode of belonging together« (Arendt 1998, 242; emphasis mine). In order to speak about this either-or, it is necessary to enter the scene of the private realm and consider it up close. For it is only through such a consideration that the various facets of love are completed in their multiple metamorphoses. And the *Denktagebuch* contains a series of fragments that can serve exactly this purpose.

This especially pertains to the somewhat longer entries that the headings join together into an essay structured by a diary-like rhythm—a kind of serialized essay about love: in December 1950, an entry of two and a half pages (in the printed version of the book) on the topic of »love and marriage« (*Liebe und Ehe*); in May 1953, around two pages with the heading »On love« (*Ad Liebe*); and in April 1955, just a bit more than one page, written in English, on the topic »Ad passions.« In the spaces between these deliberations, there are to be found countless shorter entries on different aspects of love, such as the relationship between passion and feeling, solitude and love, pain and pleasure; or on *pathos* and passion, on love as an absolute, as the highest form of recognition, and on the different readings of *volo ut sis*.

The first entry on »love and marriage« (II/26, 49) begins with a remarkable assertion: »Love is an event out of which a history or a destiny can emerge« (Liebe ist ein *Ereignis*, aus dem eine *Geschichte* werden kann oder ein *Geschick*).[11] This event, Arendt argues, is consumed by the institution of marriage. And, she continues, »institutions that are based on events« will persist only as long »as these events have not been completely consumed [*aufgezehrt*].« In the case of love, Arendt argues, this means that marriage as an institution has rendered love »homeless and unprotected« (*heimat- und schutzlos*). And as a consequence, men and women respond to this dilemma or »protest against it« in different ways. Women do so, Arendt argues, by

> transforming love, which is an event, into an emotion, which not only degrades love because it makes something divine into something human, but also degrades all emotions because they apparently cannot stand the flame of love against which they are measured.
>
> (aus der Liebe, die ein Ereignis ist, ein Gefühl machen, was nicht nur die Liebe degradiert, weil ein Göttliches zu einem Menschlichen gemacht wird, sondern auch alle Gefühle degradiert, weil sie offenbar dem Feuer der Liebe, an dem sie gemessen werden, nicht standhalten) (II/26, 49).

11 Mine emphasis.

And men do so by »rethinking« love »into friendship« (*in Freundschaft umdenken*), although no friendship, as Arendt argues, could bear »what marriage demands« (*zumutet*). The reflections that follow unfold a complex dramaturgy in the tension between love, marriage, friendship, and loyalty (*Treue*) that upends the conventional understanding of these concepts. For example, Arendt assigns loyalty to friendship, not to marriage, while assuming the »freedom of love« and understanding marriage as »an institution created by the free decision [*Entschluss*] of two people.« By the way, in this last point she comes close to Walter Benjamin's essay, *Goethe's Elective Affinities,* and his assessment that marriage comes about through a decision and not through a choice.[12]

Today, with access to the extensive archive with the enormous number of papers, letters and manuscripts that Arendt left behind, it is not difficult to decipher the contexts of experience that shine through in these entries. For example, it is obvious to associate the statement on love as being an event out of which a history or a destiny can emerge, with Arendt's relationship to Heidegger—and not only because love as an event and the word *Geschick* clearly carry the signature of Heidegger's language and thought. But also because one of the poems that Heidegger addressed to Hannah Arendt in February 1950 after they met again in Freiburg speaks of love as an event (Arendt and Heidegger 1998, 88). And because some years later, at the end of 1957, Arendt—who wrote to Blumenfeld that Heidegger, in response to their re-encounter, »enriched the German language with several beautiful poems«—herself wrote a poem in her *Denktagebuch* that reads like an echo of the images and words from Heidegger's poems from 1950, such as the »tie of glances« (*Band der Blicke*) and the word »destiny« (XXII/37, 584). Arendt's poems that are scattered throughout the *Denktagebuch* appear like embedded particles reminiscent of the language found in the earlier notebooks because they more clearly express the author's personal state of mind. It is striking that the word »heart« wanders this way and that among the fragments on the topic of love and the poems: here, the never-ending repertoire of poetic metaphors of the heart, and there, reflections such as the thought that love »takes possession of the heart, but it does not originate from the heart« (XVI/3, 372). And this position of the heart is in turn occasion for several entries about metaphors of the heart and the interplay between language and the feelings of the soul.[13]

12 For more detail, see Weigel 2016.

13 For more detail, see Weigel 2009.

But let us return to the entry on »love and marriage«: with Arendt's reference to the freedom of love, marriage, and loyalty, it also seems appropriate to think of Arendt's marriage with Heinrich Blücher. And in this case, the commentary to the edition—which is otherwise agreeably restrained in providing biographical interpretations—refers to exactly such personal relationships: among others things, it mentions Arendt's re-encounter with Heidegger and the fact that this included getting to know him as a married man (to Elfride Heidegger); and it also points to a crisis in Arendt's own marriage because of an affair of Blücher's (Arendt 2002, 929).

However, I am not interested in identifying these kinds of events as biographical background but rather in the fact that Arendt's *Denktagebuch* bridges the distance between the space of experience and that of thought inasmuch as it is the site where experiences and observations evolve and transform into the conceptual work she is undertaking. In this way, the *Denktagebuch* illuminates the metamorphoses of love within a web of various aspects. Countless entries take up different individual strands from the first, highly compressed entry on »love and marriage« and explore them in a more intensive and differentiated way. For example, the degeneration of passion and its transformation into emotions is explained in the entry from February 1951 in several ways: because »we cannot stand the pure state of being seized by passion (*pathos*)« or because of desperation about an »end, or rather a suspension of passion« that Arendt also connects to a lack of trust (III/6, 59 f.). In September 1952, one entry argues that love has no subject; love is absolute passion and moreover the only true passion because »all other so-called ›passions‹ are desires [*Begierden*]« (XI/1, 249).

In the second longer essay-like entry under the heading »On Love« (*Ad Liebe*) from May 1953 that apparently includes a kind of monad for the passage on the dialectic of intimacy and human affairs in *The Human Condition*, Arendt finally distinguishes love categorically from emotion. Love is not an emotion but a power, she argues, to then continue with considerations that lead to the conception of love as worldlessness. As the power of life, love for Arendt is »not actually of human origin« but rather a »power of the universe« that takes possession of the person and her/his heart. The extra-human nature ascribed to love, which in the entry of December 1950 was characterized as »something divine« (*ein Göttliches*), is now in May 1953 described as a cosmic power. This makes clear that her discussion of passionate love in the *Denktagebuch* transgresses the horizon of her book on Augustine and the Christian concepts of love discussed therein. In *The Human Condition*, in accordance with her understanding of man as conditioned being, she describes human beings as earth-bound creatures who »inhabit the world« and remarks that »life on earth has been given to man« (Arendt 1998, 7), but the following *Denktagebuch* entry on the limits of human power over the world refers to something beyond, while still not defining it in theological terms:

Love is a power of the universe, insofar as the universe is alive. It *is the* power of life and guarantees its advancement against death. Therefore love »overcomes« death.

(Die Liebe ist eine Macht des Universums, sofern das Universum lebendig ist. Sie *ist die* Macht des Lebens und garantiert seinen Fortgang gegen den Tod. Darum »überwindet« die Liebe den Tod) (XVI/3, 372).

The way this power affects humankind can, in German, precisely be described with the verb *bemächtigen* (take possession of) derived from power (*Macht*). When the power of love starts to affect human beings and the world and space between them, then this *extra-human* power turns into an *anti-worldly* power. This is the reason for Arendt to connect the event of love with worldlessness: »Love burns, pierces like lightning the in-between, that is, the world-space between humans« (*Die Liebe verbrennt, durchschlägt wie der Blitz das Zwischen, d.h. den Welt-Raum zwischen den Menschen*; ibid., 372). This kind of love is possible only between two persons, yet it is also the precondition for the emergence of the third and the consequence—the turning point within the dialectical dynamic—that when »the third appears, space is restored immediately« (*Tritt der Dritte hinzu, so stellt sich Raum sofort wieder her*; ibid. 372). The way that passionate love takes possession of a person is described here in a nearly poetic passage, which in my eyes forms a core of her unwritten book on love:

As a universal (universe's) power of life, love is not actually of human origin. Through nothing else are we so securely and inescapably integrated into the *living* universe as through love, from which no one escapes. But as soon as this power takes possession of man and throws him towards an Other, and burns between these two the Betweenness of the world and its space, love becomes the »most human« of the human being, namely, a humanity that exists world-less, object-less (the beloved is never an object), space-less. For love *consumes* the world and gives an inkling of what a world-less person would be.

(Als universale (Universums-)Macht des Lebens ist die Liebe nicht eigentlich menschlichen Ursprungs. Durch nichts sind wir so sicher und unentrinnbar dem *lebendigen* Universum eingefügt wie durch die Liebe, der keiner entrinnt. Sobald aber diese Macht sich des Menschen bemächtigt und ihn einem Andern zuwirft und zwischen diesen beiden das Zwischen der Welt und ihres Raumes verbrennt, wird gerade die Liebe zum »Menschlichsten« des Menschen, nämlich zu einer Menschlichkeit, die welt-los, objekt-los (der

Geliebte ist nie Objekt), raumlos besteht. Die Liebe *verzehrt*, nämlich die Welt, und gibt eine Ahnung dessen, was ein welt-loser Mensch wäre) (XVI/3, 373).

From this description, Arendt derives three principles that shape her notion of passionate or intimate love, that is the love between two individuals: it is, first, »the power of life«; second, »the world-destroying principle«; and third, »the creative principle that goes beyond the state of merely being alive because a new world emerges from its worldlessness« (XVI/3, 372 ff.).

These characteristics form the basic idea for the place that love as passion will occupy in *The Human Condition,* although the topic of love is there for the most part replaced by the idea of *natality* as the new potency of an ever new beginning: the new world emerging from the worldlessness of intimate love. In the *Denktagebuch*, numerous entries on love will follow, though only up to the year 1955—apparently because the conception of a book had taken shape at this point and Arendt's writing shifted to the manuscript. With recourse to Freud's argument that there is a genetic connection between the different meanings of the word »love,« one can summarize by saying that Arendt's *Denktagebuch* makes this connection visible in two ways: on the one hand, in relation to the genesis and emergence of her theory of love, and on the other, in respect of the connection of the various facets and modes of love within the *conditio humana*.

Only in 1966, after more than a decade where the subject of love was nearly absent from the entries, does the *Denktagebuch* once again have several entries on the topic. This is the year in which Arendt was occupied with the English translation of her dissertation on the concept of love in Augustine. On January 16th, 1966, she writes to Jaspers:

I'm rewriting Augustine, in English and not in Latin, and in a way that can be understood by a person who has not learned philosophical stenography. It's strange—it's been so long, on the one hand; but on the other hand I still recognize myself, to a certain extent, I know exactly what I wanted to say and can even read Latin fluently, as far as Augustine is concerned.

(Ich schreibe den »Augustin« um, auf englisch und nicht auf lateinisch, und so, daß es ein Mensch verstehen kann, der philosophische Stenographie nicht gelernt hat. Es ist merkwürdig—es ist so ewig lange her, einerseits; aber andererseits erkenn ich mich, gewissermaßen, noch, weiß genau, was ich habe sagen wollen, und kann selbst Latein noch fließend lesen, wenn es sich um Augustin handelt) (Arendt and Jaspers 1985, 657—658).

Although Arendt did not complete her revision of the draft of the translation prepared by E.B. Ashton, it is clear that Augustine and the question of her dissertation gained renewed intimateness to her and again importance for her work. For one finds now entries on the topic of charity and self-love in the *Denktagebuch*—a trace leading to the project *The Life of the Mind*. The second part of this project, on »willing,« contains several passages that refer to Augustine, especially regarding the »uniting force of love« and the »transformation of Will into *Love*« (Arendt 1981b, 102, 123) whereby love is evaluated as a capacity to »redeem the Will« (ibid., 123), but also in relation to the love of justice and love as »the soul's gravity« (ibid., 104). Yet, in *Thinking* Arendt refers also to the Greek tradition, especially to Socrates' idea of love, respectively *Eros*, which she reads as a »desirous love« and translates into her concept of the »›quest‹ for meaning« (Arendt 1981a, 178).

It is in this context that Arendt also returns to the sentence »I will that you be—*Amo: Volo ut sis*,« a leitmotif of Heidegger's reading of Augustine. Arendt understands the phrase as unconditional recognition, rewriting it in the *Denktagebuch* as: »The highest form of recognition is love: *volo ut sis*« (XXVI/69, 748). The second part of *The Life of the Mind* discusses this mode of love as a kind of unconditional acceptance or acknowledgement of the beloved person: »There is no greater assertion of something or somebody than to love it, that is, to say: I will that you be—*Amo: Volo ut sis*« (Arendt 1981b, 104). What relates this kind of love to her earlier description of passionate love is the fact that the beloved is not possessed and not seen as an object:

> The willing ego, when it says in its highest manifestation, »*Amo: Volo ut sis*,« »I love you; I want you to be«—and not »I want to have you« or »I want to rule you«—shows itself capable of the same love with which supposedly God loves men, whom He created only because He willed them to exist and whom He *loves without desiring them* (ibid., 136).

And she adds the commentary: »That is how the matter presented itself to the Christian.« This gesture of taking distance coincides with the book's mode of writing. When discussing the interrelation of love and will within the history of ideas, this viewpoint differs radically from Arendt's description of passionate love in the *Denktagebuch*, for the latter obviously expresses her own ideas that evolve from working through experiences and their reconsideration on a theoretical level with the help of concepts. Although related by the unconditional character of both of these kinds of love, the *volo ut sis* and the passionate love differ fundamentally because they emerge from an entirely different origin. While *volo ut sis* originates from the will, in the event of passionate love, as described in the *Denktagebuch*, the loving person, in contrast, is possessed (*bemächtigt*) by an extra-human power. The first is a product of will, whereas the latter is the effect of the loss of will.

Yet, what remains to be thought through more intensely are the correspondences as well as the differences between the unconditioned love condensed in the formula *volo ut sis* and the passionate love that happens in the worldlessness of intimacy. Why, then, after having completed her work on *Judging* that was conceptualized as the third part of *The Life of the Mind*, would Arendt not have taken up writing a book about love?

Works Cited

Alphandary, Idit (2015). Love and Worldliness in Psychoanalysis and in the Work of Hannah Arendt. *Philosophy Today*, 59(2), 227—255.

Arendt, Hannah (1981a). *Thinking*. In Hannah Arendt. *The Life of the Mind*. Ed. Mary McCarthy. San Diego/New York/London: Harcourt Brace Jovanovich.

Arendt, Hannah (1981b). *Willing*. In Hannah Arendt. *The Life of the Mind*. Ed. Mary McCarthy. San Diego/New York/London: Harcourt Brace Jovanovich.

Arendt, Hannah (1985). *Das Urteilen: Texte zu Kants Politischer Philosophie*. Hrsg. und mit einem Essay von Ronald Beiner. München: Piper.

Arendt, Hannah, and Karl Jaspers (1985). *Briefwechsel 1926—1969*. Ed. Lotte Köhler and Hans Saner. München: Piper.

Arendt, Hannah (1996). *Love and Saint Augustine*. Ed. and interpretive essay Joanna Vecchiarelli Scott and Judith Chelius Stark. Chicago: University Press.

Arendt, Hannah (1998). *The Human Condition*. Second ed. Introduction Margaret Canovan. Chicago: University of Chicago Press.

Arendt, Hannah, and Martin Heidegger (1998). *Briefe 1925 bis 1975 und andere Zeugnisse*. Hrsg. von Ursula Ludz. Frankfurt am Main: Klostermann.

Arendt, Hannah (2002). *Denktagebuch: 1950 bis 1973*. Hrsg. von Ursula Ludz und Ingeborg Nordmann, in Zusammenarbeit mit dem Hannah-Arendt-Institut, Dresden. 2 Bände. München/Zürich: Piper Verlag.

Arendt, Hannah (2005). Epilogue. In Hannah Arendt. *The Promise of Politics*. Ed. and introduction Jerome Kohn. New York: Schocken Books.

Beiner, Ronald (1992). Preface. In Hannah Arendt. *Lectures on Kant's Political Philosophy*. Ed. and interpretive essay Ronald Beiner. Chicago: University of Chicago Press.

Bernauer, James W. (ed.). (1987). *Amor Mundi: Explorations in the Faith and Thought of Hannah Arendt*. Boston/Dordrecht/Lancaster: Martinus Nijhoff Publishers.

Blumenberg, Hans (1997). *Shipwreck With Spectator: Paradigm of a Metaphor for Existence*. Transl. Steven Rendall. Cambridge, Mass.: MIT Press.

Borren, Marieke (2010). *Amor Mundi: Hannah Arendt's Phenomenology of World*. Dissertation. Amsterdam: F&N. 31.05.2021 http://dare.uva.nl/record/346972.

Chiba, Shin (1995). Hannah Arendt on Love and the Political: Love, Friendship, and Citizenship. *The Review of Politics*, 57(3), 505—535.

Freud, Sigmund (1999). *Das Unbehagen in der Kultur*. In Sigmund Freud. *Gesammelte Werke*. Vol. 14, *Werke aus den Jahren 1925—1931*. Ed. Anna Freud. Frankfurt am Main: Fischer.

Hahn, Barbara (2005). *Hannah Arendt—Leidenschaften, Menschen und Bücher*. Berlin: Berlin Verlag.

Lacan, Jacques (2001). The Mirror Stage as Formative of the Function of the I. In Jacques Lacan. *Écrits: A Selection*. Transl. Alan Sheridan. London: Routledge.

Millett, Kate (1970). *Sexual Politics*. Garden City, N.Y.: Doubleday & Co.

Paine, Rachel (2013). I Want You to Be: Love as a Precondition of Freedom in the Thought of Hannah Arendt. In Gary Peters and Fiona Peters (eds.). *Thoughts of Love*, 107—123. Newcastle-upon-Tyne: Cambridge Scholars Publishing.

Thomä, Dieter (2007). Verlorene Passion, wiedergefundene Passion: Arendts Anthropologie und Adornos Theorie des Subjekts. *Deutsche Zeitschrift für Philosophie*, 55(4), 627—648.

Tömmel, Tatjana Noemi (2013). *Wille und Passion: Der Liebesbegriff bei Heidegger und Arendt*. Berlin: Suhrkamp.

Tömmel, Tatjana Noemi (2017). *Vita passiva*: Love in Arendt's *Denktagebuch*. In Roger Berkowitz and Ian Storey (eds.). *Artifacts of Thinking: Reading Hannah Arendt's Denktagebuch*, 124—142. New York: Fordham University Press.

Weigel, Sigrid (2005). Dichtung als Voraussetzung der Philosophie: Hannah Arendts *Denktagebuch*. *Text+Kritik. Zeitschrift für Literatur*, 166/167, 125—137.

Weigel, Sigrid (2009). Poetics as a Presupposition of Philosophy: Hannah Arendt's *Denktagebuch*. *Telos*, 146, 97—110.

Weigel, Sigrid (2015). *Amor, zoon politikon* und *vita activa*: Die antiken Begriffe von Liebe und Politik als Schauplatz der Geburt von Hannah Arendts Denken und Schreiben. In Christine Lubkoll and Claudia Öhlschläger (eds.). *Kulturpraxis—Poetologie—Theatralität*, 293—307. Freiburg im Br./Berlin/Vienna: Rombach.

Weigel, Sigrid (2016). Fidelity, Love, Eros: Benjamin's Bireferential Concept of Life as Developed in *Goethe's Elective Affinities*. In Colby Dickinson and Stéphane Symons (eds.). *Walter Benjamin and Theology*, 75—92. New York: Fordham University Press.

Young-Bruehl, Elisabeth (1982). *Hannah Arendt: For Love of the World*. New Haven: Yale University Press.

Amor Mundi: The Marrano Background of Hannah Arendt's Love for the World

Agata Bielik-Robson

When I apply the term »Marrano« to Arendt, I do not mean it in a technical sense of a descendant of the Sephardic Jews forcibly converted to Christianity, but in a metaphorical one that bears a lot of affinities with the condition of the assimilated European Jewry. In my essay, I would like to apply the Marrano hypothesis to Arendt's *amor mundi* or »love for the world,« which seems to me less secular than is usually assumed. In *The Life of the Mind*, especially in the second volume, *Willing*, Arendt locates the origins of her metaphysics of appearances in the concept of natality, a term coined by her while studying Augustine, and then later, Duns Scotus' nominalistic »turn towards the world,« but—as I will try to show in my »cryptotheological« analysis—she reads both, Augustine and Scotus, via the implicit lens of the Lurianic theology of the »hidden God« whom she learned about from Gershom Scholem: the God who retreats from the creation in order to let it become the sole object of a new piety and love, messianic and worldly at the same time. In the result, there emerges a typically Marrano Judeo-Christian combination, motivated by a new desire which Arendt calls *amor mundi* in sharp distinction from the traditional *amor Dei*.

Marrano Investment in This World

As Yirmiyahu Yovel showed in his classical work on the »Marrano experience«—starting from the fifteenth century compulsion to convert, which resulted in »undercover Judaism« on the Iberian peninsula, and ending with the Marrano influence on the process of modern secularization—the Marranos, being no longer traditional Jews, but also not yet Christians, created their own—often highly individualized and idiomatic—syncretic Judeo-Christian forms of belief, in which the implicit Judaic themes would find their way into an explicitly Christian articulation. But not just that: the *Marrano religiosity* was, seemingly paradoxically, very much oriented towards *this* world and *this* life. By wishing to procure redemption here and now, in the material context of worldly reality, the Marranos pioneered modern secularization and co-created the modern philosophy—or, perhaps, rather cryptotheology—of immanence.

According to Yovel, the forced conversion to the Christian religion removed the *conversos* away from Jewish ritual and imposed on them the Pauline emphasis on individual salvation, which they nonetheless expressed in Judaic terms. By claiming that »salvation lies not in Christ, but in the Law of Moses« (Yovel 1989, 20), the Marranos proved to be neither Jewish, since they could no longer practice the halakhic law in its orthodox form, nor Christian, since they also refused to follow Paul's full sublation of law into love and grace. Yet, they were also both: what they took from Christianity was a model of the Pauline *katargein*, which would abrogate and internalize, or simultaneously negate and preserve the Mosaic Law, by distilling from it a messianic promise of redemption. This redemption, however, was not directed towards the Christian immortal afterlife. Oscillating in the nowhere land between the two religions, the Marranos filled this in-between with a renewed interest in the worldly finite existence; having been ejected from both transcendence-oriented religious systems, they discovered the realm of immanence—and the immanent life—as their new home. The orthodox Jews, therefore, continued clinging to their »life in deferral« (*Leben in Aufschub*), delayed and suppressed by the ritualistic execution of the transcendent legislation, while the Christians would go on cherishing their promise of personal immortality; the Marranos, however, found their own promised land in *worldly life*, lived in all its riches and to the full. It was their Kingdom and the Glory, and it was in a finite immanent life that they put their messianic *esperanza* (Yovel 2009, ix). The modern Marrano constellation, therefore, revolves around this *world* which is perceived, on the one hand, as a place of life, which may be good despite being finite, and, on the other, as a place of stable laws that allow *this* life a decent fulfillment. For these two reasons, for Yovel, the most accomplished Marrano was Spinoza: the first modern thinker to lift immanence from oblivion, elevate a singular *conatus* of every living thing to an object of theologico-philosophical reflection, and bestow it with redemptive qualities, where salvation may be a matter of love, but not only that; Spinoza's *amor intellectualis Dei* is less love in the Pauline sense of an all-embracing grace than it is the »third knowledge«

which gains ultimate understanding of the eternal laws governing the living matrix of *natura naturans*; and it is also less a love of God, as the original name suggests, than a love of the World conceived as a natural expression of the deity. In this way, the Marrano rule—»The salvation lies not in Jesus, but in the Law of Moses«—finds its most sophisticated revision in Spinoza's science of the natural law of immanence, which at the same time constitutes the creative divine decree (Yovel 1989, 184).

Marranos, therefore, although not simply secular, could also not be accused of *worldlessness*, which is the standard objection levied by Arendt against a Christianity whose »main political task« was »[t]o find a bond between people strong enough to *replace the world*« and create a sense of brotherhood based on the affect of love-charity which:

> is quite adequate to the main Christian principle of worldlessness and is admirably fit to carry a group of essentially worldless people through the world, a group of saints or a group of criminals, provided only it is understood that the world itself is doomed and that every activity in it is undertaken with the proviso *quamdiu mundus durat* (»as long as the world lasts«). [...] Worldlessness as a political phenomenon is possible only on the assumption that the world will not last (Arendt 1998, 53—54).

In *The Human Condition*, initially titled *Amor Mundi*, Arendt's chief purpose is to defend the world—the reliable, stable, and *lasting* sphere that Greek antiquity saw as eternal—against two other principles: God and Man. In Arendt's account, *the eclipse of the world*, which began with the birth of Christianity and accelerated in the modern age, is a far more dangerous phenomenon than »the eclipse of God,« famously diagnosed by Martin Buber. If modernity can be accused of a nihilistic »loss of faith,« it is not because of secularization—understood as a turn to worldliness—but, on the contrary, because it never invested any faith in the world:

> Modern loss of faith is not religious in origin—it cannot be traced to the Reformation and Counter Reformation [...]—and its scope is by no means restricted to the religious sphere. Moreover, even if we admitted that the modern age began with a sudden, inexplicable eclipse of transcendence, of belief in a hereafter, it would by no means follow that this loss threw man back upon the world. The historical evidence, on the contrary, shows that *modern men were not thrown back upon this world but upon themselves*. [...] World alienation, and not self-alienation as Marx thought, has been the hallmark of the modern age (ibid., 253—254; my emphasis).

Secularization, therefore, understood literally as *Verweltlichung*, is merely an illusion: after the demise of God, it is not the World that came back to the fore, but rather Man and his inner concerns—care of the self, future salvation, promise of immortality. But, could Arendt's »spiritual investment in the world,«[1] deliberately chosen against the acosmic tendencies of both Christian and seemingly »secular« modern thought, be seen as an oblique manifestation of the »Marrano religiosity«—a new *tertium* which reassumes the pagan notion of the World but adds to it a religious element of faith? Just as Spinoza's *amor intellectualis Dei* is less about God and more about the World, so perhaps is Arendt's *amor mundi* less a love as a private and »worldless« affect »which cannot withstand the implacable, bright light of the constant presence of others on the public scene« (Arendt 1998, 51) and more a faith in the Hebrew meaning of *emunah*: trust in the reliability of the covenant, in this case—solid relation with the world as the arena of a good finite life. Could it be then that when she praises »the Renaissance's new-awakened love for the earth and the world, with its rebellion against the rationalism of medieval scholasticism,« which subsequently fell victim to »the modern age's triumphal world alienation« (ibid., 264), she implicitly joins the Marrano lovers of the worldly, as described by Yovel?

The credibility of this hypothesis increases with the help provided by Scholem who, in his analyses of the Marrano theology, demonstrated how this turn towards the world was prompted by the Marrano appropriation of the Lurianic metaphysics, which involved the image of the withdrawn—*tsimtsem*—God and the world as the only possible arena of redemptive action. Arendt's enthusiasm for Scholem's reading of Jewish mysticism—itself deeply influenced by Scholem's own choice of Isaac Luria's theology of *tsimtsum*—found in her 1948 essay, »Jewish History, Revised,« is very telling in this context. For Arendt, the discovery of the kabbalah, with its rebellious and subversive power oriented against the orthodox heritage, as potentially the most valid relic of Jewish tradition, is a revelation, but not because it brings something completely new and unknown to her. On the contrary, this is a revelation of a thought that has always been known to us, yet in an inchoate form: »it accompanies my work in an unexpressed but not unconscious manner,« as she confesses in a private correspondence with Scholem.[2] This indeed is for Arendt a *revision* of the Jewish tradition

1 Arendt's position can indeed be described as the reversal of the apocalyptic standpoint of Jacob Taubes who, in *The Political Theology of Paul*, famously declared: »I have no spiritual investment in the world as it is« (Taubes 2004, 103).

2 In a letter from the 20th of May 1944, Arendt writes to Scholem: »I've been thinking much about you lately, and not just because I've spoken with a lot of people about your book. The real reason is

in the most emphatic sense of the word: instead of *directio Dei*, which she strongly associated with the Christian worldlessness, she suddenly detects here the opposite trajectory of *directio mundi*: the withdrawal of God in the act of *tsimtsum* makes a human person in the world a »protagonist of the cosmic drama« as an »instrument of supreme action«—when God becomes inactive, man become empowered *in His stead*. Kabbalah, therefore, »can lead modern men in their ethical and political life,« because it empowers human agents in the unprecedented manner of a collective Messiah:

> But in spite of cautious restraint and careful avoidance of all conflicts, mystical thought had always prepared its followers for action, thereby breaking with the mere interpretation of the Law and with the mere hope for the coming of the Messiah. In this direction, however, the school of Isaac Luria was bolder than all predecessors when it dared to give a new interpretation of the exile existence of the people: »Formerly [the Diaspora] had been regarded either as a punishment for Israel's sins or as a test of Israel's faith. Now it still is all this, but intrinsically it is a mission: its purpose is to uplift the fallen sparks from all their various locations.« For the first time, the role of the »protagonist in the drama of the world« was defined in terms which applied to every Jew. [...] Of all mystical trends of the past, Jewish mysticism seems unique in its exclusive concern with reality and action; hence, Jewish mysticism alone was able to bring about a great political movement and to translate itself directly into real popular action (Arendt 2007, 309, 311).

»Jewish History, Revised« is not a marginal text within Arendt's intellectual oeuvre, although it is often treated as such; to declare, as she did in her letter to Scholem, that the kabbalistic pro-worldly intuition »accompanies my work in an unexpressed but not unconscious manner« is no small confession.[3] Rather, it points directly to the complex hidden nexus of presuppo-

that I can't get your book out of my mind because it tacitly (please don't think I'm saying ›unconsciously‹) accompanies me in all of my own work« (Arendt and Scholem 2017, 21). In the original German, this crucial fragment sounds even more emphatic: »weil mir Ihr Buch gar nicht mehr aus dem Kopf geht und mich in einer unausgesprochenen (aber bitte nicht unbewussten) Weise in all meinen eigenen Arbeiten begleitet« (Arendt and Scholem 2010, 47).

3 In her reading of Arendt's review, Vivian Liska points to a surprisingly strong misreading of Scholem's oeuvre that goes beyond a simple misunderstanding: it is rather a typically Bloomian misprision of an alien work that strikes a chord with the forgotten ideas of one's own, thanks to this encounter returning with the exciting power of the repressed. Despite Arendt's enthusiasm for Scholem's account of Jewish mysticism, the review is indeed strangely at odds with the reviewed content: whenever Arendt thinks she is simply repeating Scholem's words, she is, in fact, strongly misreading his text according to her own wish to see the confirmation of her hunch that, despite the anti-cosmic teaching of the Rabbinic Judaism, Jews are fit for action in this world: »Arendt opposes rabbinic Judaism and Orthodoxy, which she accuses of merely interpreting the law and encouraging submissiveness. Unlike Scholem, however, she is not so interested in an antinomian, transgressive, and anarchist ›redemption through sin‹ as in mysticism's stimulus to action. The

sitions and beliefs that Yovel associates with the »Marrano experience.« In what follows, I will argue that Arendt displays three typically Marrano moments complicating her apparently secular approach to the affairs of this world: 1) *the cryptojudaic moment*: she almost never refers openly to any Jewish sources, yet she very often misreads the Christian tradition according to the hidden Judaic trajectories (as I will show in her readings of Augustine and Duns Scotus); 2) *the cryptotheological moment*: seemingly secular and interested only in the public realm, Arendt lines her choice with an intense, as she herself calls it, »faith in the world,« which, as I insist, should indeed be taken literally, that is, as *faith*; and, last but not least, 3) *the Lurianic moment*: in her enthusiastic appraisal of Scholem's work on Jewish mysticism, Arendt immediately understands that this is not the traditional mysticism of the otherworldly, but that it offers a theological bridge to and justifica-

---

Sabbatean movement endowed Jewish mysticism with antinomian forces, although until then it had ›kept itself within the Law‹ (309). Arendt, however, perceived the movement's political importance as residing in another of its aspects: its impetus to collective action impelled the rabbis to turn away from ›the mere interpretation of the Law‹ (309), which for centuries had kept them outside the sphere of history and politics. Furthermore, the new collective political action created a bond that could replace Halakhah, which had formerly been ›the only tie of the people in the Diaspora‹ (309). In her discussion of that antinomian messianic movement, she prioritized not the transgression or deactivation of the Law but the empowerment of man on the ›public scene of history‹ (311). Mysticism's esoteric side hardly fits in with Arendt's view of politics as establishing a public sphere—a crucial element of her later political thinking. She circumvents the problem by indicating that mysticism appealed to all those who were ›actually excluded from action‹ and felt that ›they were helpless victims of incomprehensible forces‹ (306). It made them feel that they were part of a larger whole and participated in influencing it. *A crucial quotation from Scholem seemingly resonates with her own imperative of human empowerment.* Through a mystical understanding of the *mitzvot*, Scholem writes, ›The religious Jew became a protagonist in the drama of the world; he manipulated the strings behind the scene‹ (304). *Arendt, however, translates Scholem's description of the mystic's approach to Halakhah into modern terms* and superimposes it onto her own understanding of man as a *zoon politicon*. Indeed, she singles out the aspect of intervention in the world suggested by Scholem's view of the Kabbalah« (Liska 2017, 21; my emphasis; the inner pagination refers to »Jewish History, Revised«). In Liska's account, Arendt's misprision of Scholem is an effect of secularization, but perhaps this pro-secular and pro-cosmic thrust also bears Marrano features, especially in one striking crypto-reference to Spinoza, which Liska very aptly notices in Arendt's text: »Arendt undoubtedly deviates here from Scholem's description of the mystics' idea of the hidden God of Gnosticism, which presumes a clear-cut separation between God as creator and God as revealer. Arendt transforms the Gnostic concept into the concept of an impersonal God, a God as force rather than as ›personality.‹ *Her quasi-Spinozan view of emanation offers a key example of her secularization of the writings of Scholem*, who had remarked explicitly that the Jewish mystics' understanding of ›creation out of nothing‹ simply means ›creation out of God.‹ According to Scholem, their understanding of emanation, therefore, ›stands farthest removed‹ from what the term stands for ›in the history of philosophy and theology‹« (ibid., 23; my emphasis).

tion for the inner-worldly type of messianism, which lends a new power to political involvement. Thus, although Arendt has often been critical of traditional religious orthodoxies as encouraging an escapist form of otherworldly piety, this does not make her simply a secular or even an—as is sometimes claimed—anti-theological thinker.

Is this Marrano attribution justified? In her interpretation of Arendt's essay, »The Jew as Pariah: A Hidden Tradition,« Martine Leibovici ponders a possible analogy between the figure of the pariah, a marginalized victim of assimilation, and the Spanish *converso*, and tests a hypothesis according to which the assimilated European Jew can indeed be regarded as a variant of a modern Marrano (which she, after having noticed some affinities, eventually rather rejects, by finding them insufficient). She notices an important coincidence, earlier spotted by Amnon Krakotzkin, that Arendt writes her essay around the same time that she commented on Scholem's *Major Trends in Jewish Mysticism*, in which she got particularly captivated by the »Marrano opening«: the historical moment when Jews left their ghettos and began to mingle with Western culture and politics. Unlike Krakotzkin who claimed that Arendt became fascinated with the kabbalistic »hidden tradition« embraced by Scholem, Leibovici argues that Arendt's interest in Scholem's work was purely political (see Leibovici 2000; Raz-Krakotzkin 2001). But I would like to propose a compromise solution: agreeing with Leibovici that Arendt does not share Scholem's religious perspective, I nonetheless want to claim, following Krakotzkin and Liska, that her creative revision of Scholem's concept of the »hidden tradition« also has a theological dimension which can indeed be associated with the turning towards the world of the Marrano religiosity. The transfer of transcendent attributes to the immanent world—a move which Yovel ascribes to Spinoza—occurs also in Arendt, for whom the world becomes a place of true fulfillment, also containing some strongly revised quasi-mystical elements.[4]

4 On the obsession with the word »hidden,« which I interpret here as a discovery of a positive meaning of this term in the Lurianic conception of *tsimtsum*, see again Vivian Liska who finds the praise for it in Arendt surprising when one considers her dislike for non-public secrecy: »One element, however, does not quite seem to fit: she repeatedly affirms in her text an aspect of mysticism that runs counter to the Enlightenment idea of transparency and the openness of the public sphere. On almost every page of her text, the word ›hidden‹ appears in an affirmative sense at least once: she writes of the ›hidden God‹ (304), of the mysticism that goes hand-in-hand with the idea of the ›hidden path‹ (305), of emanation as a limitation of self-determination (305), of the ›hidden experiments of the Jewish mystics,‹ and the ›secrecy of their speculations‹ resembling the ›discovery of the philosopher's stone‹ that is kept ›hidden‹ (306), of the mystic's ›efforts

Directio Mundi: Judaizing Augustine and Duns Scotus

Arendt once confessed that when she was young, she was fascinated by Kierkegaard, her first theoretical love, and that because of him she wanted to study theology, but since in the Germany of the 1920s, theological faculties were dominated by Protestant Christianity, she chose philosophy *instead*. We know her early poem inspired by Kierkegaard, which she wrote when she was eighteen:

No word breaks the dark— / No God lifts his hand— / And wherever I look / The land rises up. / No form dissolving. / No Shadow floating. / And still I hear it: / Too late, too late (quoted in Josefson 2019, 22).

This little poem contains Arendt's metaphysics in the nutshell, as it indeed is a *nux*, a condensed seed from which all later on will arise, even if planted in the ground of philosophy. God is no longer present in the world, his presence belongs to the past-perfect »had been,« and it is too late to grasp him directly—but his absence is not to be deplored: the worldly forms are not dissolving fleeting shadows, they are solid entities in which we can trust. Later on Arendt will say, against the last ditches of the Neoplatonic denigration of appearance that she detected in Heidegger's philosophy, that »Being and Appearing coincide« (Arendt 1981a, 20). But the sense that the only true reality, metaphysically speaking, is what appears right now, instead of the by-gone presence of the Creator in the state of retreat (*tsimtsum*), accompanied her from the very beginning as, in Derrida's felicitous formulation, *la foi originaire*: her original »faith in the world.« In her book on Arendt, Julia Kristeva

---

to attain a higher reality that was hidden rather than revealed in the tangible world of everyday life,‹ of the ›laws which, too, work hidden from the eyes of ordinary men‹ (305—6), and of the hiddenness of the mystic's belief in an ›impersonal force as opposed to the God of revelation,‹ a force that is ›concealed rather than revealed in the revelation of the Bible‹ (305)« (Liska 2017, 22). Liska stipulates that this sudden appreciation of hiddenness derives from the way in which Arendt associates it with the Heideggerian *Verborgenheit*, a »letheic« moment of truth in which Being withdraws. This is more than probable. Yet, even here the adversarial moment in her relation with Heidegger also comes to the fore. Once again, in a Marrano manner, she insinuates a Lurianic trace into the Heideggerian motif of the withdrawal of Being: while Heidegger deplores it as a cause of history understood as »errancy« and »error«—»Being qua Truth breaks into the continuum of error« (Arendt 1981b, 192)—for Arendt, already at this early stage of her thought, this offers precisely a chance of plurality and newness which deviates from the monotone monopoly of one Truth. It is precisely because she encounters Scholem's text on the Lurianic *tsimtsum* that she can begin to reverse the Heideggerian negative thinking on *Verborgenheit*, something she was instinctively looking for, but only now found the means to articulate.

quotes Arendt's conversation with Alfred Kazin, in which she said: »I have never, since a child, doubted that God exists,« and then Kristeva comments: »And yet her insistence on the narrated action [...] reveals, in the end, a rare atheism that is devoid of nihilism [...] while rejecting nihilism, she rethought the religious tradition (›believing in God‹), by constantly questioning transcendence« (Kristeva 2001, 97, 104).

Indeed, Arendt's choice of faith can be seen as a case of »rare atheism,« aimed at turning the vertical structure of the religious cult more horizontal, but perhaps it is better to call it a maverick form of Marranism, which, having applied the Lurianic lesson of *tsimtsum*, questioned transcendence as no longer operative in the creaturely world, and paved a way towards an innovative *theology of immanence*. Perhaps, it is no accident that Hans Jonas dedicated his 1961 essay on immortality—where he for the first time reinvented the »Lurianic myth« later to be found in *The Concept of God after Auschwitz*—to »H.A.,« clearly suggestive of »Hannah Arendt«?[5]

This Marrano faith in the world is what stands behind her; it is, in Scholem's words, »non-secular secularism« or, more literally, a pro-worldly and pro-cosmic form of belief in the potentialities of *saeculum* which cannot be reduced to a simple irreligious atheism (Scholem 1976, 46). Arendt's other term for her non-secular secular position is *amor mundi*, the »love for the world.« Initially, this was the working title of the book which she eventually published as *The Human Condition*; after that, she used it only a few times, in her *Denktagebuch*,[6] as well as in the text constituting an epilogue of *Introduction into Politics*, which was unpublished during Arendt's lifetime. There Arendt wrote that »[i]n the last analysis, the human world is always the product of man's *amor mundi*, a human artifice whose potential immortality is always subject to the morality of those who build it and the natality of those who come to live in it« (Arendt 2005, 203).

Apart from Kierkegaard, her youthful love, Augustine and Duns Scotus are Arendt's two favorite theologians. This double choice may seem strange because, at first glance, Augustine and Duns don't have much in common: Augustine, the first Christian Platonic, still preserving traces of his earlier

5 This conjecture comes from Rafael Zawisza.

6 The whole entry reads: »*Amor mundi*—warum ist es so schwer, die Welt zu lieben?« (»*Amor mundi*—why is it so hard to love the world?«) (Arendt 2016, I, 522). But precisely because it is so hard, it cannot simply be a question of a natural attitude: it must be chosen and maintained by a deliberate »spiritual investment« or »faith.« If love of the world were self-evident and spontaneous, no special religious effort would be necessary.

Gnostic leanings, is known for his hatred of this world—Duns, on the other hand, is the first modern theologian whose nominalism turns our attention away from God and towards the worldly reality. For Augustine, the *directio mundi*—the tendency to »return to the world of appearances,« as Arendt calls it in her unfinished third volume of *The Life of the Mind*, which was to be devoted to the faculty of judgment and which was eventually previewed posthumously as *Lectures on Kant's Political Philosophy*[7]—is precisely what the true piety must denounce as the wrong orientation. Only the wish to know one's immortal soul, and God who created it, hits the mark, but to direct one's interest and curiosity toward the world of fleeting phenomena will always miss the mark and stray from the proper religious concerns. Contrary to this, not only does Duns Scotus not treat our stepping into the world as disorienting or missing something essential; he actually advocates *amor mundi* as the right expression of our love for the Creator, which is to be mediated by the admiration for the creaturely spectacle: the beauty of singular appearances—contingent, transient, capricious, arbitrary, but, in its constant change and self-transformation, constituting a likeness, *tselem*, of the infinite will of God himself. Duns Scotus, therefore, having wrestled with the last powerful system of contemplative Neoplatonism created by Thomas Aquinas, inaugurates the modern secular world, by proposing an affirmative concept of contingency: »I say that contingency is not merely a privation or defect of Being like the deformity which is sin. Rather, contingency is a positive mode of Being, just as necessity is another mode« (quoted in Falque 2016, 127).

The finite contingent worldly being is not a defective result of the Fall or a cosmic error: it is born this way because it was wanted this way. God willed his creation as the constantly moving and changing image of its infinite will and hence gave birth to the world as dynamic: contingent and finite. No chain of mediators weakened the divine light, as in the Neoplatonic system of emanation, which perceives the lowest form of material existence as merely the contemptible by-product of the Fall and subsequent Dispersion. God gave birth to this world directly, straight from his will.

---

7 »Judgment deals with particulars, and when the thinking ego moving among generalities emerges from its withdrawal and returns to the world of particular appearances, it turns out that the mind needs a new ›gift‹ to deal with them. [...] Taste, the discriminating, discerning, judging activity of love of beauty, is the *cultura animi*, the possession of ›a mind so trained and cultivated that it can be trusted *to tend and take care of a world of appearances whose criterion is beauty*‹« (Arendt 1992, 4, 104; my emphasis).

It is precisely the motif of birth which, in Arendt's theological imagination, brings Augustine and Duns Scotus closer to one another. Natality is Arendt's *thema regium*, running like a common thread through all her works, from the doctorate on Augustine's *Liebesbegriff*, through *Human Condition*, up to *Life of the Mind*:

> [T]he decisive fact determining man as a conscious, remembering being is birth or »natality,« that is, the fact that we have entered the world through birth (Arendt 1996, 51). Every man, being created in the singular, is a new beginning by virtue of his birth; if Augustine had drawn the consequences of these speculations, he would have defined men, not, like the Greeks, as mortals, but as »natals« (Arendt 1981b, 109).

Arendt is the first thinker to have developed the *philosophical concept of birth*, and we can safely assume that it was because she was a *woman* thinker, but not just that, a *women Jewish* thinker, tending to read male thinkers of the Western philosophico-theological tradition with a peculiar, female-Marrano, bias. Thus, while in Augustine, the birth defined as *initium* is rather a marginal issue, subservient to his grand theodicy, in Arendt it gains a theoretical autonomy as a new approach to philosophical anthropology: the birth is the properly anthropogenic factor that transforms the biological material into a human conceived as a *natal*.

In Arendt's theological imagination, life is always a *given life*, life transmitted in the act of birth; if she often comes across as hostile to the notion of sheer survival, which she associates only with the biological self-preservation of *animal laborans*, it is only for the sake of supporting a life articulated and maintained by the tradition of life, and not just left to its natural devices. The concept of life as gift shows that, in the words of Arendt's friend, Walter Benjamin, »our coming was expected on earth«[8]: that we are not accidental products of blind natural forces that throw us—as in the biological notion of *der Wurf*, »the throw,« or, for that matter in Heidegger's concept of *Geworfenheit*—into the world. The idea behind natality is that, while natural being is meaningless, our existence *matters* because it was *wanted*; our birth is the result of will turned into love. Hence, once again rereading Augustine towards the end of her life, Arendt defines love as an autotelic activity constituting the last transformation of the Will: »Love is the soul's gravity [...]; there is no greater assertion of something or somebody than to love it, that is, to say: I will that you be—*Amo: Volo ut sis*« (Arendt 1981b, 104). Arendt finds the

8 »Our coming was expected on earth. Like every generation that preceded us, we have been endowed with a *weak* Messianic power, a power to which the past has a claim« (Benjamin 2007, 254).

same variation on the will transformed into love in Duns Scotus, her favorite scholastic:

The willing ego, when it says in its highest manifestation, »*Amo: Volo ut sis*,« »I love you; I want you to be«—and not »I want to have you« or »I want to rule you«—shows itself capable of the same love with which supposedly God loves men, whom He created only because He willed them to exist and whom he *loves without desiring them* (Arendt 1981b, 136).

In her reading of Duns, Arendt once again performs a distinct Marrano clinamen which pushes his nominalist teachings into a positive *directio mundi*. While most of the commentators emphasize the negative moment of the nominalist God's arbitrary and capricious infinite Will whose only justification is *quia voluit*—»because He wanted it that way«—Arendt interprets the Ockhamian *quia voluit* motif outside its traditional Christian context and sees in it not an existential threat to the created reality, but a moment of the highest affirmation. Unlike Kierkegaard, therefore, whom the very idea of the world being totally dependent on the divine will imbues with fear and trembling, Arendt turns the threat of arbitrariness into the blessing of an affirmative »letting-go«: God willed us to exist and let us be—»here-below« in the thickness of our concrete contingent phenomenal being—without »desiring« for us to be anything else.

»Things Are a Mission«: Living, Thinking, Saying

Arendt's metaphysics of appearances culminates in her late concept of self-presentation, according to which all that is alive possesses the narcissistic »urge to self-display [*Selbstdarstellung*]«: while the phenomenal being is already good in its contingent and finite *modus essendi*, life constitutes a self-affirmation to the second power of the worldly manner of existence.[9] In *The Life of the Mind*, Arendt writes:

This instinct is entirely gratuitous in terms of life-preservation; it far transcends what may be deemed necessary for sexual attraction. These findings suggest that the predominance of outside appearance implies, in addition to the sheer receptivity of our senses, a spontaneous activity: *whatever can see wants to be seen, whatever can hear calls out to be heard, whatever*

9 Which, again, may derive from Arendt's reading of Rosenzweig for whom life adds a value of active self-confirmation on the objective goodness of the finite creaturely being (Rosenzweig 2005, 239—240).

> *can touch presents itself to be touched*. It is indeed as though everything that is alive [...] has an *urge to appear*, to fit itself into the world of appearances by displaying and showing, not its »inner self« but itself as an individual (Arendt 1981a, 29).

A certain positive narcissism, therefore, would be the feature of all living beings, already transcending the realm of the simple naturalist *conservatio vitae*: the impulse to show oneself as beautiful, to be acknowledged in existence, and finally—to be loved. This narcissism, however, has nothing to do with an expression of the »inner self«: the self-display is not a partial articulation of some hidden and ineffable *ego absconditus*. The urge to appear pushes every »living surface« into visibility and monstrability and is met by a symmetrical urge of *Seinlassen*: letting-things-be, withdrawing for the sake of an other, making room for her *phaintesthai*; a double-move of life which loves itself and loves others in order to let them be: *amo—volo ut sis*.

The natural vehicle for this kind of love, simultaneously narcissistic and kenotic in its will to let others be, is, for Arendt, language. For Arendt, to be alive is to maintain oneself in the »constant effort to be born,« but not in the naturalist sense: the highest achievement of human—denaturalized—life is *thinking*; here sublimation not only does not indicate renunciation of life, but, to the contrary, realizes life in its fullness, or as Freud would have said it, »without loss« (Freud 1989, 453). Thinking is the true »life of the mind,« one which does not produce knowledge in the scientific understanding of the term, but constantly initiates new ideas; it is the unnatural power of birth made fully operative in the sphere of thoughts, words, and deeds: »With word and deed we insert ourselves into the human world, and this insertion is like a second birth, in which we confirm and take upon ourselves the naked fact of our original physical appearance« (Arendt 1998, 176—177). Just as the »urge to self-display« in all organic living beings already manifests the confirmation of the physical act of being, its sublimated form in thinking takes this confirmation to the even higher—third power—level.

Thus, in a late appreciative essay on her former teacher, »Martin Heidegger at Eighty,« Arendt writes, somewhat against his explicit »thanatic« intentions: »the idea of a *passionate* thinking, in which thinking and being alive become one [...] [and] which rises out of the simple fact of being-born-into-the-world [...] can no more have a final goal [...] than can life itself« (Arendt 2018, 423—424). Her praise of Heidegger, therefore, is qualified: only by annexing him to her concept of being-born-in-the-world (as opposed to his being-*thrown*-in-the-world), which emphasizes the joy of living and thinking fused into one, can she appreciate the intensity of his intellectual passion. As we know from Arendt's critique of Heidegger in *The Life of the Mind*, thinking-without-loving ends in the dead-end of a solitary mind staring mutely at nothingness—while loving-without-thinking, which was the case of Rahel Varnhagen, to whom Arendt devoted her habilitation thesis, ends in a libidinal mess. It is only when living/loving/thinking/saying fuse into one activity that life can celebrate its—at least partial—release from the confines of natural *zoe*, without at the same time indulging in the phantasmatic projections of personal immortality. As if in a polemical inversion of the Anselmian-Cartesian ontological argument, according to which only God himself can imbue the finite mind with the idea of infinite being, Arendt claims otherwise: human life is finite but it is precisely for that reason that it can have a concept of infinity, or, in Kristeva's nice summary: »It is because we are mortal and because we believe we are mortal that we are able to contemplate eternity« (Kristeva 2001, 156). To contemplate eternity, however, is not the same as wanting to appropriate it in the form of immortal life: it is rather—and here Rosenzweig's inspiration comes to the fore once again—to see one's phenomenal existence as *strong*: strong in the sense of Scottian univocity, which attributes the same being to God and his creatures, but also strong in the poetic sense of a *stärkeres Dasein* which lies in the power of language.

According to Arendt, the only thing that can keep us *in between* the paralyzing horror of the mortal doom, which he attributes to the Heideggerian account of human finitude, and the escapist phantasy of immortal life, for which she never stopped blaming Christianity, is *beauty*. Beauty is the defining moment of the ambivalence of all finite being, somewhere between doom and redemption, or rather, in the vertiginous point where they both meet, as in Hölderlin's famous formula. Beauty is a feature of the finite singulars that are given over to time (Rilke's *die Zeit, die zerstörende*), yet, precisely because of that, call for eternalization in their transience; beauty, therefore, can show the world as the horror of death, transience, destruction and, simultaneously, as worth being preserved: caught in the special Moment of innerworldly contemplation and then memorized in language, however imperfectly. As Jim Josefson rightly points out in his highly innovative interpretation of Arendt's thought, the »freedom of the beautiful« does not close its eyes to the horrors of existence—it is neither a simple theodicy nor an equally straightforward condemnation of being, but something that allows us to abide in *this* world. Beauty may thus be a Rilkean »beginning of terror«

in its intimation of the world as inescapably finite and transient, but it also reconciles us with finitude by making it bearable: this is why it »blocks« the escapist flight towards transcendence and always allows one to return to the cave. Beauty plays an essential *pro-cosmic* role.[10]

Beauty, however, does not only reside in the eye of the beholder: while it calls for eternalization, it wants to be preserved and shared through language and its power of saying. Arendt's attitude towards »saying« seems ambivalent, at least in *The Human Condition*: on the one hand, it is a necessary vehicle of giving an ontological stability to a fleeting moment—yet, on the other, it somehow tarnishes the glory of the beautiful experience. Using the foil of the Pauline opposition between spirit and letter, Arendt writes:

> Without remembrance and without reification [...] the living activities of action, speech, and thought would lose their reality [...]. The materialization they have to undergo in order to remain in the world at all is paid for in that always the »dead letter« replaces something which grew out of and for a fleeting moment indeed existed as the »living spirit« (Arendt 1998, 95).

But this ambivalence, dictated by the Pauline dogma, is not the only lens through which Arendt approaches the issue of language: when compared to a »dead letter,« language may indeed seem to weaken the intensity of the living moment, but when seen as a gain in reality, it makes the »living spirit« ontologically *stronger*. In its kenotic willingness to let things be and display themselves (again, *amo: volo ut sis*), it also becomes a matrix of their »second birth.« The truly singular poetic idiom realizes *amor mundi* in letting-things-be in a new way that no one has tried before; in complying with their »urge to self-display« in the singular manner which intensifies their *selbstdarstellende* tendency, by showing what has not yet been shown; and, last but not

10 The only bone of contention between Josefson and me is how we perceive this role. For Josefson, the experience of beauty blocks the very escapist move away from immanence and thus substitutes for the metaphysical desire: »Arendt's entire project rests in the anti-metaphysical claim that being is appearance and the conviction that such being can only be known through a comportment of wonder toward the phenomenality of the world that is essentially aesthetic« (Josefson 2019, 252). I would rather claim that the initial evacuation from the transient world of appearances is inevitable as long as we are thinking beings, but then beauty facilitates a return to the phenomena. But Josefson is right when he writes: »Arendt's point in all this is not just to debunk metaphysics but to *reconnect* thinking to the world of appearances« (ibid., 177; my emphasis), because a tendency to evacuate oneself from the realm of radical contingency constitutes a permanent moment of the »human condition,« so the work of *reconnection* has to be undertaken again and again. In *The Life of the Mind*, Arendt not only criticizes the metaphysics of escape, but offers her own version of a non-escapist metaphysics which indeed involves the »freedom of the beautiful« and the appreciation of appearances through love.

least, in adding to their *phainesthai* the extra-power of demonstration. *Amo: volo ut sis*—is here not just a passive faculty of pure contemplation of alterity; it is an active idiosyncratic force of bringing about what has not yet fully appeared, a maieutic »nursing« of all appearances that are then given a chance of a permanent birthing, the gift of the Augustinian *initio* which allows them to step out from the hopeless natural cycle of becoming and perishing. In this manner language—the loving abode of all phenomena, or, as Kristeva, inspired by Arendt, calls it: »semiotic khora,« itself of »no-essence« (Kristeva 1987, 84)—can also *appear*, i.e. come to the surface in the delight of self-display, despite having nothing to show on its own. The Bloomian »strong poet« lends his strength of creative initiation to things he names, akin to the Whitmanian »Adam early in the morning«: she uses language as though she was naming things for the first time and showing herself in the unique showing of all other beings, not just encountered as singularities but also displaying themselves as such thanks to the poet's idiosyncratic »slant« (Bloom 2015, 68). The power of naming, in which self-love and love for others come into a perfect balance, is the linguistic joy of spreading the unique spectacle of the world; its *phainesthai* to the second power, augmented and intensified in the idiomatic lens. *Amo: volo ut sis*. A reciprocity of a disseminated gift: »As I was talked into being by the loving speech of those who expected me on earth, I let you be.«

Poetry as a means to achieve »stronger existence,« *starkeres Dasein*, which strengthens *both*: things and the poet, emerges as the major theme of the early text of Arendt, co-written with her husband, Günther Stern, on Rilke's *Duino Elegies*, where she muses on the relationship between language and things. If beauty is a call—*Auftrag*, task—the mission of a poet is to give birth to the singularity of each and every thing. Rilke writes:

> Yes, Springs needed you. Many stars
> waited for you to see them. A wave
> that had broken long ago swelled toward you,
> or when you walked by an open window, a violin
> gave itself. All that was your charge.
> But could you live up to it? (Rilke 1977, 7)

On which Arendt comments:

> Things are a mission; [...] the human being actually hangs in the air, un-related to anything. [...] The detour consists in what Rilke calls »rescue« (*Rettung*). The background to this res-

cue is as follows: things are transient and therefore need rescuing. Rescuing is not simply a spontaneously human act, but a task and an urge imparted by things (*drängender Auftrag* […]), and also—and herein consists the detour […]—an »escape« (*Hinüberretten*) into the »stronger existence.« The »other relation« is for Rilke the »unsayable,« but things are capable of being said (»Sind wir vielleicht hier, um zu sagen: Haus, Brücke, Brunnen, Tor, Krug, Obstbaum, Fenster«—[…] »Perhaps we are here in order to say: house, bridge, fountain, gate, pitcher, fruit-tree, window« […]). Rescuing, however, is naming, in other words, preservation from destruction. […] Being extolled basically means being transformed into a stronger being: »aber zu *sagen*, verstehns / o zu sagen, so, wie selber die Dinge niemals / innig meinten zu sein« (»but to *say* them, you must understand, / oh to say them more intensely than the things themselves / ever dreamed of existing«) (Arendt and Stern 2007, 6—7; original emphasis).

This mutual gain of »stronger existence«—both, for the things who now manifest themselves in an undreamt-of novelty and for the poet who talks himself into existence with his »mission«—is the final compensation for the Herderian condition of *Nichtverständigtsein*, »not-being-advised-about-the-world,« which separates man from the animal kingdom of better instructed and less fragile beasts bold enough to see and confront the open with »all their eyes.« The lack of instruction—the »gaping hole,« »emptiness« and »hanging in the air« of the human being destined for permanent neoteny—turns here into a surplus of the linguistic faculty *to say all things* in a way that could not have been intended or anticipated even by God, the supposed creator of the world. In the end, every being shows itself to be a lovable alterity, one of the »countless singulars«: infinite despite being finite.

The idea of language perceived not as a »dead letter« tarnishing the glory of the »living spirit,« but as a power of naming which endows things with a »stronger being,« can be regarded as Arendt's Marrano *clinamen* from the mainstream Paulinism dominating the Western discourse. It is possible that her reflections on Rilke's poetic mission and the rescuing power of naming, offering a »second birth« to things, were also inspired by Rosenzweig's *Star of Redemption*, where love—turned into an *amor mundi*, an intense neighborly love attaching itself to all that exists—operates mostly in poetic language: »it is language which erects the visible bridge from man to that which is not man, to the ›other‹« (Rosenzweig 1999, 80):

The bond of the complete and redemptive tie between man and the world is, at first, the neighbor, only and constantly the neighbor. […] [Love] slides from one carrier to the other, to the one that comes next, from one neighbor to the next neighbor, and it is not at rest before it has made the whole circuit of Creation. But it only apparently surrenders its power to the plural; in reality, it leaves traces of this wandering from place to place by introducing everywhere, into the plural of things, the sign of singularity (Rosenzweig 2005, 252).

This paragraph derives from the long chapter in which Rosenzweig himself wrestles with the Pauline notion of *agape* and—in a gesture precursory to Arendt's treatment of Augustine—tries to give it a more pro-cosmic, worldly spin, oriented towards concrete »neighbors« understood in the radically nominalist manner of *locum tenens*, a *Platzhalter*, which is simply »anything and everything.«[11] Love, transformed in this manner into *amor mundi*, »sows the seeds that are called to give names« (Rosenzweig 2005, 258), thanks to which beings of this world are being born again: taken out of the undifferentiated »plural of things« (ibid., 252) and offered the human gift of *initio* that makes them properly and irreducibly singular. If »things are a mission,« then the mission is accomplished in an act of »saying« that responds to the »call« of phenomenal beauty not only by »preserving« but also by rescuing and augmenting its momental glory.

Conclusion: A Pro-Cosmic Thrust

Both Arendt's reading of Augustine—focusing on natality as the break in the natural cycle of becoming and perishing and ignoring his Neoplatonic acosmic otherworldliness—and her late reading of Scotus bear Marrano features. Despite all the changes and breaks in her intellectual career, one aspect seems to persistently »accompany her work in an unexpressed but not unconscious manner«: a pro-cosmic thrust which she eventually names *amor mundi* and which I see as the defining moment of the modern »Marrano religiosity.« The shift towards the *positive nominalism*, which accentuates the loving and enabling aspect of God's voluntaristic power at the expense of his terrifying and paralyzing arbitrariness, is a move which Arendt shares with other »philosophical Marranos« of her time—Benjamin, Adorno, Jonas, Derrida, all very much concerned to rescue the »honor of the singular name« as precisely the element of the sacred that wandered into the profane, or the Lurianic spark of the divine that found an expression in the world of

11 In that sense, in terms of her innovative take on the nominalist tradition, Rosenzweig can also be regarded as Arendt's precursor. On the notion of *positive nominalism*, see my essay: Bielik-Robson 2014.

appearances. While all the Christian thinkers whom she intensely read and misread (to use Harold Bloom's expression), from Augustine to Heidegger, display a tendency towards *acosmism*, she always finds a way to turn them back from their otherworldly transports and profess an *amor mundi*: »faith and hope for the world.«

Amor mundi is a distinctly and deliberately *theological* term, conceived by Arendt as a counterpart to the traditional concept of *amor Dei*, and it signifies a game-changing transformation occurring in the cryptotheological matrix of modernity: the shift from God to the World. Following Vivian Liska, I claim that Arendt's review of Scholem's *Major Trends in Jewish Mysticism* is not a marginal commission but a text that comes with a revelatory power of what Jacques Derrida, a propos his own »Marrano experience,« calls a *revenant* (see Derrida 2012, 28): an uncanny recognition of what she always knew, »in unexpressed but not unconscious manner.« Thanks to this *nachträglich* recognition, Arendt is confirmed in her theological choice, which she, up till then, had considered too *unheimlich* and idiosyncratic in the acosmic climate of Weimar theology. She thus invents, in consequence, a concept of *amor mundi*, now explicitly directed against the dualistic Christianity of *Theologie der Krise* with which she, despite her theological leanings, could never identify. And for obvious reasons: the rising specter of Marcionism in such leading Weimar theologians as Adolf von Harnack and Karl Barth meant an increase of anti-Judaic sentiments (Jews being perceived by Marcion as the »carnal Israel,« following the illegitimate archon Jehova), while their anti-Hegelian turn, favoring a more Gnostic-dualistic version of Christianity, inevitably ended up in the metaphysical denigration of the worldly realm. What she thus associated with the religion of her times was the very opposite of her own theological intuition, which she could not locate in any existing source, neither orthodox Jewish or Christian—until she read Scholem's account of the Lurianic kabbalah.

But why did Arendt then drop the concept of *amor mundi* and go for a different title of her *magnum opus*—*The Human Condition*? Was it once again a Marrano caution on her part, preferring to hide the theological content which could have been too easily misunderstood? Or, was her »love for the world« greater than her youthful love for theology? Perhaps. Poised between the two possible misunderstandings—the theological interpretation that would inevitably be pushed towards the Christian acosmism, on the one hand, and the purely secular interpretation that would completely ignore her »spiritual investment in this world« on the other—she chose the latter as less harmful. But we don't need to stick to her compromise. The Marrano methodology allows one to read her *amor mundi* precisely in the way she intended it, even if she lacked means to articulate her non-normative and heterodox theological intuition, i.e. as an intense and passionate *faith* in the worldly reality and a *messianic mission* of giving things »stronger existence,« which only such faith could fulfill. We can thus understand better her non-secular secularity or her, only seemingly paradoxical, *theology of worldliness* which invests spiritually in the phenomenal realm, despite all its limitations, in order to avoid an escapist resentment against »everything given«:

> Modern man has come to resent everything given, even his own existence. The alternative to this resentment, which is the psychological basis of contemporary nihilism, would be a fundamental faith in the few elementary things that indeed are invariably given us, such as life itself, the existence of man and the world [...] The stubbornness of reality is relative. *Reality needs us to protect it.*[12]

By claiming that »the stubbornness of reality is relative,« Arendt betrays her adherence to the nominalist tradition, from Duns to Kierkegaard, and not to the pagan concept of the world as the eternal absolute, which she seemingly extols in *The Human Condition*. Yet, in contrast to the Christian nominalists, who delegate the decision of the world's existence solely to the divine will—»If God Himself had not willed repetition, there would never have been a world« (Kierkegaard)—she, in the Marrano-secularizing vein, urges us human subjects to assume the burden of the faith in the world that would sustain and protect its reality, or, in Kant's words, »take care of the world of appearances.« When the World is no longer a correlate of absolute certainty, and God has withdrawn into his otiose hiddenness, only Man remains to take on that task that is simultaneously worldly and messianic.

12 The first part of the epigraph derives from: Arendt 1951, 438; the second from the brief note on the margin of the letter from David Riesman, from the 8th of June 1949, quoted in Young-Bruehl 2004, 254—255; my emphasis.

Hannah Arendt, ca. 1930.
Courtesy of the Hannah Arendt Bluecher Literary Trust / Art Resource, NY.

Works Cited

Arendt, Hannah (1951). *The Burden of Our Time*. London: Secker & Warburg.

Arendt, Hannah (1981a). *Thinking*. In Hannah Arendt. *The Life of the Mind*. Ed. Mary McCarthy. San Diego/New York/London: Harcourt Brace Jovanovich.

Arendt, Hannah (1981b). *Willing*. In Hannah Arendt. *The Life of the Mind*. Ed. Mary McCarthy. San Diego/New York/London: Harcourt Brace Jovanovich.

Arendt, Hannah (1992). *Lectures on Kant's Political Philosophy*. Ed. and interpretive essay Ronald Beiner. Chicago: University of Chicago Press.

Arendt, Hannah (1996). *Love and Saint Augustine*. Ed. and interpretive essay Joanna Vecchiarelli Scott and Judith Chelius Stark. Chicago: University of Chicago Press.

Arendt, Hannah (1998). *The Human Condition*. Second ed. Introduction Margaret Canovan. Chicago: University of Chicago Press.

Arendt, Hannah (2005). *The Promise of Politics*. Ed. Jerome Kohn. New York: Schocken Books.

Arendt, Hannah (2007). Jewish History, Revised. In Hannah Arendt. *Jewish Writings*. Ed. Jerome Kohn and Ron H. Feldman. New York: Schocken Books.

Arendt, Hannah, and Günther Stern (2007). Rilke's *Duino Elegies*. In Hannah Arendt. *Reflections on Literature and Culture*. Ed. Susannah Young-ah Gottlieb. Stanford: Stanford University Press.

Arendt, Hannah, and Gershom Scholem (2010). *Der Briefwechsel*. Ed. Marie Luise Knott, David Heredia. Berlin: Jüdischer Verlag.

Arendt, Hannah (2016). *Denktagebuch 1950—1973*. Ed. Ursula Ludz and Ingeborg Nordmann. München: Piper Verlag.

Arendt, Hannah, and Gershom Scholem (2017). *The Correspondence of Hannah Arendt and Gershom Scholem*. Ed. Marie Luise Knott. Transl. Anthony David. Chicago: The University of Chicago Press.

Arendt, Hannah (2018). Heidegger at Eighty. In Hannah Arendt, *Thinking Without a Banister: Essays in Understanding, 1953—1975*. Ed. and introduction Jerome Kohn. New York: Schocken Books.

Benjamin, Walter (2007). *Illuminations*. Transl. Harry Zohn. Ed. and introduction Hannah Arendt. Preface Leon Wieseltier. New York: Schocken Books.

Bielik-Robson, Agata (2014). The Promise of the Name: »Jewish Nominalism« as the Critique of Idealist Tradition. In Agata Bielik-Robson. *Jewish Cryptotheologies of Late Modernity: Philosophical Marranos*, 233—254. London/New York: Routledge.

Bloom, Harold (2015). *The Deamon Knows: Literary Greatness and the American Sublime*. Oxford: Oxford University Press.

Derrida, Jacques (2012). Avowing—The Impossible. Transl. Gil Anidjar. In Elisabeth Weber (ed.). *Living Together: Jacques Derrida's Communities of Violence and Peace*. New York: Fordham University Press.

Falque, Emmanuel (2016). *Crossing the Rubicon: The Borderlands of Philosophy and Theology*. Transl. Reuben Shank. New York: Fordham University Press.

Freud, Sigmund (1989). Leonardo da Vinci and a Memory of His Childhood. In Sigmund Freud. *The Freud Reader*. Ed. Peter Gay. New York: W.W. Norton & Co.

Josefson, Jim (2019). *Hannah Arendt's Aesthetic Politics: Freedom and the Beautiful*. Cham, Switzerland: Palgrave Macmillan.

Kristeva, Julia (1987). *Tales of Love*. Transl. Leon S. Roudiez. New York: Columbia University Press.

Kristeva, Julia (2001). *Hannah Arendt*. Transl. Ross Guberman. New York: Columbia University Press.

Leibovici, Martine (2000). La tradition cachée chez Hannah Arendt: un nouvel avatar du marranisme?. *Pardes*, 29, 187—204.

Liska, Vivian (2017). *German-Jewish Thought and Its Afterlife: A Tenuous Legacy*. Bloomington: Indiana University Press.

Raz-Krakotzkin, Amnon (2001). Binationalism and Jewish Identity: Hannah Arendt and the Question of Palestine. In Steven Aschheim (ed.). *Hannah Arendt in Jerusalem*, 165—180. Berkeley: University of California Press.

Rilke, Rainer Maria (1977). *Duino Elegies and the Sonnets to Orpheus*. Trans. A. Poulin, Jr. Boston, MA: Houghton Mifflin Co.

Rosenzweig, Franz (1999). *Understanding the Sick and the Healthy: A View of World, Man, and God*. Transl. Nahum Glatzer. Cambridge, MA: Harvard University Press.

Rosenzweig, Franz (2005). *The Star of Redemption*. Transl. Barbara Galli. Madison: University of Wisconsin Press.

Scholem, Gershom (1976). *On Jews and Judaism in Crisis: Selected Essays*. Ed. Werner Dannhauser. New York: Schocken Books.

Taubes, Jacob (2004). *The Political Theology of Paul*. Transl. Dana Hollander. Stanford, Calif.: Stanford University Press.

Young-Bruehl, Elisabeth (2004). *Hannah Arendt: For Love of the World*. New Haven/London: Yale University Press.

Yovel, Yirmiyahu (1989). *Spinoza and Other Heretics: The Marrano of Reason*. Princeton, N.J.: Princeton University Press.

Yovel, Yirmiyahu (2009). *The Other Within: The Marranos: Split Identity and Emerging Modernity*. Princeton, N.J.: Princeton University Press.

Part II: Encounters With Theology

Between Adamite Dreams and Original Sin: Hannah Arendt's Cryptic Heterodoxy?

Rafael Zawisza

»Was mir fremd ist, ist die Immanenz«—with these words, Hannah Arendt described her perception of Baruch Spinoza's philosophy.[1] They come from a lost letter written to Karl Jaspers in the late summer of 1949. They were preserved because Jaspers quoted this sentence in his reply from the 1st of September of that year (Arendt and Jaspers 1985, 176). The disagreement about Spinoza permeated their letters from that time, with Jaspers dramatically defending the philosopher and praising him »as one of the few human beings and thinkers whose existence is like a guarantee that there is something good in human beings after all«[2] (Arendt and Jaspers 1992, 139), and Arendt adamantly retaining her »mistrust, even towards the tranquility«[3] (ibid., 142), which is the indelible hallmark of Spinoza's image.

For a thinker regarded as persistently secular, the phrase »what is alien to me is the immanence« (ibid., 140) must sound incongruent with her whole post-war work that was devoted to the worldly realm of human affairs and politics and very much *not* to a transcendent God. By employing a cryptotheological perspective, I do not intend to deny that Hannah Arendt was primarily a secular thinker; but, at the same time, this methodology allows me to claim that hers was a secularism deriving from theological sources.[4] Thus,

1 English: »What is alien to me is the immanence.« The initial idea of reading Hannah Arendt's early work in the context of Carl Schmitt's theories from the 1920s was presented on the 18th of November, 2015, during a seminar entitled *Thank God We Are Creatures: Hannah Arendt Versus Political Theology* at the Institute for Human Sciences in Vienna where I was a Józef Tischner fellow at that time. Since then, I incorporated the discoveries made during my stay in Austria into my doctoral research project (financed by the National Science Centre, Poland, grant no. 2016/20/T/HS1/00244), and I largely revised the previous perspective. I want to express my gratitude to Manuela Kölke and Mark Farrier whose insightful comments on the manuscript and editorial experience enabled me to improve the essay and rethink terminological dilemmas concerning translations.

2 Jaspers to Arendt, August 4th, 1949.

3 Arendt to Jaspers, September 29th, 1949.

4 Agata Bielik-Robson writes that »cryptotheology« can be seen as the discursive »instantaneous bilingualism« that uses »the special *slant* of Jewish religious thinking« for »non-religious purposes,« and yet, by pointing at the world's »ontological insufficiency,« cryptotheological thought

it complicates the question of the origin and legitimacy of the secular world. I claim that the separation of politics from religion and, consequently, the immanence of a human plurality from any transcendent origin, cannot be fully understood without reference to Arendt's doctoral dissertation, *Der Liebesbegriff bei Augustin* (1929). In that work, she lays the foundations for her later political anthropology, and here we can observe the moment when her departure from Western ontotheology begins to make space for an irreducible human plurality composed of enigmatic singularities. Her dissertation is also the locus where her natalist reorientation of philosophy takes place, even though she had not yet formulated the concept of *Gebürtlichkeit* as such.

This text is thus a prelude for rethinking the Arendtian legacy and reflecting on a question that has been lingering since the *Denktagebuch* was first published in 2002: If it is true that Arendt cut ties with theology at an early age[5] and remained a secular thinker throughout her life, why then did she, in her »thought journal« entries during the 1950s, constantly revive a theological imagination and return to the concept of God in order to theorize about politics and human diversity? In her *Introduction into Politics*—which should have exhibited her absolute commitment to the worldly realm—why does God appear in the second sentence as *the negative* from which the image of humanity emerges? There she states that »[p]olitics is based on the fact of human plurality. God created *man*, but *men* are a human, earthly product, the product of human nature« (Arendt 2005, 93; original emphasis).

---

emphasizes »the need for redemption« (Bielik-Robson 2014, 4, 24; my emphasis). We will see how Arendt's secular orientation is empowered by that peculiar slant.

5 Samuel Moyn writes about »Arendt's youthful flirtation with theology« and her »later turn to the secular« (Moyn 2008, 71). In my essay, I contest Moyn's interpretation of *Der Liebesbegriff* (Moyn 2005, 77—87) by claiming that since Arendt never actually embraced a theological discourse, there was, consequently, no need to give up on it. To the contrary, Arendt's secularized reading of theology made possible a passage into secularity via cryptotheology. I insist on the fact that Arendt contrabanded her »crypto-theological ethics,« as Moyn calls it, into her later philosophy, but it then went through the second secularizing »retouch« in order to be genuinely *universal*—according to the demand posed in *Der Liebesbegriff*. Using Moyn's own locution, one may say that his intention to present »mature« Arendt as a purely secular thinker results in ignoring the complexity of Arendt's early philosophical project. Paradoxically, Moyn reads the early Arendt in complete accord with Catholic interpreters, who never cease to stress her indebtedness to Augustine, her »humble« (see ibid., 82) acceptance of Christianity and its dualistic ethics (ibid., 80—81, 84).

***

The logic of Arendt's thought in *Der Liebesbegriff* is the following: in the first two chapters, she argues that is not the individual confrontation with death (oriented towards salvation and very similar to the Heideggerian *Sein-zum-Tode*) or the individual search for the ultimate origin (oriented towards creation) that enables the development of worldly ties with one's neighbors. Hence, in the third chapter entitled »Vita socialis,« Arendt observed that there must be a conceptual chiasmus connecting an individual to common life and found the germ of that bond in birth. Natalist reorientation relocates the individual in the vast horizon of generational interconnectedness.

A constant concern of early Arendt is that the social bond lacks reliability if it is grounded in God or in the cosmos, in other words, in something which is not tangible enough. Another of her arguments against divine legitimacy of any worldly community is that the only analogue of the divine absoluteness in the human world is to be found in the absolute inwardness of the individual facing God (or death). When facing ultimate things, »every original relationship had been forgotten along with the self [*jede ursprüngliche Bezogenheit in der Selbstvergessenheit mitvergessen war*, 75[6]]« (Arendt 1996, 98). Arendt notices that confronting a human creature directly with the source of Life—»referring back [*Rückbezug*, 75]« (ibid., 98) to God—means the total isolation (*Isoliertheit*) (Arendt 1929, 75) of the individual and this confrontation always leads to »self-denial [*Selbstverleugnung*, 75]« (Arendt 1996, 98), in which the true relevance of the neighbor is lost as well. The traditionalist view would still insist on the centrality of God, underlining that the problem is with the fallen nature of man. Arendt, instead, suggests that those realities—God and the world—were not meant to be compatible.[7] The doctrine of original sin only retroactively justifies something which was more original. The lesson from the paradise lost can be, then, that bringing absoluteness back to human affairs can only result in further destruction.[8]

6 Note that whenever only page numbers appear in this way following the German original in square brackets, it always refers to the first edition of Arendt's dissertation (Arendt 1929).

7 In this sense, what for Karl Barth was a dramatic abyss, was for Arendt just a matter of fact. I agree, then, with Jim Josefson's perspective (see his essay in this volume), that Arendt domesticated the abyss hollowed-out by the dialectical theologians—this abyss is the world.

8 »[I]n the realm of human affairs sovereignty and tyranny are the same« (Arendt 1990, 153). In January 1951, Arendt wrote in her notebooks that European political theories wrongly followed the model of God the Almighty, whereas political thinking should have as its premise the impossibility of omnipotence, which is already ruled out by way of human plurality (Arendt 2016, I, 54).

The concept of God—because of its connection to creatureliness and origins—remains operative in Arendtian speculation, unlike the religious faith, which, especially in its Christian elaboration, leads towards »the inner dialectics of faith« (ibid., 99). That is why Arendt, in order to avoid the contradictions characteristic of inwardness, seeks for another »origin [*Ursprung*]« in a »ganz losgelösten Erfahrungszusammenhang« (Arendt 1929, 75), which is rendered in the English translation as »empirical context, different in origin« (Arendt 1996, 98). It is a rather bizarre kind of empirical data, one which demands acknowledging the fact that all humans have a common descent. Although this fact is tangible, it is rarely accepted as *the* overriding political principle.

To make the common origin of humankind central, it is necessary to rearrange thinking and refocus attention away from classical metaphysics and its conception of the hierarchy of beings. This re-location of theology and philosophy can be traced back to Franz Rosenzweig, who once defined revelation as »orientation«; this word also appears in *Der Liebesbegriff*, where Arendt uses »beobachtende Orientierung« (Arendt 1929, 75) to describe how (Judeo-)Christian revelation changes the basic perception of one's neighbors. This German term becomes slightly diluted in the English translation: »by observation we can define the society of believers [...]« (Arendt 1996, 98). The word *beobachten* very specifically refers to the point of observation. In this spirit Arendt asks: »Von welchem Blickpunkt aus wird das pure Zusammen der Gläubigen zu einer fides communis, d. h. zu einer Gemeinsamkeit des Glaubens selber, die sich mit allen Menschen verbrüdert (jeder ist der Nächste) auch mit dem Ungläubigen?«[9] (Arendt 1929, 76). At this crucial moment *Blickpunkt*, or »point of view,« is less noticeable in the English translation.[10] The specific relatedness to others that comes from a traumatic encounter requires a certain orientation. Arendt regards the Christian type of revelation as something that alienates one from the world, whereas that of Judaism has secured a necessary »harbor.« A philosophy oriented towards »a pre-existing reality in the world« (Arendt 1996, 98) must work through the human experience as its fertile ground. This reality, realness of the world was sought for by Arendt from »the common ground of experience [*Erfah-*

9 English translation: »How does the mere concurrence of believers turn into a common faith, that is, into a community of faith itself that regards all people, even unbelievers, as brothers, since everyone is my neighbor?« (Arendt 1996, 99).

10 It returns in the next paragraph as »the difference in viewpoint [*die Differenz des Blickpunktes*, 76]« (Arendt 1996, 99).

rungsgrundlage, 76]« (ibid., 99), forming a kind of tunnel leading through »a historically pre-existing reality [*eine geschichtlich vorgegebene Realität*, 76]« (ibid., 99) to »the factuality of history [*die Faktizität der Geschichte*, 77] and to the past as such« (ibid., 99), which is ultimately anchored in »Adam,« that is, in the common origin of humankind.

An Overcoming of Original Sin

I claim that Arendt's praise of natality and human plurality had already begun in her doctoral dissertation. Seen in this perspective, her philosophical anthropology cannot be assimilated by contemporary biopolitical discourse because Arendt's vitalism is not an unquestioning embrace of the immanence of the self-regenerating process of life and death. Arendtian natalism emphasizes the way that every human birth brings to the world its own relative transcendence, that human action, whose novelty is ontologically rooted in the fact of birth (Arendt 1958b, 247), interrupts the natural cycle of becoming, and that »man's ›nature‹ is only ›human‹ insofar as it opens up to man the possibility of becoming something highly unnatural, that is, a man [*die ›Natur‹ nur insofern ›menschlich‹ ist, als sie es dem Menschen freistellt, etwas höchst Unnatürliches, nämlich ein Mensch zu werden*[11]]« (Arendt 1979, 455). In contrast, »the ever-recurrent cyclical movement of nature [...], where no beginning and no end exist« (Arendt 1958b, 96) renders birth and death *exchangeable* as the two extremities of life. For Arendt, however, human birth disturbs the cycle, becoming its internal counterpoint because even if death—taking into account a purely chronological perspective—ultimately has the last word, it is the messianic power of natality during a lifespan that can prevail and alter the linear perspective. Moreover, it is exactly through the overcoming of original sin that Arendt saves the non-sovereign transcendence[12] of human life within the natural life, which itself remains the epitome of absolute immanence.

Although Arendt describes *Der Liebesbegriff* as an »attempt at an inquiry of purely philosophical interest« (Arendt 1996, 6), she nonetheless brings to it

11 See Arendt 1958a, 248.

12 It is as early as 1930 that Arendt in her review of Karl Mannheim's *Ideologie und Utopie* defended »philosophy's transcendence« (Arendt 1994, 30), arguing that transcendence is not identical with absoluteness, especially in the case of human transcendence within nature.

theological material, extracting from it what belongs to the »pretheological sphere« (ibid., 5), which I identify with an anthropological potentiality prior to any religion yet that upon which every religion was built. Arendt also intervened in theological and theologico-political debates of her time, even if she refrained from direct polemics in her dissertation.[13] Arendt's voice is confusing: her distance from Christianity can be understood as coming from her secularity, her Jewishness, and her heterodoxical Marrano religiosity. She presented a *cryptotheological critique of Christianity* as the apparent overcoming of Judaism, but it is also an overcoming of Christianity. It was necessary for her to operationalize that because Christianity suppressed natality by monopolizing its significance and limiting it to the divine figure of Jesus, whereas in Arendt's *heterodox secularity* the fact of birth shines with its own glory.[14]

Arendt wanted to remove »originally alien contexts« (ibid., 98) from Augustine's work; it is clear throughout the dissertation that her intention was to detach the Judeochristian message from »the Hellenization of Christianity« (to use Adolf von Harnack's term), namely the dependence of Christian theology on Graeco-Roman philosophy. For that reason, Arendt is skeptical about the notion of *physis* and so distances herself from the Stoic concept of natural law (ibid., 5).[15] Any such cosmic scale »degrades« the »concrete uniqueness« of the neighbor due to a »sublime indifference regardless of what or who he is« (ibid., 43). This also occurs when the love of the neighbor is mediated through and depends on God. When Arendt deploys her main argument against metaphysics, she claims that this and other obstacles are created by the overestimated concept of *summum bonum*, God as the highest good (ibid., 44). She sees the greatest mistake of traditional metaphysics as being its vision of God, which she regards as having a false premise. Consequently, this conception of God creates, quite logically,[16] the only imagined

13 The subtlety of Arendt's stance is overlooked by Peter Eli Gordon who claims that she did not participate in the debates about political theology (Gordon 2007, 856—857).

14 For a reading of natality as a concept relating to Jewish and Christian themes, see my text: Zawisza 2020.

15 Her view on the matter seems to be consistent with her later thought because, in a brief note on Marx from December 1952, it is implicit that, for her, the notion of »human nature« has lost its foundation when the ancient cosmology collapsed with the beginning of the modern age: »The nature of humankind is, for the young Marx, simply a human nature. [...] As if he still believed in the Cosmos!« (Arendt 2016, I, 274) (my translation).

16 Not making any claim about the link between religion and totalitarianism, one can wonder whether Arendt's early deconstruction of Christian theology did not give her an ability to discern analogous structures in their operativity. In *The Origins* she calls the totalitarian type of reasoning »the

relation of human beings to God, namely, one of obedience, subservience, order, and hierarchy. This *ordo* of Being, which Arendt simply mocked in *Der Liebesbegriff*, was legitimized through Neoplatonism and later incorporated by Thomism.

With the concept of original sin, this hierarchical metaphysics became merged with a Manichaean perception of existence as evil and with the tragic Greek notion of life, according to which death is the just retribution for birth, for coming-into-being.[17] There can be an infinite debate about the subtleties of the concept of original sin, but all in all, it means that »man is responsible for all that is bad in the world« (Blumenberg 1985, 53). Hans Blumenberg analyzed the concept from the standpoint of philosophical anthropology, pointing out its »crudity« (ibid., 135) and vulgar dualism: man must be evil so that God can be absolutely good. Original sin was used to explain not only the fallibility of human nature, but also the cruelty and violence encountered in nature. Blumenberg writes:

> According to the exemplary conception developed by Augustine, the physical defects of the created world are simply the just penalties for the evil that proceeded from human freedom. […] To be sure, the converted Gnostic had to provide an equivalent for the cosmic principle of evil in the bosom of mankind itself (ibid., 53).

Blumenberg claims that the driving force of Augustine's speculations is »his Gnostic trauma« (ibid., 54), namely a haunting thought that God might, at least to some extent, comprise the root of evil (a thought that Jewish kabbalists speculated about). However, Augustine did not prove that God is just, on the contrary, he always used the absolute goodness of God as the initial and unquestionable »premise« (ibid., 133). The whole Augustinian acrobatics with concepts, both his dialectic and rhetoric were employed »in order to close this gap« (ibid., 133—134) created by the shadow of the evil God. Blumenberg even claims that the concept of freedom, as such secondary for Augustine, was created because of »the problem of the justification of

systems of paranoiacs,« in which »everything follows comprehensibly and even compulsorily once the first premise is accepted. The insanity of such systems lies not only in their first premise but in the very logicality with which they are constructed. The curious logicality of all isms, their simple-minded trust in the salvation value of stubborn devotion without regard for specific, varying factors, already harbors the first germs of totalitarian contempt for reality and factuality« (Arendt 1979, 457—458).

17 Agata Bielik-Robson has written a very profound analysis of the modern Jewish protest against the tragic Greek paradigm haunting European philosophies of life, elucidating it through the opposition of »individuation *as* sin versus individuation *through* Sin.« See especially her essay about Hermann Cohen in Bielik-Robson 2014.

God« and was »accomplished at the expense of man« (ibid., 133). Hence, there is no »pathos of human responsibility for the world« (ibid., 134), even if the hyper-moralistic concept of original sin carries the potential for it. This is not because the damage is conceived of as being so irreparable that the only solution given to humankind other than salvation is to obey the hierarchical powers who are responsible for suppressing what is regarded as dangerous: freedom, spontaneity, novelty, and unpredictability. Those qualities, together with goodness, became reserved only for God and the earthly sovereigns, which creates another problem—that of metaphysical and political »terror« (ibid., 135).

Arendt's rejection of the Stoic concept of nature parallels Blumenberg's observation that the Stoic »concept of providence, although foreign to the biblical world of ideas, is assimilated as theological property and made into an essential anti-Gnostic principle« (ibid., 132). The absoluteness of God, or cosmos, or nature, all result in aporias and contradictions on the anthropological level, because humans have to pay the price for theodicy. As already mentioned, Arendt openly admits that the whole problem with the (in)significance of the neighbor in Christianity lies in the concept of God as *summum bonum* (Arendt 1996, 44), the concept which became dogma for Augustine in order to provide a solid barrier against the Gnostic trauma.

When God is no longer at the center of theological reflection and when the notion of God is unburdened from the Greek philosophical vision of the absolute, then one can dismantle the crude dualisms dominating Augustinian thought, where »there are always, in fact, only the two cities—the good and the bad, the one based in Christ and the one based in Adam. In a similar sense, there are but two loves: love of self (or the world) [*amor mundi bzw. sui*] and the love of God [*amor Dei*, 79]« (ibid., 102). This moralistic blackmail is visible in a quote from Augustine's *The City of God*, where he posed the two alternatives: either one feels »contempt for God« or »contempt for self« (ibid., 102, footnote 19.).[18]

Arendt's philosophical revolution—elevating natality over mortality—was preceded by the shift from »God« to the »world,« which coincided with reconfiguring the conceptual constellation in anthropology. Instead of

18 This and other outcomes of Arendt's deconstruction can be easily understood through psychotheology, elaborated by Eric Santner, whose description of Frank Rosenzweig's project fits perfectly to the aim of *Der Liebesbegriff*: for it is a »therapy for metaphysical thinking,« which clears the path for »the possibility of truly inhabiting the *midst of life*« (Santner 2001, 55, 129; original emphasis).

negating or reversing Augustinian thought, Arendt decided to present her own vision of humanity on the same canvas that he did. It is as if she painted over some parts so that God faded away into the background, and because of this, the contours of creaturely silhouettes were sharpened, like in a still life, where fruits and bodies are exposed as flesh.

The flesh of the world is grasped through literalness; hence it is the real act of human birth to which Arendt refers.[19] For Arendt, human birth is endowed with a gravity not lesser than for Augustine, but whereas for him the transmission of life was the channel for original sin,[20] for Arendt, it is »the miracle of being« (Arendt 1979, 469)[21] or »the great mystery« (Arendt 1958b, 10), as she introduced the concept of natality for the first time in *The Human Condition*. It is no coincidence that she refers to Augustine at the very beginning of the book, evoking his phrase *grande profundum* to underpin the highest significance of birth.

The »sudden turn« in *Der Liebesbegriff* is expressed in the language of an Adamite heterodoxy:

> In the society founded [*gegründet*] on Adam man has made himself independent [*unabhängig*] of the Creator. He depends on [*angewiesen*] other persons and not on God. The human race [*genus humanum*] as such originates in Adam and not in the Creator. It has come to be by generation and relates to its source [*Ursprung*] only through all its generations. [...] The world's independence from God [*die Unabhängigkeit dieser Welt von Gott*] rests on

19 Trying to capture Arendt's moment of literalness, I build on Sigrid Weigel's essay on the topic of *Buchstäblichkeit* in Benjamin and Arendt, where Weigel points at the »corporeality and figurativeness of language« as well as at the »physical-spatial dimension of meaning.« The force of Arendt's »linguistic gestures,« as Weigel calls them, comes from the oscillation between what is specific and what is conventional, see Weigel 2014, 305—306.

20 Arendt says that it is through birth that original sin comes into the world (Arendt 1996, 102) although footnote 20 on the same page indicates that she knew that, for Augustine, reproduction was sinful. This demonstrates that she skipped the dogmatic content and focused on its result: the denigration of birth.

21 This phrase appears unexpectedly in the closing chapter of the second edition of *The Origins* (1958) entitled »Ideology and Terror.« Unlike in the first edition (1951) where the remembrance of the Shoah was at the center, Arendt found this time a fully positive response to the totalitarian threat: the radical philosophy of birth. »Ideologie und Terror« was published in Germany in 1953, but Arendt started to work on it during the summer of 1950 (see Young-Bruehl 2004, 251). In the fragment, Arendt clearly uses the critical language deriving from *Der Liebesbegriff*: »Ideologies are never interested in the miracle of being. They are historical, concerned with becoming and perishing, with the rise and fall of cultures, even if they try to explain history by some ›law of nature‹« (Arendt 1979, 469).

historicity, that is, on mankind's own origin, which possesses its own legitimacy[22] [*in dem eigenen Ursprung der Menschheit, der seine eigene Legitimation hat*, 81]. The world's sinfulness derives from its origin independent of God (Arendt 1996, 103).

Arendt tries to distill here a philosophical anthropology, or what Hans Blumenberg called *Beschreibung des Menschen*, which is present in Augustine if one can forget for a moment about God, creation and salvation. However, it does not mean that this gesture is simply a non- or anti-religious reading, or a secularization. It is rather an example of philosophical Marranism that continues Franz Rosenzweig's *Neues Denken*, a thinking that oscillates between religion and nihilism. Arendt not only extracted secular meaning from theological narrative, but also intervened with her own understanding of it. Its Judaizing effect is visible in the way it opposes the Christian tradition, which sees in the Fall a purely negative occurrence: the destruction of the divine order. Moreover, Arendt rescues plurality from an equally negative judgment by »reminding« Augustine that the Fall, if read literally, »only« brought about a state of life where giving birth becomes labor and human beings are mortal. The act of procreation, the generational transmission of life, and life as such given through birth—contrary to what Augustine claims—are not touched by any corruption, except natural decay.

What Arendt achieves through her »dialectic dualism«[23] is the firm separation of God and world, but this is also present in many Christian thinkers from Augustine to Karl Barth and on. What truly distinguishes Arendt's vision is that she legitimizes this separation in the form of a chiasmus: through generations, humans still perpetuate the luminous newness from before the Fall, but since it now occurs in the earthly realm, every individual searching for the source of life first refers back to their birth and then to the non-divine origin in Adam. This way the Fall loses its status as the only anthropogenic caesura, giving up its place to other caesuras: abandoning the realm of nature by humankind (first couple) and abandoning the mother's womb by an infant (every birth).

22 Compare her argumentation from *On Revolution*: »What saves the act of beginning from its own arbitrariness is that it carries its own principle within itself« (Arendt 1990, 212).

23 This interpretative category was proposed and tested by Agata Bielik-Robson in her first study presenting *messianic vitalism* as a theoretical perspective that elucidates the innovative presence of Jewish thinking in contemporary philosophy (Bielik-Robson 2012). For a revised English version, see Bielik-Robson 2019.

The Community of Fate

Despite Hans Jonas' dismissive opinion about Arendt's dissertation being apolitical,[24] I claim that her anthropological understanding of »the pretheological sphere« can be strongly associated with her grounding idea for the conception of human rights. In 1951 she wrote:

> The Rights of Man can be implemented only if they become *the prepolitical foundation* of a new polity, the prelegal basis of a new legal structure, the, so to speak, *prehistorical fundament* from which the history of mankind will derive its essential meaning in much the same way Western civilization did from its own *fundamental origin myths*[25] (Arendt 1951, 439; my emphasis).

To speak about the radical equality of all human beings and about the one origin of mankind was far from being an apolitical declaration in the Weimar Republic in 1928,[26] when racist ideologies spread the pseudo-scientific theories aimed precisely at destroying what Arendt wanted to legitimize. The unyielding universalism of her natalist anthropology was also provocative because Arendt adapted and »demilitarized« into her own texts notions that, at that time, had immense resonance among the extreme right.[27] For instance, she speaks about the human race, but without racial prejudices; she warned, like the Weimar critics of modernity, of wordlessness (*Entfremdung von der Welt*) (Arendt 1929, 84) and she referred to *Heimat* as a remedy, but *Heimat* for her did not mean the German Reich but the whole world, *In-der-Welt-sein* (ibid., 83, 87), it meant *doppelte Vertrautheit* (ibid., 81), a familiarity both with the world and a distant origin, *Ursprung*.

If original sin can still have some universal significance, independent of any religious creed, it is to be found in an »Aufeinanderangewiesensein[28] des ganzen genus humanum« (ibid., 81), the necessary (*notwendig*) and fateful

24 »My dissertation topic, gnosticism, was potentially a thousand times more political than Hannah Arendt's, the concept of love in Augustine« (Jonas 2008, 70). Jonas continues: »A comparable example might be the early Christians, who turned their backs on the world or went into the desert to escape the world and to seek to perfect themselves in direct contact with God—that was philosophy for Hannah Arendt« (ibid., 69).

25 The quote appears in »Concluding Remarks«, which in the second edition were replaced by »Ideology and Terror«.

26 The year of Hannah Arendt's doctoral defense.

27 Martin Jay's recognition of Arendt's place in the Weimar era overlooks her critical stance and sometimes leads him to make simplifying parallels of her position with fascist thinkers as well as identifying Arendt with decisionism (Jay 1985).

28 Arendt would later return to this notion in her *Denktagebuch*, see Arendt 2016, I, 26, 38.

(*schicksalhaft*) bond of interdependence, which cannot be undone. Because of mortality, human beings are united into a *Schicksalsgenossenschaft* (ibid., 87), a community of fate. Unlike Heidegger, for whom death is a strictly solitary phenomenon, Arendt perceives death as one of the things that *might* unite people. Because of mortality she defines man as *kreatürliches Sein* and *Gefährdetsein* (ibid., 87), a creaturely and endangered being. Neither death nor the simple unity of God are enough to ground human solidarity (ibid., 76). That is why Arendt decided that birth can better explain the non-autarkic nature of every individual (*Unmöglichkeit der völligen Isolierung des Einzelnen*) (ibid., 84).

As we can see, from the dogmatic statement that the human being »is sinful prior to any free choice« (Arendt 1996, 103), Arendt understood that »sin« obviously has to have a different meaning than personal guilt. Thus, the philosophical sublation of sinfulness into *Miteinandersein* (Arendt 1929, 78) serves to protect and strengthen the twofoldness (*Doppeldeutigkeit*) of human beings as a »mixed multitude«[29] which she calls *Vermischtsein*[30] (ibid., 87): freedom is protected together with, and not against, rootedness.[31] The prospect of death annihilates both, that's why the true anchor of vitalism is the concept of natality. Each birth reminds any other human being (*Mensch*) about the »nur ihm eigenen Ursprunghaftigkeit,« the exceptional relation of humankind to its origins (ibid., 81). Arendt's task is to find the obligatory bond that is inherent in the rooted, earthly existence of humanity, in its »essential social ties with humankind [*dem notwendigen Verwurzeltsein in der societas des genus humanum*, 80]« (Arendt 1996, 102). The lesson of Christianity is that freedom (as transcendence) enables a certain (potentially absolute) distance from the world. But whereas for Augustine it is the point of departure towards salvation, in Arendt this transcendence turns these necessary

29 The term derives from Paweł Maciejko's magnificent study about the Frankists (Maciejko 2011). Maciejko regains contemporary usefulness of the concept of »mixed multitude« (*erev rav*) from the context of the fierce, internal debates about Jewish identity.

30 One can only speculate if this is another polemical, metapolitical statement in Arendt's argumentation, which is seemingly so apolitical. If we take into account that the verb *vermischen* refers to intermarrying among different ethnic groups, and that the word *Mischling* means not only »mongrel,« but »a person of mixed parentage« (which became a dismissive category among the German fascists and then in the Nazi legal vocabulary where it especially referred to the so-called *Halbjuden* or *Vierteljuden*), we can see how critical it was to claim that *every* human being is a *Mischling*, in a way that, without negating it, predates and *transcends* any ethnic origin. If the paradigm of *transcendence-within-immanence* has a strictly political meaning, it is exactly when the Judeochristian »glad tidings« tend to unequivocally annul racism at its core.

31 Arendt later formulated this as the paradox of freedom ontologically rooted in the biological act of birth.

bonds into *freely chosen ones*, so that the individual can truly be rooted (*verwurzelt sein*), otherwise living *with* and *for* each other (*ein Mit- und Füreinander der Menschen*) would be replaced by simply living *next* to each other (*ein einfaches Nebeneinander*) (Arendt 1929, 77).

Arendt stresses many times in »Vita socialis« that humanity's common ancestry is something from which there is no escape; to express that, she uses the German verb *entziehen* (ibid., 77), meaning »to avoid,« »to evade something.« Here lies the obliging force of the Adamite provenance, not overcome by Christianity: »Death shows that the past has not been eradicated by salvation. Mortality remains the common fate« (Arendt 1996, 107).[32] In the same way, it is essential that the equality of human beings—as interconnected and mortal—is an irrevocable fact which »exists« (ibid., 100). In German it is expressed more radically: this equality *besteht* (Arendt 1929, 77)—it remains, it perpetuates itself, it survives, just like original sin.

We can't be sure whether this tone of voice was directed against Carl Schmitt or just against the general political mood of the Weimar Republic at the time, that is, its potent trends promising a new world *ex nihilo*. However, it is clear that in the late 1920s Arendt wanted to limit decisionism by using the notions of *Herkunft* (heritage) and *Bestimmung* (vocation, fate, determination) (ibid., 77). The chain of generations can help in guarding against the radical delegitimization of all obligations, since the earthly community is »a society from and with the dead« (Arendt 1996, 103) and those generational ties are for life, *without exception*. Her crucial argument against decisionism says that *civitas terrena* »is not arbitrarily founded [*willkürlich gesetzt*] and not arbitrarily dissolved [*aufhebbar*, 77]« (ibid., 100), but is grounded (*begründet*) (Arendt 1929, 77) in the common Adamite descent, which is characterized as self-evident (*selbstverständlich*) and explicit (*ausdrücklich*) (ibid., 81, 80).

32 It is politically relevant that Arendt underlines the inerasable dependence of Christianity on Judaism and locates the true origin of universalism not in the Christian »faith« but in the pre-historical »past« of Genesis: »For the neighbor's relevance is not tied to Christianity. The binding power of the common faith in Christ is secondary. Faith in Christ redeems the past and only the common past can make the faith a common faith. The past alone is common to all« (Arendt 1996, 107). In this Judaizing reading of Christianity, we can exactly see what Agata Bielik-Robson calls »the Marrano strategy« whose goal, among others, is »to oppose the widespread ›supersessionist‹ prejudice of Jewish anachronism« (Bielik-Robson 2014, 30). Arendt's insistence that *Christianity is always a Judeochristianity* indicates how aware she must have been of the danger of the radically Marcionite (anti-Judaic) understanding of Christianity, refashioned by Karl Barth and Friedrich Gogarten. The intellectual background of the theological debates of that time was very inventively depicted by Benjamin Lazier although the author did not include Hannah Arendt among the interlocutors (see Lazier 2008).

For this reason, I do not share Samuel Moyn's worry that Arendt, by speaking about »the divinity of birth as such« (Arendt 1990, 211),

> finds something religious, one might say, in the very secularity she prizes. Like the language of political miracle that Schmitt targeted, this appeal to the divinity of birth fits ambiguously, and perhaps conflicts flagrantly, with Arendt's more basic attempt to strive for a purely secular politics. Does this last fact then wreck any attempt to present Arendt as a secularist? Might it even show that whatever her fervent hopes of transcending political theology, the latter must always—as Schmitt originally suggested—have the final word (or last laugh)? (Moyn 2008, 96).[33]

Moyn overlooks that if Arendt praises any miracles, back in the 1920s and later, she always spoke about those »within the reach of man« (Arendt 1958b, 247). Her characterization of Christianity in »Vita socialis« is full of reservations because even if Christian revelation offered the highest ideal of humanness, it also brings the risk of the »overcoming of what is self-evident« (*Aufhebung der Selbstverständlichkeit*) (Arendt 1929, 86) and that could eradicate all obligations which scares Arendt politically, because this eradication reintroduces full decisionism into morality and the isolation of individuals. Hence, Arendt connects faith to the world and not to salvation. Against Moyn's suspicion, I claim that if *a* theology is smuggled here at all, it is only for the purpose of legitimizing the *cryptotheological passage to secularity*.

Adamite Heterodoxy?

It is evident that in *Der Liebesbegriff* Arendt rejected the »dogmatic subservience to scriptural and ecclesiastical authority« (Arendt 1996, 4), thus, she detached her analysis not only from official Christian theology, but also from any binding authority of the Bible as it was transmitted to us in the canonical version(s). I interpret the following sentences not as Arendt's personal religious belief, but as *a speculative exercise*, blurring the boundary between theology and philosophy. Both of them have to unlearn the centuries of praising the absolute.

When Arendt claims that »[t]he redeeming death of Christ did not redeem an individual but the whole world (*mundus*), understood as the man-

33 I here follow Elisabeth Moltmann-Wendel's suggestion that natality constitutes a challenge to the paradigm of political theology (Moltmann-Wendel 1998, 290—295)

made world [*als die von den Menschen konstituierte Welt*, 77]« (ibid., 99), it stems from Marranic crypto-Judaizing or some other heterodoxy. Here she does not extract a secular meaning from theology, but directly intervenes in the midst of Christian creed, considerably transforming its sense. Another example is when Arendt delimits the usefulness of the notion of God in community-building: »The simple sameness of the God [*die einfache Selbigkeit Gottes*, 76] in whom they all believe does not as yet bring about a community of the faithful« (ibid., 99). Arendt claims that plurality cannot be *directly* derived from the source of Being, however that origin might be understood. To say that »God is not enough« at first brings about a disorientation, but the goal is to re-orient Western thinking, which up until now has been too much grounded in unattainable absolutes (e.g., God, nature, cosmos).

To harbor thinking in »the common ground of experience« (ibid., 99) means to go back to Adam and from that point again to the world. This radicalizes the concept of the neighbor by breaking with the exclusivity of the Christian community of faith and by a recounting of all creaturely life under a very secular and even more universal formula: »everyone is my neighbor« (ibid., 99). From the active remembrance of the common origin should emerge »a new law on earth« (Arendt 1979, ix). The equality of mankind springs not from God and not from nature, but from this Law and cannot be *aufgehoben* (Arendt 1929, 80), »canceled out,« because it was »not arbitrarily founded« (Arendt 1996, 102).

Regardless of whether Arendt was aware of it or not, her anthropology, in this case, works against Schmitt's political theology (1922). Schmitt later extended this paradigm into an analysis of the Catholic political form (1923) that rests on *complexio oppositorum*—the universal intellectual »tool« that serves to reconcile contradictory views, resolves conceptual aporias and moral paradoxes and, in the end, strengthens dogmatism; it does all this while allowing the church a »limitless ambiguity« when it comes to its application (Schmitt 1996, 7). Despite Schmitt's claims that the Catholic dogma does not see human nature as evil, institutional Catholicism clings to the conception of original sin; in it, the vision of human corruption is simultaneously posed as a problem and structurally elaborated, just in order to find a »resolution« to the problem in the hierarchical order (Catholic political form). This order legitimized the sovereign monarchical power through the claim that only such power keeps the human beast under control. It is characteristic that Arendt does not respond directly to this conundrum.[34] Rather, she demonstrates—like Franz Rosenzweig—that Christian metaphysics and dialectic do not do justice to the neighbor in her earthly existence. Here Arendt's debt to Rosenzweig comes to the fore since it was he who contested the philosophical absolutism of the Hegelian system by referring to the figure of the neighbor and using a theological arsenal.

Hegelian dialectic can be seen as the philosophical appropriation of *complexio oppositorum*—the reconciliation of the opposites—to achieve different goals. In Arendtian usage it was revised, yet without dialectic Arendt would not be able to build the chiastic figures of thought. The core concept of transcendence-within-immanence prevents the divine absoluteness from entering immanence, but on the other hand, it allows »the sanctity of human spontaneity«[35] (Arendt 2016, I, 66) to migrate over in a sublated form: as the non-sovereign transcendence of human freedom.

What Arendt disliked in Spinoza's philosophy was the risk that immanence can become absolute, since it coincides with divinity (*Deus sive Natura*). From her point of view, absolute immanence equalizes birth and death. If they are considered exchangeable, *homo temporalis* falls prey to »time as a continuous flow« (Arendt 1990, 205). There is an alternative reading of this idea, offered by Agata Bielik-Robson who demonstrates that whereas Arendt criticized equalizing birth and death (since such stance sides with indifference coming from the cosmic, inhuman point of view), there is also in Arendt »the notion of interchangeability between the beginning and the end« (Bielik-Robson 2015, 555): death is replaced by birth in the role of the most decisive anthropogenic caesura. Furthermore, a life turned toward its origin can benefit from the »reversed temporality« where the end, death, is no longer mistaken for life's destination. It is not a coincidence that, in order to explain this, Bielik-Robson chooses to evoke the heterodox imaginary

34 This becomes evident in *On Revolution*, where Arendt only once mentions the conception of original sin, calling it a »proposition« (Arendt 1990, 87). What interests her is not so much evil but violence in politics, resulting from the imitation of God's *potentia absoluta* in the worldly realm. Arendt also observed that Machiavelli's »so-called realistic insight into human nature« was in fact the expression of his helplessness, namely it was meant to justify the use of violence in politics by a certain elite, who could in this way get closer to divine absoluteness (ibid., 39) and solve what Samuel Moyn called a »substitutional dilemma« (Moyn 2008, 77).

35 This entry from April 1951 is a reflection on Augustine, but its second part resembles a reflection of Arendt's from *The Origins*, that is why I propose to read this sentence literally. As mentioned before, Arendt returned to Augustine again when the manuscript of the book was finished and the rediscovery of her early achievement, natalism, became the hallmark of her philosophy (see footnote 21).

suggesting that the natal self, meditating on their origins, ceases to focus on »afterlife« and, instead, discovers the plenitude in the midst of earthly life (see ibid., 551—560).

In the history of Christianity, various groups called »Adamites«[36] were accused of heresy, because they contested the necessity of a hierarchical order. By organizing structures not dictated by the already sanctioned social roles (estates), their refusal to accept the consequences of original sin was practical. Even without stating any direct inheritance, one can recognize a logical parallelism between some of the ancient Gnostics—who called their autonomous communities *ἀβασίλευτος*, »without a king«—and a great adversary of Carl Schmitt, Hans Kelsen, who wrote: »Democracy is, according to its ideal, a fatherless society« (quoted in Kalyvas 2008, ii). This means that as long as people can organize themselves peacefully and suppress their own violent impulses, hierarchy and order are not necessary. Arendt hoped that through mutual pledges it would be possible to enforce »the consistent abolition of sovereignty within the body politic« (Arendt 1990, 153).[37]

It was theoretically preceded by a cryptotheological stratagem, which Arendt found in Hugo Grotius, and which she earlier used herself in *Der Liebesbegriff*. Namely, in her view Grotius' »intention was clearly to bind and limit the sovereign will of an absolute prince who claimed to incarnate divine omnipotence on earth, by declaring that even God's power was not without limitations« (ibid., 192—193). Thus, the non-absolute concept of God serves to limit the human appetite for the absolute power that seemingly comes from God. But even *potentia absoluta* can be employed for the same purpose, only if one understands that the divine oneness and omnipotence is unsurpassable for humankind. This—conversely—could mean that »power under the condition of human plurality can never amount to omnipotence, and laws residing on human power can never be absolute« (ibid., 39).

It is this cryptotheological argument that led Arendt to refuse the conditions dictated by Schmitt in the discussion about evil. While Schmitt claims that »the antithesis of man ›by nature evil‹ and ›by nature good‹« is the »decisive question for political theory« (Schmitt 1996, 8), formulating an

36 One of the most suggestive, even if nowadays contested, views on the cryptic Adamite heterodoxy is the classic book by Wilhelm Fraenger entitled *Hieronymus Bosch: Das tausendjährige Reich* (Fraenger 1947). It is noteworthy that Schmitt was interested in Fraenger's research and they exchanged letters.

37 This point is very similar, if not identical with »association theories« criticized by Carl Schmitt in *Political Theology*, where he wrote about the community »constituted from below« and »associational self-government« (Schmitt 1985, 24—26).

either-or type of intellectual blackmail, and whereas the Catholic response (which Schmitt highly respected) to this question is »*as-well-as*« (ibid., 7), Arendt's stance utilizes her negative dialectic: *neither-nor*. Throughout *On Revolution* it is clear that the problem of human violence is treated in full seriousness: although we cannot *overcome* violence and precisely because of that, we have to *cope with it*. Arendt rejects both optimism—which she characterized as »a semi-religious trust in human nature« (Arendt 1990, 174—175)—and pessimism, finding in the American political invention a dialectical mediation between the two extremes. True realism comes down to an observation that »whatever men might be in their singularity, they could bind themselves into a community which, even though it was composed of ›sinners,‹ need not necessarily reflect this ›sinful‹ side of human nature« (ibid., 174). In the phenomenon of self-government as a community constituted spontaneously from below, Arendt—inspired by Rosa Luxemburg—saw the manifestation of natality in the political realm. Revolutionary councils are not »a romantic dream« as long as their creators abstain from building a »paradise on earth« (ibid., 263—264). Instead, the goal is to establish in politics something unnatural: equality. If compared to »the dream of a ›promised land‹ where milk and honey flow« (ibid., 139), political equality achieved through mutual promises may be seen as a lesser boon. Yet, it depends on the point of view.

In *The Origins* Hannah Arendt wrote about »the *terror* of the ideal of humanity and of the Judeo-Christian faith in the common origin of man« (Arendt 1979, 235; my emphasis), elucidating this bold statement with the following observation: »the more peoples know about one another, the less they want to recognize other peoples as their equals, the more they recoil from the ideal of humanity« (ibid., 235). This complicates Arendt's dogmatized image of an apostle of plurality. According to her, diversity of physical differences and divergent lifestyles is highly ambiguous, to the extent that it can traumatize with the force of »overwhelming monstrosity« (ibid., 185) characteristic of our species. But as Eric Santner says, it is »the trauma that has the potential to open us to the force of trauma in the lives of others, *who thereby become our neighbors*« (Santner 2005, 109; original emphasis). Arendt's name for this perspective on human life was *Gefährdetsein*, »endangered being.«

From Faith in the Fact to Faith in the World

What poses a challenge for traditionalism is that Arendt cannot be accused of claiming that humankind is good by nature and that humans are equal by birth. Nor did she accept the religious cliché that everyone is equal before God[38] because that endangers the »worldly significance [*weltliche Bedeutsamkeit*, 79]« (Arendt 1996, 101) of the other in her uniqueness. Rather, Arendt's dictum is that by birth humans are unequal, but because of that they endow themselves with equality on the political and juridical level to compensate for what nature stinted them on.

Although Arendt writes about »the obligatory equality [*verbindliche Äqualität*, 77]« (ibid., 100), which has its root (*radix*) in Adam, she is aware that it has never been institutionalized and remains an Adamite dream: »Equality had always been the prerequisite of worldly interdependence, but it was never grasped thematically in establishing society on earth« (ibid., 101). However, the interdependence is implicit in everyday exchange between people, which involves belief and trust. In her close reading of Augustine, Arendt came to the following conclusion: »this belief that arises from our mutual interdependence precedes any possible proof. The continued existence of humankind does not rest on the proof. Rather, it rests on necessary belief, without which social life would become impossible« (ibid., 101).

If that sounds paradoxical, one can translate this into the reality of our era, when the common origin of humankind is an obvious fact, but its obviousness still does not imply any political obligations. As the case of refugees demonstrates, the »mere presence in this world« (Arendt 1979, 286) does not guarantee any legal status. Only now, in the wake of ecological catastrophe, might this idea gain juridical and political incarnation. What Arendt suggests here is that knowing the mere fact is not enough. We need a *faith* in this fact that can become operative and transform life on earth into a (dis)harmonious unity in peace. Faith in the common origin of humankind is analogous to faith in the world.

To come to that point, however, humanity has to discreetly contraband a transcendence, which will guarantee that coming to terms with finitude does not immediately turn into naturalism. The echo of *Der Liebesbegriff* is

38 It is telling that in the very first entry to the *Denktagebuch*, Arendt refers to original sin, rejecting one of its manifestations, namely the phrase »we are all sinful«—she considered its banality demoralizing and its naturalism an obstacle to think about equality politically (see Arendt 2016, I, 4).

clearly audible in the numerous passages of the *Denktagebuch* where Arendt writes that plurality was not created by God because God created Man (Adam), not mankind. How to unpack this heterodox message? I suggested elsewhere that the Adam to which Arendt referred can be read as the kabbalistic *adam qadmon*, the image of Man created by God, who is not only »a mediator between God's oneness and human plurality,« but also »a condensation of human dreams about a [...] diverse unity« (Zawisza 2018, 20).[39] As in photography, God's oneness literally becomes *the negative of plurality*, and this negativity guards the human Adamite origin as independent from the absolute. Thanks to negative dialectic embedded in the Lurianic vision of creation (*tsimtsum*) the idea of unity is indirectly transmitted[40] from God to *adam qadmon* before it explodes into the multiplicity of beings, who inherit the image of oneness. Since the image brings about a terrifying obligation, the simple fact of a common descent is strongly repressed and that is why this fact must be accompanied by faith.

Why the Lurianic hypothesis is a very plausible cryptotheological approach to Arendt's speculative exercises, becomes clear when we take into account that in April 1951 she writes down that the mainstream traditions of Judaism and Christianity were »averse« towards human plurality: in Judaism, the idea of God's chosenness undermines, according to Arendt, the plurality of peoples, and in Christianity the doctrine of original sin is responsible for degrading plurality to the level of the animalistic and perceiving it as a sign of sinfulness (see Arendt 2016, I, 70—71). Whatever the difficulties were, Arendt admits that the idea of a single human being generating all of humankind is »the guarantee« that people will not »degenerate« (*entarten*) into races (ibid., 70).

Having a non-absolute conception of God at hand in *Der Liebesbegriff*, Arendt could achieve what for Augustine was impossible, namely to find a

39 The status of this »primordial man« was largely discussed among the kabbalists. Gershom Scholem noticed that in the book *Bahir* this idea embodied the »pleroma of all aeons and potencies« (Scholem 1987, 139), while for the later kabbalists from Provence (who invented the term *adam qadmon*) it was only »a configuration of the supreme potencies,« which themselves are interpreted by Scholem as a synonym of »vitality« or »life« (ibid., 339).

40 Although for the *man, as creature,* his »true and God-given being [*ihr wahres, von Gott geschenktes Sein,* 81]« has its source »in the most distant and unworldly past« (Arendt 1996, 103)—which we can picture as our divine or cosmic origin—the *historical man* lives in another dimension thanks to his natality, the generationally transmitted life, which »does not denote the direct extraction from the Being [*die direkte Herkunft aus dem Sein,* 81] without which man, if he is at all, would not be. Rather, it is the origin of the whole race transmitted indirectly to the individual by generation« (ibid., 103).

»conjunction« between God and the world »in antithetical form« (Arendt 1996, 4), which secures the realness of the created world and thus forms the foundation (*Grund*) (Arendt 1929, 76) from which ethical responsibility can derive. The binding force of obligation cannot be dependent on God because it must have universal validity for all people, including unbelievers. Moreover, this validity is not real enough if the world is considered to be transient: »How can duties be derived from a past that is to be totally eradicated?« (Arendt 1996, 104). This way the faith in the world, its ontological solidity, supports necessary faith in the fact that life comes from the same origin. The world is thus this pre-theological sphere, which reappears with its »earthly pathos« (Arendt 2016, I, 22) when the absolute voluntarily leaves humanity to its fate. The question whether this negative conjunction, this chiasmus, still forms a passage to divinity, cannot be easily answered. Isn't the »divinity of birth as such« really the last remnant of the old glory? Isn't it the lost spark of pleroma in the earthly realm, with no way back? And even if so, doesn't it simply mean that the divine decomposed for good?

Writing about Hannah Arendt's language as a theologically tinged and hybrid discourse, Susan Neiman warns us that even the most enquiring look must be prepared to face Arendt's »consequent ability to live with *creative confusion*« (Neiman 2001, 71; original emphasis). We find a perfect example of that cryptic way of speaking in Arendt's note from December 1952, where the question about the passage from absolute oneness to plural worldliness is raised. At first, Arendt observes that God is the equivalent of one, solitary individual, »but as soon as *many* people are there, a specific de-divinized sphere [*ent-göttlichte Sphäre*] begins. Just what God couldn't create« (Arendt 2016, I, 275; original emphasis). The next fragment about *the* passage, at first gives us a firm negative response, nonetheless, its internal interruption, made by Hannah Arendt, creates again a confusion—as if she suddenly bit her tongue: »Because in this sense there is no passage [*Übergang*] from the One into plurality, or *better*, because in plurality the in-between [*das Zwischen*] is established as an *only* human, non-ideal realm [*Bereich*] which the idea as such can neither foresee nor dominate« (ibid., 275; original emphasis).

Works Cited

Arendt, Hannah (1929). *Der Liebesbegriff bei Augustin: Versuch einer philosophischen Interpretation*. Berlin: Julius Springer.

Arendt, Hannah (1951). *The Burden of Our Time*. London: Secker & Warburg.

Arendt, Hannah (1958a). *Elemente totaler Herrschaft*. Frankfurt am Main: Europäische Verlagsanstalt.

Arendt, Hannah (1958b). *The Human Condition*. Chicago/London: University of Chicago Press.

Arendt, Hannah (1979). *The Origins of Totalitarianism*. San Diego/New York/London: Harcourt Brace Jovanovich.

Arendt, Hannah, and Karl Jaspers (1985). *Briefwechsel 1926—1969*. Herausgegeben von Lotte Köhler und Hans Saner. München: Piper.

Arendt, Hannah (1990). *On Revolution*. London/New York: Penguin Books.

Arendt, Hannah, and Karl Jaspers (1992). *Correspondence, 1926—1969*. Eds. Lotte Kohler and Hans Saner. Transl. Robert and Rita Kimber. New York: Harcourt Brace Jovanovich.

Arendt, Hannah (1994). Philosophy and Sociology. In Hannah Arendt. *Essays in Understanding, 1930—1954*. Ed. Jerome Kohn. New York: Harcourt, Brace & Co.

Arendt, Hannah (1996). *Love and Saint Augustine*. Ed. and interpretive essay by Joanna Vecchiarelli Scott and Judith Chelius Stark. Chicago: University of Chicago Press.

Arendt, Hannah (2005). *The Promise of Politics*. Ed. and introduction Jerome Kohn. New York: Schocken Books.

Arendt, Hannah (2016). *Denktagebuch 1950—1973*. Zwei Bände. Eds. Ursula Ludz and Ingeborg Nordmann. München: Piper Verlag.

Bielik-Robson, Agata (2012). *Erros: Mesjański witalizm i filozofia*. Cracow: Universitas.

Bielik-Robson, Agata (2014). *Jewish Cryptotheologies of Late Modernity: Philosophical Marranos*. London/New York: Routledge.

Bielik-Robson, Agata (2015). L'amour fort comme la mort: les Juifs contre Heidegger (sur la question de la finitude). Transl. Laurent Vannini. *La Règle du Jeu*, 58/59, 529—560.

Bielik-Robson, Agata (2019). *Another Finitude: Messianic Vitalism and Philosophy*. London: Bloomsbury Academic.

Blumenberg, Hans (1985). *The Legitimacy of the Modern Age*. Transl. and introduction Robert M. Wallace. Cambridge/London: MIT Press.

Fraenger, Wilhelm (1947). *Hieronymus Bosch: Das tausendjährige Reich: Grundzüge einer Auslegung*. Coburg: Winkler.

Gordon, Peter Eli (2007). The Concept of the Apolitical: German Jewish Thought and Weimar Political Theology. *Social Research*, 74(3), 855—878.

Jay, Martin (1985). The Political Existentialism of Hannah Arendt. In Martin Jay. *Permanent Exiles: Essays on the Intellectual Migration From Germany to America*, 237—256. New York: Columbia University Press.

Jonas, Hans (2008). *Memoirs*. Ed. Christian Wiese. Transl. Krishna Winston. Waltham/Hanover: Brandeis University Press/University Press of New England.

Kalyvas, Andreas (2008). *Democracy and the Politics of the Extraordinary: Max Weber, Carl Schmitt, and Hannah Arendt*. Cambridge/New York: Cambridge University Press.

Lazier, Benjamin (2008). *God Interrupted: Heresy and the European Imagination Between the World Wars*. Princeton: Princeton University Press.

Maciejko, Paweł (2011). *The Mixed Multitude: Jacob Frank and the Frankist Movement, 1755—1816*. Philadelphia: University of Pennsylvania Press.

Moltmann-Wendel, Elisabeth (1998). Natalität und die Liebe zur Welt: Hannah Arendts Beitrag zu einer immanenten Transzendenz. *Evangelische Theologie*, 58(4), 283—295.

Moyn, Samuel (2005). *Origins of the Other: Emmanuel Levinas Between Revelation and Ethics*. Ithaca, N.Y.: Cornell University Press.

Moyn, Samuel (2008). Hannah Arendt on the Secular. *New German Critique*, 35(3), 71—96.

Neiman, Susan (2001). Theodicy in Jerusalem. In Steven E. Aschheim (ed.). *Hannah Arendt in Jerusalem*. Berkeley: University of California Press.

Santner, Eric L. (2001). *On the Psychotheology of Everyday Life: Reflections on Freud and Rosenzweig*. Chicago: The University of Chicago Press.

Santner, Eric L. (2005). Miracles Happen: Benjamin, Rosenzweig, Freud, and the Matter of the Neighbor. In Slavoj Žižek, Eric L. Santner, Kenneth Reinhard. *Neighbor: Three Inquiries in Political Theology*. Chicago: University of Chicago Press.

Schmitt, Carl (1985). *Political Theology: Four Chapters on the Concept of Sovereignty*. Transl. George Schwab. Cambridge, Mass.: MIT Press.

Schmitt, Carl (1996). *Roman Catholicism and Political Form*. Transl. G.L. Ulmen. Westport, Conn.: Greenwood Press.

Scholem, Gershom (1987). *Origins of the Kabbalah*. Ed. R.J. Zwi Werblowsky. Transl. Allan Arkush. Philadelphia/Princeton: Jewish Publication Society/Princeton University Press.

Weigel, Sigrid (2014). Buchstäblichkeit: Walter Benjamins und Hannah Arendts Denken auf den Spuren der Sprache. In Nicolas Berg and Dieter Burdorf (Hg.). *Textgelehrte: Literaturwissenschaft und literarisches Wissen im Umkreis der Kritischen Theorie*, 289—307. Göttingen: Vandenhoeck & Ruprecht.

Young-Bruehl, Elisabeth (2004). *Hannah Arendt: For Love of the World*. New Haven/London: Yale University Press.

Zawisza, Rafael (2018). Thank God We Are Creatures: Hannah Arendt's Cryptotheology. *Religions* 9(11), 371.

Zawisza, Rafael (2020). Hannah Arendt's Marranic Evasions and the Truth of Her Cryptotheology. Barbara Bokus and Ewa Kosowska (eds.). *Truth and Falsehood in Science and the Arts*, 172—188. Warsaw: Wydawnictwa Uniwersytetu Warszawskiego.

Hannah Arendt's Debt to Rudolf Bultmann

Jim Josefson

In a July 13, 1953 letter to Karl Jaspers, Hannah Arendt wrote, »As you know, I learned a lot from Bultmann and owe him a lot. I don't want to forget that debt« (Arendt and Jaspers 1992, 221).[1] In what follows, I hope to illuminate Arendt's political theology by accounting for this debt.[2]

In order to make that argument clear, however, I want to first sketch the outlines of that political theology as I see it.[3] As *political* theology, it involves an attempt to secularize theology or take the mythology out of God-talk while leaving the spirit of theology intact, that is, the transcendence or freedom involved in what Kierkegaard called »the religious« and Benjamin called »messianic.«[4] Arendt developed this political theology primarily from Christian sources like Augustine and Bultmann and that makes her a prime example of what Agata Bielik-Robson calls »Philosophical Marranos« (Bielik-Robson 2014, 23—55). Arendt's negative theological politics, similarly, sketch how politics might also be secularized in Bultmann's sense, that is, how political theory might be purged of mythology while leaving the spirit of politics intact.[5] That *spirit* is the love of the world that prompts us to create

1 Arendt was responding to an article Jaspers had published attacking Bultmann's theology. Jasper's article, Bultmann's response and Jaspers' answer are collected in: Jaspers and Bultmann 1954 (translated into English as Jaspers and Bultmann 2005). Another indication of Bultmann's importance to Arendt can be seen in Edna Brocke's account of visits to her aunt in Tegna, Switzerland: »My husband and I would visit her there regularly, each year meeting different friends of hers who were visiting her at the same time, and we were able to have long, extensive debates about Rudolf Bultmann and other theologians, about Zionism and the state of Israel, about German poetry and its significance in the postwar era« (Brocke 2007, 515).

2 While Arendt's debt to Bultmann has been ignored, her debt to Heidegger has been thoroughly explored. See for instance Villa 1996; Taminiaux 1997.

3 For accounts of Arendt's personal belief in God see: Arendt 1968, 67; Baron 1980, 62; Kazin 1978, 199.

4 This goes further than saying only that Arendt draws on religion's utopian aspirations. See Habermas 1983, 170—86.

5 For a radically different reading of Arendt's »covert theology,« see Rieff 1952, 119—126.

the conditions for the possibility of sharing it with others.[6] While more orthodox accounts of Arendt emphasize recovering those conditions in terms of the separation of public and private and creating an institutionalized public sphere, the political theology I present here emphasizes recovering the spirit of the political and leaves these conditions a more open question.[7] That is, while Schmitt and Benjamin sought to revivify political concepts for a *particular political purpose* by revealing their theological roots, Arendt, in my view, had no partisan political purpose, only the *essentially theological purpose* of returning human beings to the faith proper to the human condition of finitude. Therefore, she declined to overtly join the »theological-political predicament,« not just because she refused to define politics technologically (Van Camp 2011, 28—30), but because she sought conditions for the possibility of human transcendence that were positive (not rooted in death, fatalism, or nothingness), worldly (rooted in tangible reality rather than idealist hopes), and free (rooted in exercising finite human capacities rather than obeying truth). By showing how this political theology is indebted to Bultmann, I hope to reveal it to be more than an »amorphous religiosity« rooted in the miracle of natality (Villa 1996, 269) but less religious in the orthodox sense of a respect for a divine order.[8]

Our roadmap for this inquiry is Arendt's letter acknowledging her debt to Bultmann, in which she responded to an article Karl Jaspers wrote that was critical of Bultmann. In the letter, Arendt indicts theology (»not only in Bultmann«) for the »conspicuous neglect [...] of Jesus' preaching as opposed to Christ [...], an exclusive regard for the functional and a pushing aside of the real ›substance‹.« This »substance« is the palpable worldly reality that both theology and politics (in different ways) should be concerned with, according to Arendt's own political theology. To sum that up, she writes, *»faith communicates itself, wants to be understood and so understands itself«* (Arendt and Jaspers 1992, 221; emphasis mine). In order to understand these three moves I turn now to Bultmann's own writings from the period.

6 This framing greatly expands on themes found in Bernauer 1987, 1—19.

7 For orthodox accounts, see Margaret Canovan 1992; Disch 1996.

8 See the discussion about this reconstructed by Mavis Louise Biss (Biss 2012). The latter is Moyn's worry (Moyn 2008, 95—96).

Faith Communicates Itself

The task of theology, according to Bultmann, the problem it seeks to solve, turns out to be very similar to the task of political theory according to Arendt. Theologians are ahead in this game because since Paul they, at least, have focused on the conditions for the possibility of salvific faith. Political theorists would not focus on the conditions for the possibility of salvific action until Arendt published *The Human Condition*. However, that leaves most of the heavy lifting of specifying these conditions (on both counts) undone, and there are several difficult problems involved. Luckily (we shall see), theology's head start on the question of faith means it could provide a template for answering the question of action. In other words, and this is my core contention, Bultmann's answers to the problem of faith may have provided Arendt with that template.[9]

What distinguishes Bultmann's thought is that he resisted Karl Barth's attempt to replace theological knowledge with nothing but the conversion experience. To Bultmann, this objectified Christianity into a kind of Hellenic Christ-cult in which an empirical experience was equated with revelation, thereby violating his enduring neo-Kantian commitment to the difference between *Erfahrung* and *Erlebnis* (see Dennison 2008, 122—123). Of course, this meant Bultmann needed, then, to tackle the difficult task of explaining the conditions for the possibility of *Erlebnis*, an unmediated experience of Jesus, despite the fact that we know of Jesus only through world-views. He is, as dialectical theology says, *not* a given object.

In my view, this is a similar problem to the one facing Arendt, who must find a different ground for political freedom than in some given objective truth. The key to both Bultmann's and Arendt's solutions, we will see, is that, if faith (or freedom) cannot be a kind of knowledge, then it must be »something that determines the whole of the Christian's existence« (Bultmann 1987a, 67). In Bultmann's view, such an existence must, in that case, be a kind of authentic being-in-the-world, one that pushed him away from Barth and towards Heidegger (Chacón 2012, 84—87).[10] Such existence cannot involve a metaphysical belief system, not only because it must be lived in faith rather than known, but particularly because Paul, in I Corinthians, specifically warns about what Bultmann identified as rival Gnostic factions that »rob

9 See Chacón 2012, 81—82. I agree with Chacón that dialectical theology leads to a secularization of theology (ibid., 83).

10 Chacón provides a good account of Bultmann's decisionist leap of faith (Chacón 2012, 87).

God of what is his, of his right of judgment, his majesty, his freedom« (Bultmann 1987a, 68—69).

Such freedom, for Bultmann, means that God is always a *subject*, acting on human beings through the gifts of grace, and never an *object* of knowledge. The faith that receives and *is* such a gift is then not »waiting« or »silence« but a »laying hold of the Word of God« that engages with events through communication and action. It is a moment of decision that is not decisionist, freed as it is »from my speaking and action as a system or programme. I confront it in freedom, so far as it is *something to hand*, done, and said« (ibid., 70; emphasis mine). As something ready-to-hand, to use the Heideggerian analog, the knowledge involved is not a conceptual possibility, determined by correct application of a principle, but *God's* possibility, one synthesized by God's love. And such »love is to be understood only as the ultimate human possibility, absolutely beyond the area of healthy bourgeois religious mediocrity« (ibid., 78). You might say, it does not involve the synthesis of the traditional contents of a community (an intersubjective or phronetic knowledge) because its source is God rather than a community.

That means the church has no characteristics or knowledge that makes it the church. *It is only the space in common for persons united by the same source, the same* res publica (*public thing*). As Bultmann put it, »[t]he divine origin is therefore not a structural element but is present as a vivifying force. In other words, one does not *possess* spirit, one *is* spirit or one is not.« The kind of »resurrection of the dead« involved, then, is not a magical life after death but the empty tomb, a space that was closed off by tradition, law, and the privacy of the body and is now open to move about. The church, then, is the body of Christ that moves about this open space, a possibility opened up simply by the fact that that body is not dead but with us. The preaching of God's love »is preaching the resurrection of the dead,« therefore, simply because the object of that love is absent as an object of knowledge but present as the possibility of love. There is no *a priori* rule that defines what is appropriate to this sphere. It is only the space in common, the space shared by people united by (to use an Arendtian phrase) a shared *inter-est* (ibid., 78). Any more specific meaning of the resurrection, especially any notion of its essence, falls into a confusion of dogmatism that shatters faith, that is, the substance of things hoped for (ibid., 82, 85).

What we see here is a new perspective on Arendt's use of the word »space.« Arendt scholars tend to think of this either as an institutionalized political space or as a more or less impromptu space (such as a park) that is appropriated because of the absence of an official one.[11] This also leads to interpretations of the public sphere as an empty stage, one that makes room for agonistic action.[12] However Bultmann, quite differently, conceptualizes space in terms of the convoking power of a common thing, a common love, or a common revelatory source. That is, the space is not created by the boundaries of a building, the boundaries of group membership, the bounds of tradition, or the ties of overlapping beliefs. All of these, according to Bultmann, would actually fill the paradoxically absent center of Christianity that makes possible the freedom of the believer, who believes in the significance of something she cannot see by allowing it to communicate through her own revelations.

Now, Arendt can be read in a similar way, by taking care that the same sorts of boundaries cannot be allowed to destroy the freedom of politics.[13] That requires the public sphere to be resituated from the »table« around which people may act to the »table« that itself »relates and separates« them as a *res publica*, a public concern (Arendt 1998, 52—53). Tellingly, from her discussion of this table, Arendt moves immediately to the problem of Christianity, which had not lost tables as spaces in which to gather, but they had lost the »table« itself, »their interest in the common world and felt themselves no longer related and separated by it.« What they required, according to Arendt, was not a space open enough in which to act but »a bond between people strong enough to replace the world,« a bond that Augustine provided with »charity.« The problem, for Arendt, with such charity is its »worldlessness« (ibid., 53). What is required for a *genuine* public sphere, Arendt then explains, is »a community of things which gathers men together and relates them to each other,« and such things must have »permanence,« »transcendence,« or »immortality« (ibid., 55). These are, in my view, not just words for durability or fame. Rather, they are words for the existential situation identified by Bultmann.[14] The public thing must be loved, but it cannot be known or possessed, since it is alive in the secularized sense of Bultmann's »resurrection of the dead.« Such public things are not dead things that are used to satisfy private interests; rather, they are read like Scripture, as if they have something transcendent to say, as if they communicate to us and call us

11 See Canovan 1992; Disch 1996; İlhan Demiryol 2018.

12 See Honig 1993; Villa 1996.

13 See Arendt 1961; Arendt 1998, 197—198.

14 This point contradicts the orthodox reading of Arendt that makes her politics performative, elitist and guilty of polis fixation.

to reveal that communication. Therefore, when Arendt turns to discuss the destruction of the public realm by private interests of money and property, she does not mean it, as I read her, as a pietist indicting us for sin and calling us to purity (ibid., 56—58). Rather, like Bultmann, she calls us to the transcendence of reading things like tables as if they are Kierkegaard's bespoke *logos*. Only, of course, for Arendt this is neither a Christian nor a theistic *logos*. Again, this is *political* theology. The secular faith in the public thing (*res publica*), which communicates something the reader loves but does not know, makes both the thing and its lover transcendent. In other words, »*this faith communicates itself.*« It receives an unmediated experience of something revelatory, and, because it cannot *recall* that revelation as truth, *repeats* it by repeating its communicative appearance in word and deed.[15]

Faith Wants to Be Understood

Another important theme in early Bultmann that we can see in Arendt's thought concerns the relationship between historical events, truth and freedom. The problem for Christian theology is that transcendence must be connected somehow to Christology, and this connection must cohere with at least the broad outlines of orthodox dogmatics. These problems are further complicated by the findings of historical Biblical criticism, which demonstrate that both the Bible and dogma are shot-through with mythological content. Put more simply, the transcendence of the Christian conversion and life must involve a freedom to act independently of both human nature and divine law, and that freedom cannot be rooted in an autonomous capacity *inside* the person (e.g. reason or will) but instead on the historical appearance of such a capacity *outside* of the person (e.g. Jesus).

Bultmann's dialectical theology deals with these problems just as Kant dealt with the problem of pure reason. It finds in the finitude of man precisely the required conditions for the possibility of transcendence. In Kant, this finitude involves a dialectic in which truth is not determined by the concept of the thing-in-itself (the *noumena*) but by the concept of phenomenal reality. Dialectical theology, Bultmann tells us, involves »a dialectic in which

15 Such faith, then, is emphatically not *belief* in any orthodox sense. Indeed, from this perspective belief in dogma violates both the Kantian insistence on the incommensurability of religious experience and objective knowledge and the Jewish prohibition on idolatry.

the concept of truth is not determined by the concept of a true statement but by the concept of reality.« That is, theological statements are not universally valid, but they are true when they provide »the answer to the question posed by the concrete situation in time to which the sentence itself belongs when it is being spoken.« Such a truth refers to the *address* of the statement and not the truth of a conception (Bultmann 1987c, 146—147). This means that Scripture does not convey a set of metaphysical truths to everyone. Rather, it documents God's grace, His dispensation of faith to the persons involved in the text. If that is the case, then God's grace in the present must be nothing other than a similar graciousness »to *me*.« Here, we see Bultmann following Kierkegaard's *repetition* rather than the *recollection* of a universal truth, only now the repetition does not just act but hopes for a return to understand the meaning of it all. But this meaning is historical and not metaphysical, and so theological statements about it are similarly historical acknowledgements of God's work rather than claims to knowledge (ibid., 148). Furthermore, if a human being is essentially historical in this way, then that being is actually »a potentiality to be« rather than a natural being or a pure subjectivity. Such a »man does not choose *something for himself*, but chooses himself in his *possibility*« (ibid., 149). Here we have the obvious foundations for Bultmann's conception of the Gospel as *kerygma* and for his dialogue with Heidegger during the same period.

Another element in Bultmann's theology that is especially important to Arendt's dissertation is Bultmann's arguments about the relationship between the human being's status as a finite creature, which is a condition for man's very possibility and not just man's sinfulness. Given that the Gospel is God's personal address to the individual person, his or her creaturely condition of being-in-the-world is a setting for revelation (transcendence) and not just a stage for Arendt's supposed virtuosity. According to Bultmann, as we just saw, the New Testament can only be read historically, as accounts that reveal possibilities for human existence under the address of the kerygma, which we can understand only so far as we can comprehend these possibilities in our own existence. These are possibilities realized by the exegete based upon his own experiences, conceptions and ability to interrogate the kerygma. For example, Bultmann tells us that we must ask: »Out of what conception of existence did this statement originate?« (ibid., 151). That kind of understanding is unavoidably mythological or poetic. The task of the exegete, then, is to not treat such language as progressively solving a universal ontological conundrum. It is also not to debunk the text of mythological claims that violate the findings of science. Instead, the task is to unpack the original experience of transcendence the authors attempted to communicate to us in their native idiom with the assumption that this idiom is neither truer or more primitive than our own (ibid., 152).[16]

Here, in the terms Arendt used in her letter to Jaspers, »*faith wants to be understood.*« Such faith, as Arendt also expressed in the letter, »assumes that the revealed existence and acts of God are as palpable a reality as the reality of animals is for zoology« (Arendt and Jaspers 1992, 221). As we already saw, in Bultmann, such reality is a communicative appearance, which a faithful person repeats by communicating faithfully. But now, in this second moment, faith wonders as to its meaning. Its search for the kerygma, in my view, is like the search for the »*Ur*-phenomena« Arendt found in Benjamin or what she called in her Kant Lectures, the »nonappearance in the appearances.«[17] This nonappearance has none of the sorrow we see, for instance, in young Gershom Scholem, where lament at finitude is considered essential to religious transcendence (see Ferber 2013). Instead, Arendt follows Bultmann towards the positivity of Kierkegaard's repetition.

Arendt worked through these issues notably in her engagement with John Duns Scotus. She pointed out that the implication of creation *ex nihilo*, for Scotus, is not that God is absent but contingent. This contingency follows from the assumption that, given God's freedom, God could have created a universe »in which neither our mathematical truths nor our moral precepts would be valid.« Therefore, pantheism is ruled out because the necessary character of the world can never be used to infer the necessary character of the divine. Contingency, then, is not a defect of Being but *another aspect* that we may transcendentally deduce to exist if the freedom of God and man is to exist (Arendt 1981b, 135). As Arendt summarizes Scotus' position, »Being in its universality is but a thought, what it lacks is *reality*; only particular things (*res*), which are characterized by ›thisness‹ (*haecceity*) can be said to be real for man« (ibid., 120). This means that the »thisness« of particular and contingent appearances are placed above the universal, just as the revelation of God given in reality must be placed above our thoughts about it. For, given the utter finitude of human beings we can never encompass

16 I feel the need to point out that Bultmann's Christian theology is *simultaneously* heretical and orthodox in a way that is much more inventive than other negative theologians like Barth. That he is neither a liberal Christian nor a conservative Evangelical or Catholic makes him, exactly like Arendt, impossible to place in any conventional ideological spectrum.

17 Arendt 2007, 12; Arendt 1992, 80. See also my works: Josefson 2019; Josefson 2020.

even »thisness« in thought (ibid., 144). Rather, we must have faith in reports of events given by others, whether they are reports of the Resurrection or of a past history that exists outside our own experience (ibid., 129—130). Now, while Scotus thought such faith was the accomplishment of the will, Arendt points out that the will has the inherent problem of nullifying its own freedom by deciding (ibid., 141). Therefore, Scotus only provided »the speculative conditions for a philosophy of freedom,« since Arendt concludes that the will by itself is inadequate for securing those conditions by itself (ibid., 145—146).

Arendt turned to Kant's *Critique of Judgment* to identify the other required but free capacities, which explain how it is possible for human beings to see the infinite in the finite, the invisibles in appearances, and freely judge them such that they can enter the invisible world of thought. This is especially important for Arendt because when it comes to appearances of action, which have a clear kerygmatic character, »*whatever can see wants to be seen, whatever can hear calls out to be heard, whatever can touch presents itself to be touched*« (Arendt 1981a, 29; original emphasis). Her judgment, therefore, does not reason or judge (it neither condemns nor judges the validity of claims, and thereby it *repeats* God's grace); rather, it freely understands this form of address and rescues it through memory and metaphor. The faith that freely does so, Arendt tells us, is actually involved in every mental activity, even cognition and sensibility, which means that, for her, there is something free and transcendent at the root of a human being, even one oriented by wants (ibid., 87, 52).

Faith Understands Itself

Furthermore, this *free* desire, for Arendt, leads faith to »*understand itself.*« If communication is the present moment, where delight in the given is expressed through another gift, and the hope to be understood is oriented towards a future meaning, then the moment when faith understands itself is oriented towards the past whereby we can be assured that understanding may be given since it was given before. In this third moment, faith tastes faithfulness and acquires a taste for faith. Bultmann influenced Arendt's insights on that point, especially in the anthropology of Paul he was developing in 1925 (Bultmann 1955, 196 ff.). There, Bultmann points to the distinctive worldview presented by Paul's conceptions of man as »creature« and God

Hannah Arendt in a Paris café, 1930s.
Courtesy of the Hannah Arendt Bluecher Literary Trust / Art Resource, NY.

as »Creator« that, he insists, is not inferior to the understanding of God as the *Logos* and man as part of that rationally ordered whole (Bultmann 1987c, 153). His point is in equal parts indebted to Kant and Kierkegaard. The Kantian transcendental deduction asks about the »condition for the possibility of understanding,« which involves the »pre-understanding,« but when the object of inquiry is not an object in the common natural world, »this pre-understanding is not something the exegete *recalls*« as the road to the Good (ibid., 156—158). The Kierkegaardian perspective insists that all such recollection is fundamentally pagan, a pre-understanding of the *logos* that forbids the repetition of the Word made Flesh. It holds, instead, that a genuine pre-understanding is rooted in scriptural possibilities that are repeated in the kerygma, an address that is utterly personal and new even as it is repeated in the unique historical circumstance of the addressee.

You might say that what Bultmann is doing here is like Arendt's »pearl diving« (Arendt 2007, 38—51). He seeks to find the »rich and strange« that has been missed by orthodoxy with its tendency to subsume everything under dogmatic rules and pious clichés. The key to the interpretive enterprise, then, is for the reading to be based in a genealogical analysis rather than a scholastic or metaphysical one. This was the topic of Bultmann's seminar on the anthropology of the Apostle Paul that Arendt attended (Heller 2015, 51). In »The Significance of ›Dialectical Theology‹,« Bultmann explained what such anthropological investigation gets at: »the concepts of Pauline anthropology are interpreted on the basis of a conception of existence wholly different from that out of which they came« (Bultmann 1987c, 160). The point, then, is to give us the freedom to move about the text and recover the experience it memorializes in the »now« (ibid., 160).[18]

If this analysis is part of Arendt's debt to Bultmann, then the implication is that Arendtian concepts should never be read ontologically (for example, the being of labor is...) but anthropologically in Bultmann's sense, as possibilities that become part of the reader's possibilities. That means that, from this perspective, there is no problematic »phenomenological essentialism« in Arendt.[19] The truth about action or world, in that case, is never something to be recalled but only repeated, possibilities seized when one is seized by a »*Thou*.« For Arendt this Thou involves a moment of political freedom rather than the kerygma, but the moments are similar. Such politics becomes politics because of its object. Just as in theology, the object is something unknowable that calls us to new possibilities because it occasioned an opening up of possibilities for a person in the past; in politics, the object is an unknowable public thing that calls us to action because it occasioned action for another person in the past. This gives action its condition of possibility (natality is something Given) and plurality (a relation between persons each with her own possibility).[20] This reveals Arendt's political theology as one that is concerned with a Given and a Giver, which are the conditions for the possibility of being claimed by the world, that is, for freedom. This comportment might

18 Bultmann cites Heidegger here.

19 See Benhabib 2003, xliv, 123—126, 157, 172; Loidolt 2018, 190—193.

20 See esp. Arendt 2005; Arendt 1961, 142—143.

be framed simultaneously as a secular relation to a holy thing and a spiritual relationship with a secular thing.

These conclusions are further supported if we turn to Bultmann's »The Eschatology of the Gospel of John« from 1928. It is the only work by Bultmann cited in Arendt's dissertation (see Arendt 1996, 58, footnote 48). There, Bultmann expands on the analysis of »world« arguing that »world« should not be read as a universal system of *physis* that incorporates both God and human beings. For John, Bultmann insists, God is neither part of the world, nor is he coextensive with it in a pantheist sense. He holds, instead, that the »world created by the Word,« which makes the world something created or creaturely, is not an objective state of affairs caused by another object. The world refers primarily, then, to mankind. Human beings *are* the world rather than in it, in that case, and they stand in a more or less responsive posture to the Word that brought them into being and continually serves to properly direct or orient them as to their condition as creatures. In other words, the Gnostic framework of an abyss of separation between man and God is inaccurate, for the dualism at work in John is not the ideal versus the flesh but two orientations to creation: one which uses it and one which is grateful for it (Bultmann 1987b, 165—166). This involves what Bultmann calls an »*eschatological now*« such that eternal life is just this inexhaustible gratitude and hell is life without it (ibid., 171—172, 176). The echoes of Kierkegaard's *øjeblik* are clear in Bultmann's prose: »Therefore that *now* of ›the Word became flesh‹ is always present in the *now* of the proclamation, in the *moment*« (ibid., 177). In other words, the truth of the Gospel is not a »recollection« or »reconstruction« but the kerygma in which Jesus »is always coming again« (ibid., 177).

These insights from Bultmann's analyses of Paul and John are influential throughout Arendt's work, but they are especially important to her dissertation. Arendt's task there is »to show how Augustine's definition of the Creator and of eternity as the twofold ›before‹ grows out of these two intentions whose diametrical opposition he must reconcile« (Arendt 1996, 58). The two intentions express what Arendt calls the »Christian distinction between world and universe, in which the former is understood as the human world constituted by men« (ibid., 58)[21] (which comes from Paul) and the latter is understood as a timeless whole in which each part, including human beings, participates (which is Greek). They are opposed because in creation God makes a new beginning by introducing human beings and time, which con-

21 Here is where Arendt cites Bultmann.

tradicts the sempiternal cyclical order of *physis*. With time, God is associated with the absolute past (creation) and the absolute future (death or return). This means that, as Arendt says, »Being relates to human life as that from which it comes and to which it goes, and is ›before‹ (*ante*) man in the twofold sense of past and future« (ibid., 55). So, the »twofold ›before‹« of God is imitated by the twofold before of man, where, with memory and hope, human beings can place both the past and future before themselves in the present. In so doing, a person can take something out of the past and make it his possibility for the future, and he can »concentrate through remembrance and anticipation his entire life into the present,« and so he can »participate in eternity and thus be ›happy‹ even in this life« (ibid., 57). Of course, Arendt quotes Augustine as saying that such happiness only comes from salvation or participating in eternal life, yet her presentation suggests that something like eternal life is possible, and therefore a happiness that does not require a salvific miracle that triumphs over nature and death. We only need to concentrate on something present while being oriented by the past and future in order to understand ourselves, our place in the story. As she puts it, death can be the negation of life, but it can also be the completion of life, »the point where life meets eternity or even as eternity itself. Eternity is then achieved by life.« In this »second meaning, the end becomes eternity as the point of cessation in a radically positive sense and a bid for a lingering gaze and reflective calm« (ibid., 73). Here, life is moving towards Being in the sense of its eternal existence, but the being involved is merely *reality*, which we taste with gratitude.

Now, much of the dissertation presents a critique of Augustine's concept of love; however, the argument of the preceding paragraph is the actual core of the book. In it she follows Bultmann's demythologizing to separate Augustine's moment of revelation from its mythological coral reef. She also borrows from Bultmann's notions of the Creator/creature relationship and world, in order to find in Augustine the possibility for a post-Christian kerygma or *øjeblik* that is political rather than eschatological. It involves an acceptance of creatureliness that forswears idolatrous knowledge and, instead, returns to and loves the world. That love, then, is nothing but the moment in which a person focuses on some particular part of reality (a *res publica*) with a »lingering gaze and reflective calm« that reveals and realizes both the particularity of reality (its natality and plurality) and the particularity of the lover. One might say, in that case, that faithfulness to the world reveals the invisible particularity of the object of faith, desires to understand

and communicate that particularity to the world, and in so doing, ultimately, *understands itself*. Arendt's only difference with Bultmann, then, is that she has completed the demythologizing Jaspers asked for. Therefore, Jaspers was certainly right that the dissertation represented Arendt's efforts to »justify her freedom from Christian possibilities which also attract her« (Arendt and Jaspers 1992, 690) but Jaspers' evaluation misses (in my estimation) Arendt's argument for the same reason he misses Bultmann's. That is, he thinks she is doing philosophy when she is doing political theology. However, her political theology delivers neither a self nor God, giving both up to silence in favor of the world, yet self and God return in messianic (perpetually awaited) form. Perhaps she could perform such a balancing act between disillusionment and mythology because, since her sources are so often Christian rather than Jewish, she could demythologize them with greater freedom. They all become simply appearances in the world, given by the gracious Giver, such that the mythological lament and hope about the scattered divine light can both be given up in favor of a new alternative »between myth and exodus« (Bielik-Robson 2014, 416—417). Perhaps, because this »faith communicates itself, wants to be understood and so understands itself,« it can speak to modernity like no other.

Works Cited

Arendt, Hannah (1961). What Is Freedom?. In Hannah Arendt. *Between Past and Future: Six Exercises in Political Thought*, 143—171. New York: The Viking Press.

Arendt, Hannah (1968). *Men in Dark Times*. New York: Harcourt, Brace & World.

Arendt, Hannah (1981a). *Thinking*. In Hannah Arendt. *The Life of the Mind*. Ed. Mary McCarthy. San Diego/New York/London: Harcourt Brace Jovanovich.

Arendt, Hannah (1981b). *Willing*. In Hannah Arendt. *The Life of the Mind*. Ed. Mary McCarthy. San Diego/New York/London: Harcourt Brace Jovanovich.

Arendt, Hannah (1992). *Lectures on Kant's Political Philosophy*. Ed. and interpretive essay Ronald Beiner. Chicago: University of Chicago Press.

Arendt, Hannah, and Karl Jaspers (1992). *Correspondence, 1926—1969*. Ed. Lotte Kohler and Hans Saner. Transl. Robert and Rita Kimber. New York: Harcourt Brace Jovanovich.

Arendt, Hannah (1996). *Love and Saint Augustine*. Edited and interpretive essay Joanna Vecchiarelli Scott and Judith Chelius Stark. Chicago: University of Chicago Press.

Arendt, Hannah (1998). *The Human Condition*. 2nd edition. Introduction Margaret Canovan. Chicago: University of Chicago Press.

Arendt, Hannah (2005). Introduction *Into* Politics. In Hannah Arendt. *The Promise of Politics*. Ed. Jerome Kohn. New York: Schocken Books.

Arendt, Hannah (2007). Introduction: Walter Benjamin: 1892—1940. In Walter Benjamin. *Illuminations*. Transl. Harry Zohn. Ed. and introduction Hannah Arendt. Preface Leon Wieseltier. New York: Schocken Books.

Baron, Jeannette M. (1980). Hannah Arendt: Personal Reflections. *Response*, 39, 58—63.

Benhabib, Seyla (2003). *Reluctant Modernism of Hannah Arendt*. Lanham, Md.: Rowman & Littlefield.

Bernauer, James W. (1987). The Faith of Hannah Arendt: Amor Mundi and Its Critique-Assimilation of Religious Experience. In James W. Bernauer (ed.). *Amor Mundi: Explorations in the Faith and Thought of Hannah Arendt*, 1—19. Boston/Dordrecht/Lancaster: Martinus Nijhoff Publishers.

Bielik-Robson, Agata (2014). *Jewish Cryptotheologies of Late Modernity: Philosophical Marranos*. London/New York: Routledge.

Biss, Mavis Louise (2012). Arendt and the Theological Significance of Natality. *Philosophy Compass*, 7(11), 762—771.

Brocke, Edna (2007). Afterward: »Big Hannah«—My Aunt. In Hannah Arendt. *The Jewish Writings*. Ed. Jerome Kohn and Ron H. Feldman. New York: Schocken Books.

Bultmann, Rudolf (1955). *Theology of the New Testament*. Vol. 1. Transl. Kendrick Grobel. New York: Charles Scribner's Sons.

Bultmann, Rudolf (1987a). Karl Barth: The Resurrection of the Dead. In Rudolf Bultmann. *Faith and Understanding*. Ed. and introduction Robert W. Funk. Transl. Louise Pettibone Smith. Philadelphia: Fortress Press.

Bultmann, Rudolf (1987b). The Eschatology of the Gospel of John. In Rudolf Bultmann. *Faith and Understanding*. Ed. and introduction Robert W. Funk. Transl. Louise Pettibone Smith. Philadelphia: Fortress Press.

Bultmann, Rudolf (1987c). The Significance of »Dialectical Theology« for the Scientific Study of the New Testament. In Rudolf Bultmann. *Faith and Understanding*. Ed. and introduction Robert W. Funk. Transl. Louise Pettibone Smith. Philadelphia: Fortress Press.

Canovan, Margaret (1992). *Hannah Arendt: A Reinterpretation of Her Political Thought*. Cambridge/New York: Cambridge University Press.

Chacón, Rodrigo (2012). Hannah Arendt in Weimar: Beyond the Theological-Political Predicament?. In Leonard V. Kaplan and Rudy Koshar (eds.). *The Weimar Moment: Liberalism, Political Theology, and Law*, 73—107. Lanham: Lexington Books.

Dennison, William D. (2008). *The Young Bultmann: Context for His Understanding of God, 1884—1925*. New York: P. Lang.

Disch, Lisa Jane (1996). *Hannah Arendt and the Limits of Philosophy: With a New Preface*. Ithaca, N.Y.: Cornell University Press.

Ferber, Ilit (2013). A Language of the Border: On Scholem's Theory of Lament. *Journal of Jewish Thought and Philosophy*, 21(2), 161—186.

Habermas, Jürgen (1983). *Philosophical-Political Profiles*. Transl. Frederick G. Lawrence. Cambridge, Mass.: MIT Press.

Heller, Anne C. (2015). *Hannah Arendt: A Life in Dark Times*. Boston: Houghton Mifflin Harcourt.

Honig, Bonnie (1993). *Political Theory and the Displacement of Politics*. Ithaca: Cornell University Press.

İlhan Demiryol, Gaye (2018). Arendt and Benjamin: Tradition, Progress and Break With the Past. *Journal of the Philosophy of History*, 12(1), 142—163.

Jaspers, Karl, and Rudolf Bultmann (1954). *Die Frage der Entmythologisierung*. München: Piper.

Jaspers, Karl, and Rudolf Bultmann (2005). *Myth and Christianity: An Inquiry Into the Possibility of Religion Without Myth*. [Translator unknown.] Amherst, N.Y.: Prometheus Books.

Josefson, Jim (2019). *Political Philosophy in the Moment: Narrative of Freedom From Plato to Hannah Arendt*. New York: Routledge.

Josefson, Jim (2020). *Hannah Arendt's Aesthetic Politics: Freedom and the Beautiful*. New York: Palgrave.

Kazin, Alfred. (1978). *New York Jew*. New York: Knopf.

Loidolt, Sophie (2018). *Phenomenology of Plurality: Hannah Arendt on Political Intersubjectivity*. New York: Routledge.

Moyn, Samuel (2008). Hannah Arendt on the Secular. *New German Critique*, 35(3), 71—96.

Rieff, Philip (1952). The Theology of Politics: Reflections on Totalitarianism as the Burden of Our Time. *The Journal of Religion*, 32(2), 119—126.

Taminiaux, Jacques (1997). *The Thracian Maid and the Professional Thinker: Arendt and Heidegger*. Transl. and ed. Michael Gendre. Albany: State University of New York Press.

Van Camp, Nathan (2011). Hannah Arendt and Political Theology: A Displaced Encounter. *Revista Pléyade*, 8, 19—35.

Villa, Dana R. (1996). *Arendt and Heidegger: The Fate of the Political*. Princeton, N.J.: Princeton University Press.

Part III: Final Destination: Secularity

Hannah Arendt and Michael Walzer on the Exodus: Politics in the Hebrew Bible?

Martine Leibovici

In an article published in *Aufbau* on March 27th, 1942, Arendt reminds her readers of the difference between freedom and slavery as recounted by »the Passover story« and the legend of Moses that call »the heart and mind« to »the eternal rebellion [...] against slavery« (Arendt 2007c, 150). Five years later, in an article originally published in *Commentary,* Arendt expresses, albeit in a less directly political way, the same kind of calling out to the Jewish people to reappropriate their own »myth of foundation« in order to recover the »national and political meaning« of the Jewish tradition. In her view, the Jewish people, living for centuries as a pariah people deprived of political power, »did not share in the slow process of secularization that started in Western Europe with the Renaissance« (Arendt 2007a, 299) and that resulted in the severing of politics »not simply [...] from religion in general but very specifically from the Christian creed« (Arendt 1994, 379). This process reached its peak with the Enlightenment, which encouraged Jewish emancipation while having at the same time specific consequences for many Jews »attracted by Enlightenment and culture« who were eager to escape from what they regarded as the narrowness of Jewish life. For them, »[s]ecularization and even secular learning became identified exclusively with non-Jewish culture, so that it never occurred to these Jews that they could have started a process of secularization with regard to their own heritage« (Arendt 2007a, 299). After expressing gratitude to theologians and scholars who preserved »the great religious and metaphysical postbiblical tradition,« she calls for the creation of a cultural atmosphere for Jews, in which »we«—Arendt includes herself in that group—»shall have to discover and deal with this tradition anew in our own terms,« even if that tradition »no longer constitutes a holy past or an untouchable heritage« (ibid., 300).

More than fifty years later, everything happened just as if Michael Walzer, together with Menachem Lorderbaum, Noam J. Zohar and Yair Lorderbaum, had collectively planned to achieve what Arendt had called for in 1947, namely, to deal with the Jewish tradition anew »in our own terms.«

Interviewed by Michah Gottlieb in 2006 about the recent publication of the first two volumes of *The Jewish Political Tradition,* Michael Walzer expresses the hope that the books

> will challenge the claim of orthodox Jews to have a monopoly on the tradition—to be its true owners and authoritative expounders. I want all the texts that we have collected to become (what the Sinai story implies) a common possession. And then I want this possession, these texts, religious and secular, sacred and profane, to be recognized as objects of critical reflection, all of them subject to the same scrutiny, the same questioning.[1]

In his book, *In God's Shadow: Politics in the Hebrew Bible,* Walzer implements his own way of »dealing with the tradition anew in our own terms,« something Arendt never did, in part because her appeal in *Commentary* dates back to the time when she was involved in Jewish politics.[2] Nevertheless, some parts of the Hebrew Bible—the Book of Exodus in particular—are of great importance for her political reflection, and one can say that she poses to them, as Walzer would say, »the same kind of questions« about politics that he would pose to any book, without considering it as God's word (Walzer 2012, ix). Although the Bible is not a political book as such, the political dimension is widely present in it, all the more so since the Western political tradition has extracted more than one model from it. It just so happens that the Exodus also attracted Walzer's attention and, in one of his early books, he considers it to be, like Arendt, a revolutionary paradigm (I). Arendt and Walzer also share a common mistrust of political messianism, even if there is a messianic dimension in Arendt's conception of time (II). In any case, the stakes of their readings are not the same and this has consequences for the way they take the Mosaic Covenant into account. Walzer's project is to »figure out what the ideas (about politics) of the biblical writers were in their own time and place« (ibid., ix), whereas Arendt picks up on what interests her, either to excavate pearls or to identify difficulties caused by the secularization of political concepts derived from the Bible, such as the concept of law. Walzer, recognizing these texts »as objects of critical reflection,« wonders how much we can even talk about politics in the Bible, thus joining an Arendtian perspective of questioning while still revealing their different political sensibilities (III).

---

1 Michah Gottlieb, »Interview with Michael Walzer,« *AJS Perspectives* (Fall 2006), pp. 11—12, quoted in Arkush 2012, 232.

2 Arendt's engagement ceased after the death of Judah L. Magnes in October 1948, five months after the creation of the State of Israel. From July 1948 to Magnes' death, they worked closely together in order to create a group advocating for a federated state.

I. Liberation and Freedom: The Legendary Hiatus Between Past and Future or Exodus as a Revolutionary Paradigm

Arendt rediscovered »the biblical story of the exodus of Israeli tribes from Egypt« in the archives of the American Revolution. This story is one of its »two foundation legends,« besides »Virgil's story of the wanderings of Aeneas after he had escaped burning Troy« (Arendt 1990, 205). Still later, she generalizes the importance of these legends while naming their origins more explicitly: Virgil's *Aeneid* and the Exodus narrative are »[t]he two foundation legends of western civilization, the one Roman and the other Hebrew« (Arendt 1981, 203).[3] Both legends begin with an act of liberation told from the perspective of a future that will redeem us: the promised land in the Bible and the foundation of a new city in the *Aeneid*. In spite of their differences, they teach a common lesson: »freedom is no more the automatic result of liberation than the new beginning is the automatic consequence of the end« (Arendt 1990, 205).[4]

In other words, according to Arendt, Judaism—and not just Athens or Rome—transmitted important political elements to the Western political tradition and, more specifically, to the revolutionary tradition. In *Exodus and Revolution*, Walzer also focuses his attention on »Exodus *as* revolution« and sees it as »a paradigm of revolutionary politics,« by which this »big story [...] became part of the cultural consciousness of the West.« From English Puritans to American revolutionaries, from the Civil rights movement to the South American liberation theology, »a range of political events [...] have been located and understood within the narrative framework that it produces.« And like Arendt, Walzer brings the Exodus close to Virgil's *Aeneid*, while noting the difference between the two legends: »Rome, though it represents for Virgil a ›new order of the ages‹ is not, after all, significantly different from Troy,« whereas »Canaan is the very opposite of Egypt« (Walzer 1985, 7—8, 11—12), because, as Arendt also reminds us, »the conquest of a ›new promised land‹ [...] offers more than Egypt's fleshpots« (Arendt 1981, 204).[5]

---

3 Further on she writes about Canaan not being the »original Jewish home but the land of the Jew's former ›sojourn‹ (Exodus 6:4)« (Arendt 1981, 206), when there's never any question of Jews in the text.

4 See also Arendt 1981, 204—205.

5 Further, like later Walzer, Arendt writes that »those who had started as men of action and had been transformed into men of revolution changed Virgil's great line ›*Magnus ab integro saeclorum*

Arendt and Walzer have a different way of reading, however, and this affects their identification of the political problems posed in the text. Arendt is attentive to the presence of the Exodus legend in the self-interpretation of revolutionary actors, i.e. to the meaning they give to the ongoing revolution in which they are involved. First of all, it indicates their own fear of daring to radically break with an old order and how, in order to make this break, their courage needs support to help them face »the abyss of freedom,« which carries »in itself an element of complete arbitrariness« (ibid., 207). Interestingly, such support is provided not by theories but by ancient narratives, which allow political actors to orient themselves in new situations, provided that these narratives are appropriate to the problems posed by these situations. Arendt uses a very suggestive expression here: the Pentateuch and the *Aeneid* are »thought-things« (ibid., 207)[6] that a human being of action »rethought« in order to interpret what he or she were doing. Like theories, narratives are works of thought, but of another kind, because—as Paul Ricoeur has shown—they are much closer to action than theories are. This is the case of the Exodus legend, which metaphorized the presupposition on which the idea of a new beginning is based: a »hiatus between the end of the old order and the beginning of the new, [...] between a no-longer and a not-yet« (Arendt 1990, 205); it is a hiatus in time, not a theoretical one but a lived void »that opens up« before those who have just accomplished liberation. This void is an »*abyss* of nothingness« (Arendt 1981, 207), an impossible representation within »the currently accepted notion of time as a continuous flow« (Arendt 1990, 205) that usually pushes us to fill this gap by reintegrating its novelty into a »chain of cause and effect« (Arendt 1981, 207).

If the highlighting of this hiatus is the main lesson of the Exodus narrative and the point in Arendt's reading, »it is of no great importance in this context whether the hiatus is being filled by the desolate aimless wanderings of Israeli tribes in the wilderness or by the adventures and dangers which befell Aeneas before he reached the Italian shore« (Arendt 1990, 205). Arendt's reading is thus selective, and this is probably the reason why, from the »transitory period—from bondage to freedom,« she only retains the appearance of »great leaders,« of persons who »were not satisfied to change the world by

nascitur ordo‹ (›the great order of the ages is (re)born as it was in the beginning‹) to the *Novus Ordo Seclorum* (the ›*new* order‹)« (Arendt 1981, 207). Following Walzer's interpretation, she could have noticed that this difference was also at work in the Exodus narrative.

6 This comparative approach is similar to one Arendt made previously between action and story in *The Human Condition* (Arendt 1958, 181 et sqq.).

the gradual reform of an old order,« as if the revolutionaries in the eighteenth century, to whom she compares these great leaders, needed to identify with figures who preceded them in order to carry out their undertaking (Arendt 1981, 204—205).

Like Arendt, Walzer is attentive to the conception of time underlying the biblical narrative and contrasts it to the Greek cyclical concept, which Arendt also, although not explicitly, may have been doing. But unlike Arendt, he takes the narrative more completely into account, approaching it as a *story* that takes the form of a piece of *history,* where events happen only once along a straight line going from past to future. According to Walzer, this in-between is not an empty time but a duration, in the course of which many things occur and various political problems arise. Hence, for Walzer, the Exodus is not made up of »aimless desperate wanderings,« as Arendt characterized it, but is rather an onward march, a transition period that lasted forty years, that is, one generation. This encompassed not only the Covenant but also the transformation of the individuals from slaves to free human beings.

In *Exodus and Revolution*, Walzer refers only once to Arendt's »revolution« book, not to question the passages where she mentions the Exodus, but to criticize those in which she contrasts »tyranny and misery« (Walzer 1985, 30).[7] He negatively draws on this reference in order to stress how much the Exodus is about the interpenetration of both. In the Bible, slavery means *corvée*, »hard bondage,« mistreatment and humiliation, and also »a kind of political rule,« a tyranny, the oppression of an entire people. Although the act of liberation—the Exodus out of Egypt—breaks with both slavery and the Pharaoh's tyranny, it is not enough for human beings to cease being slaves. This problem was precisely posed by Maimonides, as quoted by Walzer: »for a sudden transition from one opposite to another is impossible [...], it is not in the nature of man that after having been brought up in slavish service [...] he should all of a sudden wash off from his hands the dirt (of slavery).« This is why it was the second generation after the exit from Egypt, and not the first, who entered Canaan: »people were born who were not accustomed to humil-

7 Walzer does not quote any passages from *On Revolution*. In a footnote he only refers to chapter II, where we can read, for instance: »The direction of the French Revolution [...] was determined by the exigencies of liberation not from tyranny but from necessity, and it was actuated by the limitless immensity of both the people's misery and the pity this misery inspired« (Arendt 1990, 92).

iation and servitude« (ibid., 27, 32, 54). Besides, the golden calf episode tells us of a kind of homesickness and the appeal of the Egyptian way of life.

Even if she does not refer to the Exodus narrative regarding that point, Arendt is nonetheless perfectly aware of the problem posed by Maimonides, namely the deep imprint that oppression leaves in the minds of the oppressed, which is still at work when they revolt and are tempted by a pure reversal of oppression. According to her, two desires, entangled in reality but distinct in intention, are at work in revolutions, the first being the condition of the second. The first desire is the longing for liberation as a negation of oppression, a desire not to be oppressed any more, which often takes the form of a »passionate hatred of masters« and that, most of the time, leads to reactive violence against the ruling classes. Such violence is unavoidable for disrupting an order of things that is felt to be unjust by a majority of people. But this first desire, Arendt adds, »has never yet resulted in revolution since it is incapable of even grasping, let alone realizing, the central idea of revolution, which is the foundation of freedom«; this is the second desire: a »passion for public or political freedom« (Arendt 1990, 125). From Walzer's point of view, one of the dangers of such a situation is the development of a widening gap between pure revolutionaries and the people for whom they struggle yet perpetually disappoint, so that the purists in power are tempted to use violence in order to force the people to be free (Walzer 2015). In Arendtian terms, we would say that the appearance of such a possibility in the transition period from slavery or oppression to freedom shows exactly how much that freedom is not »the automatic result of liberation« (Arendt 1990, 205).

II. A Common Mistrust of Political Messianism

Even if Arendt is aware of the problems arising during the transitory period, the lesson that captures her attention in the Exodus narrative concerns the human faculty of beginning, which is most clearly deployed in the revolutionary action of »[a]ll those who [...] were not satisfied to change the world by the gradual reform of an old order« (Arendt 1981, 205). As we have seen, Walzer also considers the Exodus to be »a paradigm for revolutionary politics,« except that, for him, it does not only recount the exit from Egypt and the radical break with the Pharaoh; it is also about politics that includes a long series of reforms motivated by the emergence of problems that must be gradually faced and addressed through compromises. Walzer sides with a »social democratic version« of the Exodus, according to which revolution is a process rather than an event, while acknowledging such a version as only being one interpretation among many (Walzer 1985, 7, 54).[8]

In that respect, Walzer is closer to the Jewish interpretative tradition than Arendt, even if, in the preface of *Exodus and Revolution*, he specifies that, having studied the Bible for his *bar mitzvah*,[9] he is able to read the Hebrew of the Bible, but not the Hebrew of the Midrash or of the Jewish medieval commentators that, for him, are only accessible through English translations. However, his interpretative choice is particularly opposed to embracing the terms of political messianism that is found in both a certain revolutionary tradition and in Zionism. To a certain extent, the pattern of Exodus is appropriate to Zionism, which calls on Jews to leave diaspora countries and gather in a promised land. And as far as messianism opens up to a future that commits to breaking with present oppression, it is not hard to see why Zionism and even revolutionary movements in general derive part of their energy from a kind of messianic faith. But political messianism directs such energy towards the hope of a concentrated, total upheaval in an apocalyptic moment for which we cannot just wait and see, but instead must bring about through concrete actions. Political messianism is driven by »a readiness to ›force the End‹ in order to free humanity from evil in general.« As early as *Exodus and Revolution*, Walzer, a lifelong leftist Zionist, noted that messianic Zionism »was by and large the creation of the right, of the so-called Revisionists, and it is in Israel today exclusively a right-wing creed« (Walzer 1985, 139). On this point, Walzer relies on Scholem, who has always refused to consider Zionism a messianic movement, precisely because it occurs in concrete historical situations that always impose limits on the achievement of political ideals.

In his book, *In God's Shadow*, Walzer's purpose is no longer to study »the uses of a biblical story [...] in many countries over many years« but instead, as quoted above, to »figure out what the ideas of the biblical writers were in their own time and place« (Walzer 2012, xi). Generally speaking, the God of

8 Walzer refers to Leibowitz 1976.

9 In *In God's Shadow* he pays tribute to the »superb teacher« Rabbi Hayim Goren Perelmuter, and Walzer lets us know that he has continued to study »with the members of the ›traditional/egalitarian‹ minyan at Princeton University's Center for Jewish Life« (Walzer 2012, xix).

the Bible is a god who promises.[10] He opens a future or, more precisely, a better future where mankind will be delivered and redeemed from its present sufferings and sins. Nonetheless, not every opening of a future is messianic as such, but occurs only when the anticipated futures »are radically discontinuous with the present« (ibid., 169). These ages are announced by formulas such as »in those days, at the end of days, *afterwards*,« and they lie »on the other side of a temporal chasm called by the prophets the ›day of the Lord‹« (ibid., 171, 180). Two versions of messianism in the Bible can be found in the prophetic books: one is the hope of restoring David's kingdom, from which the doctrine of the personal Messiah derives, while the other suggests a restoration of God's kingship, which is a »universal redemption, delivered through Israel and manifest in worship of God and obedience to his law« (ibid., 177). Each prophet gives his own vision either of the Lord's catastrophic day or of the messianic age coming just after. Among these visions, Walzer distinguishes between those displayed by the prophet in public that are »humanly recognizable,« such as Isaiah's, and those remaining secret, such as Daniel's apocalyptic allusions or the Christian Book of Revelation (ibid., 183). Post-biblical messianism, distinguished by Walzer from biblical messianism, developed from these texts not only a mystical, esoteric approach of the days to come but also came to imagine—here Walzer quotes Scholem—»a cosmic antithesis« between »God and the anti-divine powers.«[11] On the one hand, God in the prophetic visions remains, as far as the Bible is concerned, the only actor capable of bringing about messianic times, and it is well known that rabbis in post-biblical exile conditions have always encouraged »pious men and women« to wait and to live »a life [...] in deferment,« in Scholem's words (quoted in Walzer 2012, 183).[12] On the other hand, Walzer emphasizes the non-messianic nature of the Exodus, as evidenced by »the image of people marching« which, with two exceptions, is not found in late biblical books. However, in its move to force an apocalyptic end by acting here and now, political messianism is post-biblical, and although Walzer recognizes the im-

10 Submitting the Bible to a critical reflection requires avoiding anachronisms or treating it as an antique document to be dealt with from a mere historical point of view. Walzer insists on the necessary respect for the Bible's internal significance, by taking seriously the »sense of God's mysterious immediacy« felt by its writers (Walzer 2012, 28), without considering that sense as an ideology or the product of a mystified consciousness.

11 Gershom Scholem, *The Messianic Idea in Judaism and Other Essays on Jewish Spirituality*, Schocken Books, New York 1971, quoted in Walzer 2012, 181.

12 The exceptions are »Ezekiel's forced march through the wilderness (20:33—38) and Second Isaiah's opposing vision of a quick painless return from Babylon (49:9—13)« (Walzer 2012, 170).

portance of the words of hope carried by messianism, he remains suspicious of the type of politics inspiring »[p]olitical activists possessed by a messianic faith« who are »cut loose from all the normal constraints on political action« (ibid., 170, 184).

As we have seen, Arendt's version of the Exodus is certainly not »social democratic.« She does not take into account the march in the desert but rather emphasizes the revolutionary break symbolized by the flight out of Egypt leading to the establishment of a new beginning that reveals the discontinuous structure of time. Focusing on the »deeds of great leaders« who appeared during these transitional periods, while bringing them closer to modern revolutionaries, she admires their »radical utopian thought-trains« which enabled them to recognize the »hiatus in the continuous flow of temporal sequence« (Arendt 1981, 205). According to Bethania Assy, this »time scheme« indicates the imprint of a Jewish »messianic diagram« in Arendt. By using this expression, Assy does not directly refer either to biblical messianism or to the post-biblical messianic tradition, but to their reinterpretation by »central European intellectuals from the 1920s« (Assy 2011, 53—54)[13] who, like Rosenzweig and Benjamin, were at odds with historicism and Hegelianism, both of which had become completely inoperative after the First World War. There is indeed a great affinity between Benjamin's idea that »Redemption looks to the small *fissure* in the ongoing catastrophe« (Benjamin 1985, 50) and Arendt's concept of the *hiatus* through which something new can begin by actualizing the human faculty of natality, making it indeed possible to speak of a messianic dimension in the Arendtian conception of time. For both of them, revolutions are interruptions: in Benjamin's words, »[t]he awareness that they are about to make the continuum of history explode is characteristic of the revolutionary classes at the moment of their action« (Benjamin 2007, 261).[14]

13 On alleged messianism in Arendt and Benjamin, see my paper: Leibovici 2007.

14 After listening to Händel's *Messiah*, Arendt finds the human condition of natality wonderfully expressed by the Christian exclamation »a child is born to us« (Hannah Arendt's letter to Heinrich Blücher, May 18th, 1952, in: Arendt and Blücher 1996, 270). See also an entry around the same time in her *Denktagebuch*, Arendt 2016, I, 208. From Arendt's point of view, however, the Christian formulation is not the only one. She also finds it in the fourth Eclogue of Virgil, who thought that »mit jedem wirklichen Menschen von neuem die große Ordnung der Zeitalter anhebt (magnus ab integro saeclorum nascitur ordo)«—and she specifies in a parenthesis that this poem »gar nicht messianisch ist« (Arendt's letter to Kurt Blumenfeld, May 25th, 1959, in: Arendt and Blumenfeld 1995, 234), which is perhaps more meaningful in the context of a reflection on revolutions.

Despite the structural affinities of this conception with Benjamin's temporality, Arendt takes no explicit interest in the messianic theme as such. On the other hand, she was impressed by Scholem's book *Major Trends in Jewish Mysticism* and, in particular, by the chapter devoted to the Sabbatian movement, which directly concerned her own questions at a time when she was involved in Jewish politics and relied, as we have seen above, on the reactivation of the Passover story in order to urge Jews to act.[15] Of the review she finally succeeded in publishing in 1948, I will mention only two points. First, by responding in the middle of the seventeenth century to the call of the self-proclaimed messiah Sabbatai Tsevi to end exile and join Palestine, many Jews from all over Europe and the Middle East had indeed embarked on »a great political movement« that »Jewish mysticism alone was able to bring about [...] and to translate itself directly into real popular action« because »mystical thought had always prepared its followers for action« (Arendt 2007b, 311, 309). Here Arendt quotes Scholem: »In [the kabbalists'] interpretation of the religious commandments, these are [...] represented as [...] the performance of a secret rite [...] [in such a way that] [t]he religious Jew became a protagonist in the drama of the World« (ibid., 304).[16] Both the action and the myths underlying it could only come from the heterodox tendencies of Judaism that challenged the »life in deferment« encouraged by rabbis. Moreover, not only did messianism keep the Jewish people's flame of hope alive, it also appealed to people to act in the here and now because »the role of the ›protagonist in the drama of the world‹ was defined in terms which applied to every Jew« (ibid., 309).

Second, although her text is oriented towards highlighting the political attitudes involved in the messianic element of Judaism, Arendt also expresses her distance from the way in which mysticism encourages people to act. According to the doctrine of emanation that underlies the transformation of the Halakha into a secret rite, the one who performs the rite is a part of the divinity, participating in the secret power governing the world, not as »an independent entity« but as »an instrument for supreme action« (ibid., 306, 308). This is why mystical speculations have an esoteric character and are reserved for a small select group. But why have esoteric

15 »I've been thinking much about you lately, and not just because I've spoken with a lot of people about your book. The real reason is that I can't get your book out of my mind because it tacitly (please don't think I'm saying ›unconsciously‹) accompanies me in all of my own work« (Arendt to Scholem, May 20th, 1944; see Arendt and Scholem 2017, 21).

16 The first bracketed text is Arendt's and the rest is mine.

mystical ideas reserved for a minority been more attractive to people than »the teachings of the learned rabbis and philosophers, who maintained that their interpretations could be understood by everybody« (ibid., 305)? Arendt answers this question by reminding us that people who are likely to be receptive to this kind of doctrine are in a state of powerlessness, in which they feel themselves »helpless victims of incomprehensible forces« and thus »are naturally inclined to find some secret means for gaining power for participating in the ›drama of the World‹« (ibid., 306). Furthermore, Arendt specifies »*Today, as in the past,* these speculations appeal to all who are actually excluded from action« (ibid., 306; my emphasis). How, then, could she not be suspicious of such a doctrine? How could these mystical speculations not have consequences on the mode of action that they inspire? For all these reasons, which are certainly different than Walzer's, Arendt's reading of the Exodus cannot be considered messianic in the political sense, even if she reads in it how the faculty of beginning opens up an undetermined future and brings about something new in the world.

III. Arendt and the Western Reinterpretation of the Covenant (*brith*): Politics in the Hebrew Bible?

According to Walzer, the Covenant is the main event occurring in the desert, »the political invention of the *Book of Exodus,*« insofar as »[t]here is no precedent for a treaty between God and an entire people« (Walzer 1985, 74). Quite ironically, Walzer wants to »give modern liberal and democratic readers reasons to admire the biblical legislators« (Walzer 2012, 22). For instance, God's words are addressed to anybody of »›the mixed multitude‹ that came out of Egypt with them (Exodus 12:38)« (ibid., 2),[17] regardless of any hierarchy, any gender or age difference, including even strangers. Moreover, the fact that »Israel's law is God's alone,« not any king's or assembly's, means politically that »everyone—kings, elders, priests, judges—is [...] equally subject to the

17 Walzer does not take into account the rabbinic exegesis that interprets the mixed multitude (*erev rav*) as a source of corruption or as the image of unwelcome strangers present in the midst of the holy people. Sabbatianism reversed this interpretation by designating with this expression the riches and the rabbinic elite. This kind of argumentation reveals a current of social criticism and perhaps an emancipatory current within Sabbatianism of which Frankism was a continuation. See Paweł Maciejko's book on the Frankists: Maciejko 2011.

Hannah Arendt, after 1940. Photographed by Fred Stein.
Courtesy of the Hannah Arendt Bluecher Literary Trust / Art Resource, NY.

authority of the law« (ibid., 22—23). It is also true that God asks the people for their consent before they even know what they are committing to. Clearly this is a consent to obey: »Now therefore, if ye will obey my voice indeed, and keep my covenant, then ye shall be a peculiar treasure unto me above all people« (Ex. 19:5), and the people unanimously respond: »All that the LORD hath spoken we will do« (Ex. 19:8). Even if it means agreeing to obey commandments, evoking the necessity of a consent nevertheless presupposes a possible refusal, and the Bible is full of episodes that, if not revolts, are at least episodes of disobedience. Notably, the prophets constantly blame the people for disobedience and the Covenant must be periodically renewed in the course of Hebrew biblical history. According to Walzer, the centrality of the »covenantal idea« is one of the possible reasons why »many of the laws that [Israel's codes] include,« such as social and economics laws, »are laws-with-reasons, justified laws« (ibid., 26—27), as if the full consent at the outset was not sufficient and should be protected from the potential disobedience of the people by providing them with reasons for obedience.

Considering the importance Arendt gives to the revolutionary constitutional and foundational moment, is it not therefore surprising that she only briefly mentions that the »exodus of Israeli tribes from Egypt [...] preceded the Mosaic legislation constituting the Hebrew people« (Arendt 1981, 204)? She does indeed address the Covenant in *On Revolution*, in the chapter referring to the Exodus, but she does not link it to the legend. To understand this, we must turn to Arendt's analysis of the modern revolutionary phenomenon. For her too, something happens »in-between,« in the course of »the very act of liberation« while differing from it in nature: freedom, as an unexpected collective rather than private experience, on the occasion of which »every individual« discovers his or her own capacity and desire »to be seen, heard, talked of, approved and respected by the people about him« or her (Arendt 1990, 33, 119). Arendt quotes John Adams insisting on the diversity of these individuals: men, women and even children, but also old and young, rich or poor, wise and foolish, and so on. Without asking for anybody's approval, they establish themselves as equal participants in public affairs and experience a pleasure that is impossible to enjoy in private: public happiness, the joy of the company of others and the desire to excel in front of them. In other words, they begin to »constitute that space of appearances,« i.e. an in-between in the sense of an in-between men and women, »where freedom can [...] become a visible, tangible reality« (ibid., 33).[18]

18 Here I fully agree with Vivian Liska, when she opposes Agamben's and Arendt's understanding of the gap between past and future: »When Arendt creates a space, Agamben sees a break; [...] where she inserts an opening for the possibility of human action upon worldly reality, he conjures up a reversal that risks undoing not only time and space but the reality of the lived world itself« (Liska 2012, 93).

At the same time, a revolution does not consist of a single space of appearances but of large numbers of them, each constituting what Arendt calls a power. Depending on the place and time, these powers were named townships, clubs, soviets, councils (*Räte*). But if power »exists only in its actualization« (Arendt 1958, 200), then it is not impossible that the old order may return as soon as a good part of the citizens grow tired of spending their time in public places, which is something that will eventually happen. In order to open a future which engages generations to come, »an entirely new *system of power*« has to be established (Arendt 1990, 147; my emphasis), i.e. the foundation of a new political body. Such is the essential challenge and it involves the drafting of a new constitution, a new fundamental Law. However, a revolution is only likely to occur on the basis of a general delegitimization, a radical loss of the authority of the entire political and legal system. As Jacques Derrida writes, commenting on Benjamin, any foundation presupposes a moment of *epoché*, as if the foundation of law were suspended from a void, which is another aspect of the revolutionary hiatus (Derrida 1994, 89). This raises the problem of a new source for the law's legitimacy. In that case, once again, why does Arendt not take the Covenant into account, especially since we can find the difference between liberation and freedom in the Jewish tradition itself? Indeed, according to Shlomo Pines (Pines 1997), the words of the Bible, translated as freedom and free, are *ḥufsa and ḥofshi*, and are usually used when it comes to freeing a slave or a servant. Nonetheless, these words are found neither in the ideal regime in which God reigns, nor in the context of the Maccabean revolt, which corresponds to a kind of war of liberation, nor even in the Book of Exodus, which talks about *exit* from Egypt (*yetsi'at mitzrayim*) or about divine *redemption* (*pidyon* or *ge'ula*), words which belong to the juridical vocabulary. The word *ḥerut* (freedom) appears later in Flavius Josephus' *Judean War*, i.e. at the end of the first year before the Christian era, but more importantly at the beginning of this era, when rabbis wrote the Passover Haggadah as the passage from slavery (*av'dut*) to freedom (*ḥerut*). Rabbis would also insist on the relationship between *ḥerut* (freedom) and *ḥarut* (engraved), indicating thus its difference with *ḥufsa* (liberation), because freedom really begins with the Covenant.[19]

A number of works have recently focused on the question of law in Arendt.[20] From *The Origins of Totalitarianism* to *Eichmann in Jerusalem*, she

19 As Emmanuel Levinas says: »La liberté se grave sur la pierre des tables où s'inscrivent des lois« (Levinas 1961, 219).

20 Among them: Goldoni and McCorkindale 2012; Lefebve 2016.

knows how politically essential it is to safeguard a dimension of law in a society.[21] And, as Vivian Liska shows, in contradistinction to Agamben, »for Arendt, the political importance of Jewish antinomian messianism does not lie primarily and directly in its deactivation of the Law« (Liska 2012, 95). Nonetheless, there are, as far as the Western tradition is concerned, different concepts of law: Greek, Roman, and Hebrew. Among them, only the Roman and Hebrew concepts have been politically significant. Paradoxically, despite the »enormous influence of Roman jurisprudence and legislation upon the development of medieval as well as modern legal systems and interpretations [...], the model in whose image Western mankind had construed the quintessence of all laws« is not Roman but Hebrew and its biblical source is the Covenant: »the laws themselves were understood to be commandments« to which »men owe obedience regardless of their consent and mutual agreements.« In the Covenant, laws are words of God whose voice »tells men: Thou shalt not« (Arendt 1990, 189), their legitimacy derives from Him as a non-worldly, eternal absolute. This model inspired the idea of law as expressing the absolute sovereign's will who embodies the principle of sovereignty as such which Bodin has theorized in his *Six Books of the Republic*. The absolute sovereign who finally emancipated his power from the Church's authority, which had provided him with a religious sanction, certainly was not external to the world. But his uniqueness and his state of being both the source of laws as well as a »*potestas legibus soluta*, power absolved from the laws,« may have been for a long time »a fully satisfactory substitute for the lost religious sanction of secular authority« (ibid., 156, 159). Yet the sovereign still needed to proclaim himself a representative of God on earth to ensure obedience to his will.

The revolutionary breakthrough, during which men and women rediscovered the dignity of political activity, led religious beliefs to an »utter loss of relevance in the political realm« (ibid., 184). From then on, »religious creeds and institutions« had »no publicly binding authority« and political life had »no religious sanction«: »secularism« had become a fact (Arendt 1994, 372). Nonetheless, by endorsing the Rousseauist formulation of the law as an expression of the people's *Volonté Générale*, which Sieyès transformed into the will of the nation, the French Revolution have not only kept the same definition of the law as the expression of *one* will but they have also inherited the need for an absolute source of authority, thus revealing the perplexities of

21 On that topic, see: Leibovici and Roviello 2017; Leibovici 2018.

sovereignty itself. When the French Revolution »put the people into the seat of the king« (Arendt 1990, 156), it established a worldly and secular source of legitimacy for laws. But since the structure of the concept of sovereignty implied that this source was *one* will, the people were conceived as a unity and were supposed to want like *one* man, thus denying the fundamentally plural and agonistic character of the political domain that had manifested during the revolution. In contrast, Greek and Roman law did not require an absolute source of authority, the Roman *lex* being in particular »something which connects two things or two partners whom external circumstances have brought together. […] These ›laws‹ were […] treaties and agreements with which a new alliance, a new unity, was constituted« (ibid., 187). Inspired by Montesquieu rather than by Rousseau, »the American concept of law harks back to the Roman *lex* and to the original experiences of compacts and agreements« (ibid., 313)[22] that recognized the plural nature of the people: *We the People*. In other words, Arendt does not approach the Covenant merely from the perspective of the Hebrew Bible or any Jewish interpretation, but interprets it through a theory of sovereignty, one which is imbued with a Christian doctrine that the French Revolution in particular inherited, covering rather than preserving, in her opinion, what happened in-between the old and the new order. To build on Arendt's reflection, we can say that contrary to what happens in a theocratic religion, in the secular realm the political obligation to respect the laws of the city does not come from a heteronomic voice that would address each one of us by saying: »Thou shalt« or »Thou shalt not.« Still, because the concept of law as an expression of the General Will is built on this model, it still retains something theological. »God's command« is no longer »the source of Law« (Arendt 1979, 290) but rather the command-obedience structure of the divine law that has been secularized through the concept of General Will. In her later work, very far from the Hebrew Bible, Arendt will seek for a concept of consent and a concept of law that would not require an injunction to obedience.[23] In an observation made after the Eichmann trial, she generalized her distrust of the so-called virtue of obedience: »Much would be gained if we could eliminate this pernicious word ›obedience‹ from our vocabulary of moral and political thought« (Arendt 2003, 48).

As Walzer warns us in the preface of *In God's Shadow*, his intention is not to »construct […] an apologetic account of biblical politics« (Walzer 2012, x). In particular, this means not taking it for granted that all the political questions

---

22 Regarding all these issues, see Tassin 2007.

23 See Arendt's text *Civil Disobedience* (Arendt 1972).

we ask ourselves are embodied in the Bible. Even if all human powers are equally subjected to the authority of God's law after the Covenant has been made, the covenantal partners, God and the people, were not equals when they made the contract; accordingly, Walzer asks and elaborates: »is it really possible to say no to an omnipotent God? […] The founding myth, though it insists upon consent, has no room for argument« (ibid., 5—6), God's words are formulated in an »apodictic form (›Thou shalt not…‹)« (ibid., 27). Moreover, Walzer notes that the Covenant constitutes Abraham's descendants as a people to whom God addresses collectively, but »there is no demand on individuals that they act politically […] nor is there any explicit recognition of political space, […] the people exist as a collective, but they don't appear to act collectively« (ibid., 11—12). A member of the Hebrew people is not a citizen in the Greek sense.

Rather than *Politics in the Hebrew Bible,* the subtitle of *In God's Shadow* could have been *Politics in the Hebrew Bible?*; throughout the book, Walzer hesitates to use the word politics. He writes, for instance, that the prophet had a »political (or antipolitical) role in ancient Israel« (ibid., 72). Was it political or antipolitical? It was political, insofar as the prophets speak publicly and openly to an audience. But Walzer reconsiders this statement and wonders: »is this public speech also political speech?« (ibid., 75). Prophets denounce the iniquity of the rich, the kings, and the people, but they never call the people to act and are never interested in any kind of reform: »Prophecy was a kind of public speech that militated against deliberation. God's message overrode the wisdom of men« (ibid., 88), their radicalism was »antipolitical.« Conversely, a highly political moment occurs when the elders demand that judge Samuel steps down and appoints a king as his successor (1 Sam. 8). Until then, God was said to rule, and military victories, even though led by warlords, would be attributed to Him. The request for a king comes at a time when people are facing heavy threats, leading the elders to believe that a warrior king would be better able to protect them. There is something definitively secular and worldly in the institution of kingship: »[o]nly when God is conceived to withdraw, […] to give up his political interventions, is there room for human politics« (ibid., 202). In other words, there can be no politics without contingency, without the opening of a domain depending only on human initiatives, for better or for worse. But worldliness, according to Walzer, is still not enough to grasp what politics is about, »[i]nsofar as political questions are engaged at all, […] disagreement is the norm« (ibid., 204).

In Arendtian terms, plurality, the human in-between, is the main condition of politics as action, which is basically acting in concert and which is always »action-and-speech« together. Moreover, as is clear from her January 1951 to March 1954 *Denktagebuch* entries, Arendt is intensively thinking about plurality and contrasting it with the idea of God as the Creator. Indeed, plurality is definitively this-worldly: »as soon as there are many people, a specifically de-divinized sphere begins. The very one which God could not create. Because [...] in plurality the in-between is established as an only-human non-ideal sphere« (Arendt 2016, I, 275; December 1952).[24] As long as a society is not submitted to totalitarian undertakings, there are always breaches through which something political can happen. Everything put in place to prevent this can be called antipolitical. Moreover, for Arendt, plurality is disruptive insofar as it involves natality, the appearance of an unpredictable novelty in the world, for which she borrows the term of miracle from the biblical tradition. This is less clear in Walzer's approach, which is much more orientated toward progressive politics. Here perhaps lies the difference between Arendt's plurality and Walzer's pluralism that infers the existence of already constituted entities whose identities need to be protected and whose relationships need to be organized.

IV. Pearls of Plurality

I mentioned previously that Walzer is closer to the Jewish interpretative tradition than Arendt. According to this tradition, the Covenant is recounted twice (in Exodus and Deuteronomy) and there is not just one but three legal codes that are »all said to have been revealed by God« (Walzer 2012, 6).[25] When looking closely, significant differences can be observed between these versions. Discovering these differences has been the starting point for critical biblical studies, which attributes them to authors who wrote at different times and belonged to different sectors of Hebrew society. As a secular reader, Walzer notes this plurality of writers but also takes into account the gesture of compiling the corpus under *one* name, Bible or Torah, thus making it into *one* book while, at the same time, allowing for the many contra-

24 All translations from German are by Mark Farrier.

25 The first code is in Exodus 20—23, the second in the Leviticus, the third in Deuteronomy.

dictions to be left in it. His hypothesis is that these contradictions are »the textual residue« of »actual discussions that went on within priestly or scribal or juridical circles« and that »[t]he effect of the disputes is [...] to pluralize the law« (ibid., 28—29). Although these different positions do not appear in the text as identifiable political doctrines, nor do they correspond to the »contradictory teachings of the schools of Hillel and Shamai« whose Talmud claims that »these and these are the words of the living God« (ibid., 33), it can be assumed that the biblical writers chose not to harmonize them and to leave them, so to speak, side by side. »The result of their choice, Walzer writes, was a written law that made possible those strange open-ended legal conversations that constitute the oral law of later Judaism« (ibid., 33). I don't know how much Walzer practices Talmudic study, but he knows enough about it to have retained the principle of the accepted multiplicity of interpretations. With this reading he strives, in his own way, to restore the plurality of viewpoints that are at work in the biblical text. In other words, he »deals with the tradition anew,« but from a secular point of view, which is: »in our own terms.«

Like Walzer, Arendt is a secular reader of the Bible, but, unlike Walzer, she picks up fragments of the book without putting her own interpretation in relation to other possible ones. This gesture could be linked to one of Arendt's main observations: the thread of tradition has been broken. This is particularly true for a lot of secularized Jews regarding the Jewish tradition. Yet out of this break both a problem and a chance arise. A problem: »[w]e are in danger of forgetting.« A chance: the past could be opened up to us »with unexpected freshness and tell us things no one has yet had ears to hear« (Arendt 1961, 94). This chance manifests itself as the past brought back as »thought fragments« thanks to the art of citation, which Arendt evokes in her essay about Walter Benjamin (Arendt 1968, 193). And in so far as narratives are »thought-things« (Arendt 1981, 207), Arendt discovers such »thought fragments« in the biblical narrative, which we can access independently of religious faith and even of the Jewish interpretative tradition, provided we are able to dive for and excavate the pearls that they are.

Thus, the Exodus narrative is one of these pearls that allowed American revolutionaries to represent, i.e. to think the hiatus of time they were experiencing. But the Bible, especially Genesis and the Decalogue, is present at another level that provides a backdrop to Arendt's elaboration of some of her own fundamental categories concerning action. The importance of Augustine's words—*Initium ut esset homo creatus est* (»that a beginning be made man was created«)—for Arendt's conception of natality is well known. There are other important reflections concerning God's creation that she did not develop in her published texts but that are included in her personal workshop, her *Denktagebuch*, for instance, before considering the political efficiency of monotheism, she pays attention to it at a speculative and philosophical level (see Arendt 2016, I, 357). By taking the biblical text directly into consideration, as close as possible to its Hebrew original meaning, she argues that this meaning was altered by »Religion,« the Christian religion in particular, which translated the *Ten Words* of the *Decalogue, aseret ha'devarim*, into the *Ten Commandments*. Such a translation has indeed ensured a political efficiency, but it had a direct consequence upon the idea of God conceived »as the commander and man as the follower« (ibid., 399; July 1953). Arendt brings the Decalogue closer to Genesis, where the creation of the world does not come from a fabrication but is a reality that is born of a word. Speaking is not only meaning and the Bible highlights two essential dimensions of language. Arendt does not mention it, but it is noticeable that the first of the *Ten Words* is not a »Thou shall not...« but »I am the LORD thy God.« In her words: »Self-revelation, which already happens in the calling of one's own name« (ibid., 399). This is connected to what she states in *The Human Condition* about the »affinity between speech and revelation« (Arendt 1958, 178) of *who* I am. Moreover, Arendt interprets God's word »as the beginning of an action in the sense of a coming into being,« as an »speech act« (Arendt 2016, I, 399; July 1953), which refers to another essential dimension of language. Here speaking is not the ordering that an order be obeyed but is the beginning of an action. From Arendt's interpretation, the action is not exactly God's, or rather God's word is an action as far as it incites others to act. By detecting the overlapping of this conception of speech with the idea of command, isn't Arendt looking for a gesture similar to the one she detects in Plato with his distinction between *archein* (to begin) and *prattein* (to act)? Could she be projecting her own concerns onto the text? Or is she thinking of the response the Hebrews gave to the words of God before the proclamation of the Decalogue: »All that the LORD hath spoken we will do« (Ex. 19:8), or even to the fact that God's words are always spoken in the future tense?

Works Cited

Arendt, Hannah (1958). *The Human Condition*. Chicago/London: University of Chicago Press.

Arendt, Hannah (1961). What Is Authority?. In Hannah Arendt. *Between Past and Future: Six Exercises in Political Thought*. New York: The Viking Press.

Arendt, Hannah (1968). Walter Benjamin. In Hannah Arendt. *Men in Dark Times*. New York: Harcourt, Brace & World.

Arendt, Hannah (1972). Civil Disobedience. In Hannah Arendt. *Crises of the Republic*. New York: Harcourt Brace Jovanovich.

Arendt, Hannah (1979). *The Origins of Totalitarianism*. San Diego/New York/London: Harcourt Brace Jovanovich.

Arendt, Hannah (1981). *Willing*. In Hannah Arendt. *The Life of the Mind*. Ed. Mary McCarthy. San Diego/New York/London: Harcourt Brace Jovanovich.

Arendt, Hannah (1990). *On Revolution*. London/New York: Penguin Books.

Arendt, Hannah (1994). Religion and Politics. In Hannah Arendt. *Essays in Understanding, 1930—1954*. Ed. Jerome Kohn. New York: Harcourt, Brace & Co.

Arendt, Hannah, and Kurt Blumenfeld (1995). *»...in keinem Besitz verwurzelt«: Die Korrespondenz*. Herausgegeben von Ingeborg Nordmann und Iris Pilling. Hamburg: Rotbuch Verlag.

Arendt, Hannah, and Heinrich Blücher (1996). *Briefe 1936—1968*. Herausgegeben und mit einer Einführung von Lotte Köhler. München: Piper.

Arendt, Hannah (2003). Personal Responsibility Under Dictatorship. In Hannah Arendt. *Responsibility and Judgment*, 17—48. Ed. and introduction Jerome Kohn. New York: Schocken Books.

Arendt, Hannah (2007a). Creating a Cultural Atmosphere. In Hannah Arendt. *The Jewish Writings*. Ed. Jerome Kohn and Ron H. Feldman. New York: Schocken Books.

Arendt, Hannah (2007b). Jewish History, Revised. In Hannah Arendt. *The Jewish Writings*. Ed. Jerome Kohn and Ron H. Feldman. New York: Schocken Books.

Arendt, Hannah (2007c). Moses or Washington. In Hannah Arendt. *The Jewish Writings*. Ed. Jerome Kohn and Ron H. Feldman. New York: Schocken Books.

Arendt, Hannah (2016). *Denktagebuch 1950—1973*. Zwei Bände. Ed. Ursula Ludz and Ingeborg Nordmann. München: Piper Verlag.

Arendt, Hannah, and Gershom Scholem (2017). *The Correspondence of Hannah Arendt and Gershom Scholem*. Ed. Marie Luise Knott. Transl. Anthony David. Chicago: The University of Chicago Press.

Arkush, Allan (2012). Michael Walzer's Secular Jewish Thought. *Journal of Modern Jewish Studies*, 11(2), 221—241.

Assy, Bethania (2011). Hannah Arendt and the Jewish Messianic Tradition: Singular Event and Testimonial Narrative. *Trumah: Zeitschrift der Hochschule für Jüdische Studien Heidelberg*, 20, 53—54.

Benjamin, Walter (1985). Central Park. Transl. Lloyd Spencer. *New German Critique*, 34, 32—58.

Benjamin, Walter (2007). *Illuminations*. Transl. Harry Zohn. Ed. and introduction Hannah Arendt. Preface Leon Wieseltier. New York: Schocken Books.

Derrida, Jacques (1994). *Force de loi: le fondement mystique de l'autorité*. Paris: Galilée.

Goldoni, Marco, and Christopher McCorkindale (eds.). (2012). *Hannah Arendt and the Law*. Oxford/Portland, Oregon: Hart Publishing.

Lefebve, Vincent (2016). *Politique des limites, limites de la politique: la place du droit dans la pensée de Hannah Arendt*. Bruxelles: Éditions de l'Université de Bruxelles.

Leibovici, Martine (2007). En la grieta del presente: messianismo o natalidad?: Hannah Arendt, Walter Benjamin y la historia. *Al Margen*, 21—22, 194—201.

Leibovici, Martine, and Anne-Marie Roviello (2017). *Le pervertissement totalitaire: la banalité du mal selon Hannah Arendt*. Paris: Éditions Kimé.

Leibovici, Martine (2018). Pervertissement totalitaire et perversion de la loi: Olivier Jouanjan avec Hannah Arendt. In Claudia Hilb and Martine Leibovici (eds.). *Why Arendt Matters/Pourquoi Arendt importe*. Dossier, Paris Diderot 2018. 20.06.2021 http://lcsp.univ-paris-diderot.fr/Arendt/bravard.html.

Leibowitz, Nehama (1976). *Studies in Shemot: The Book of Exodus*. Transl. Aryeh Newman. Jerusalem: World Zionist Organization.

Levinas, Emmanuel (1961). *Totalité et infini: essai sur l'extériorite*. La Haye: M. Nijhoff.

Liska, Vivian (2012). A Lawless Legacy: Hannah Arendt and Giorgio Agamben. In Marco Goldoni and Christopher McCorkindale (eds.). *Hannah Arendt and the Law*, 89—97. Oxford/Portland, Oregon: Hart Publishing.

Maciejko, Paweł (2011). *The Mixed Multitude: Jacob Frank and the Frankist Movement, 1755—1816*. Philadelphia: University of Pennsylvania Press.

Pines, Shlomo (1997). *La liberté de philosopher: de Maïmonide à Spinoza*. Trad., introd. et notes de Rémi Brague avec la collab. de Renée Bouveresse-Quilliot et Gérard Haddad. Préf. Zeev Harvey. Malakoff: Desclée de Brouwer.

Tassin, Étienne (2007). Le peuple ne veut pas. In Anne Kupiec, Martine Leibovici, Géraldine Muhlmann et al (eds.). *Hannah Arendt, crises de l'État-nation: pensées alternatives*. Paris: Sens & Tonka.

Walzer, Michael (1985). *Exodus and Revolution*. New York: Basic Books.

Walzer, Michael (2012). *In God's Shadow: Politics in the Hebrew Bible*. New Haven: Yale University Press.

Walzer, Michael (2015). *The Paradox of Liberation: Secular Revolutions and Religious Counterrevolutions*. New Haven: Yale University Press.

The Promise Inherent in Natality: Performance and Invocation

Christina Schües

> Händels *Messias*. Das Halleluja nur zu verstehen aus dem Text: Es ist uns ein Kind geboren. Die tiefe Wahrheit dieses Teils der Christuslegende: Aller Anfang ist heil, um des Anfangs willen, um dieses Heiles willen, hat Gott den Menschen in die Welt hinein geschaffen. Jede neue Geburt ist wie eine Garantie des Heiles in der Welt, wie ein Versprechen der Erlösung für die, welche nicht mehr Anfang sind.[1]
>
> *(Hannah Arendt, Denktagebuch, Band I, p. 208)*

Hannah Arendt, the political thinker of natality, was well acquainted with the traditions of philosophy, theology, politics, and literature. The acts of Socrates and Jesus, the works of Augustine and Immanuel Kant, Martin Heidegger and Karl Jaspers, as well as the theologian Rudolf Bultmann were part of her daily and academic life. Arendt has primarily been portrayed as a political thinker, yet some readers of Arendt, including the editors of this volume, pose the question of whether her thinking is actually, perhaps obscurely, grounded in religious beliefs. I will discuss this question with regard to her central theme of natality.

From Plato to Heidegger, mortality has been a key term in the history of philosophy. Arendt, however, did not accept mortality as the leading motive for human conduct; instead, she reversed temporal order and posited natality as a primary principle of philosophical thinking. Even though she did not herself theorize in detail the concept of natality, she clearly posited it as a foundational anthropological and political category: »men, though they

1 »The Hallelujah can only be understood from the lyrics: unto us a child is born. The deep truth of this part of the legend of Christ: All beginnings are a salvation, for the sake of the beginning, for the sake of this salvation, God created man in the world. Every new birth is like a guarantee of healing in the world, like a promise of salvation of those who no longer are a beginning.« The author thanks Mark Farrier for his advice in translating the fragments from Arendt's *Denktagebuch* and for helpful comments.

must die, are not born in order to die but in order to begin« (Arendt 1958, 246).

Arendt wrote at a time when the fundamental categories of thought and judgement were not sufficient to describe what was happening, a time in which the world was collapsing and political responsibility could no longer be practiced by entering into events, but only by refraining from it. The destruction of Europe and, above all, the »determined attempt to exterminate« the Jews had transformed the »ground of facts into an abyss« (Arendt 1948, 9) into which one was drawn if they tried to »explain« something like Auschwitz by studying the history of the German or Jewish people (ibid., 10). A basic trust (*Grundvertrauen*) had been broken by historical events, namely, the trust of the people in their world.

Arendt, having survived in exile the »spectacle of hell [*Höllenspektakel*]« (Arendt and Jaspers 1985, 58),[2] attempted to ask, within the framework of the human condition: how can we again be at home in a world that now seems so fundamentally unfamiliar and alien that even trying to speak or write about it seems impossible. Arendt posits one element of the human condition—natality—as containing a promise for new beginnings and for the constitution of relationships and plurality among people. What kind of promise is inherent in natality? Can the entry point of birth be of help and hope in times of crisis?

Since religious sources play a role in Arendt's thinking and writing, and since she refers explicitly to Jewish thinking and Christianity, quoting from the Bible and other religious writings, the question is whether her approach to natality and birth actually rests on religious beliefs. Is the idea of natality as a promise inspired by religious writings? Is it even possible that her writing is theological, i.e., based on the belief in God?

1. Why *Is* a Promise Inherent in Natality?

When basic trust and faith in the world and in the faculty to judge have been fundamentally broken down, then—then in particular—does the constitution and upholding of the world need birth as a source for new beginnings. When new people are born into the world they begin within a relational

2 Arendt to Jaspers, 18 November 1945.

structure and, from then on, may create new relationships and a new path of life. Because of being born, human beings have the capacity to begin something anew; natality's function is to open up to the world and to orient itself towards the future.

Arendt takes natality, the simple fact that human beings are *born* into the world and not, as Martin Heidegger suggests, *thrown* into it, as a central element of the human condition and as the basis for the possibility of acting and speaking politically, because birth means being born *from* and *with* someone and, therefore, means being in relationship. »Re ›human condition‹: The condition of acting is natality, the condition of thinking is mortality. With regard to *life*, thinking describes the conditions through which I prefer life over death« (Arendt 2016, II, 681; April 1968).[3]

Hannah Arendt posits the concept of birth as a fundamental human condition. Taking seriously Augustine's idea of [*initium*] *ergo ut esset, creatus est homo* (»that there be a beginning, man was created«; Arendt 1958, 177),[4] most of her books end with a reference to the fact that human beings are born. In order to understand why natality contains an inherent promise, I need to tease out the philosophical importance of the concept of birth as it relates to the freedom of the will, beginning with acting and understanding.

Freedom seems more rooted in the will than in thinking. In the history of philosophy, freedom of the will has been both disregarded and mistrusted, even seen as a »curse« (Arendt 1981b, 5). The rise of secularization in modern times made people aware of the contingency of their actions. Arendt observes that the origin of the will can be found in theology and not in the tradition of philosophical thinking.[5] The awareness of the experience of being capable of volition is Hebrew in origin, but was not political and did not relate to either the world of appearance or to that of human affairs. Rather, in reference to the Apostle Paul, she notices that this experience is only concerned with one's interiority (ibid., 63). Thus, it is grounded in the discovery of the »two-in-one« that was already known to the Greeks as the activity of thinking and thus related to conscience (Arendt 1981a, 179 et passim). Augustine, the »first philosopher of the will« and the »only philosopher the Romans ever had,« formulated the distinction between the *I will* and the *I can*

3 In the original: »Ad ›human condition‹: Die Bedingung des Handelns ist die Gebürtlichkeit, die Bedingung des Denkens ist die Sterblichkeit. Auf das *Leben* bezogen, zeichnet das Denken die Bedingungen vor, unter denen ich das Leben dem Tod vorziehe.«

4 The quote comes from *De civitate Dei*, book XII, chapter 21 (Arendt wrongly put chapter 20).

5 See Arendt 1981b, 19. The Aristotelian notion of *phronesis* which lies in between desire and reason is rather a pre-form of the will.

(Arendt 1981b, 84). Volition and this distinction of the will and the counter-will became central components of the history of philosophy.[6] Augustine saw a contradiction between divine omniscience and human volition. He solved this problem with the assertion introduced above: that there be a beginning, man was created. Arendt appropriates this assertion as the central ontological and anthropological confirmation of the freedom of human beings.

The purpose of the creation of man was to make possible a *beginning*: »That there be a beginning man was created, before whom nobody was«—»*Initium* [...] *ergo ut esset, creatus est homo, ante quem nullus fuit.*« The very capacity for beginning is rooted in *natality*, and by no means in creativity, not in a gift but in the fact that human beings, new men, again and again appear in the world by virtue of birth (ibid., 217).[7]

The fact that human beings are born from someone else means that they are born into a relationship. They can therefore enact their natality, i.e. act and speak with other people and bring new beginnings—relations and

6 However, the will remained as the tie between the holy and spiritual trinity of conscience, reason, and volition.

7 Augustine's proposition is a real alternative to the Occidental tradition. In the discussion concerning free will and the human capacity for volition, Arendt follows Duns Scotus' preference for contingency over necessity, Kant's concern with freedom as unconditionality of thinking, and later, Nietzsche and Heidegger's equation of power and will that is grounded in their discussion about willing and ability (*Wollen und Können*) as contradictions. Arendt shows that, from a nihilistic perspective, both discard the will. Nietzsche invented the idea of the eternal return, and Heidegger proposed a turn from the will to the not-willing (*Nichtwollen*). Arendt only followed these lines of reasoning in her second volume of *The Life of the Mind*. Last but not least, she turns to the phenomenon of *revolution*. She took this phenomenon as an option for reinterpreting spontaneity and beginning: »The abyss of pure spontaneity, which in the foundation legends is bridged by the hiatus between liberation and the constitution of freedom, was covered up by the device, typical of the Occidental tradition [...] of understanding the *new* as an improved re-statement of the old« (Arendt 1981b, 216). And Arendt adds in parentheses that this tradition was the only one »where freedom has always been the *raison d'être* of all politics« (ibid., 216). If we followed this tradition of the progress of political theory, then the »original« concept of freedom would survive only »in utopian and unfounded promises of a final ›realm of freedom‹ that, in its Marxian version at any rate, would indeed spell ›the end of all things,‹ a sempiternal peace in which all specifically human activities would wither away« (ibid., 216). After these observations, which delineate a »frustrating« conclusion, Arendt turns to Augustine who described what could have become an ontological foundation of a political theory if people had followed up on this insight that we all actually acknowledge: human beings are finite beings, or—to put it theologically—»God created man as a temporal creature, *homo temporalis*; time and man were created together, and this temporality was affirmed by the fact that each man owed his life not just to the multiplication of the species, but to birth, the entry of a novel creature who [...] was to make possible a *beginning*« (ibid., 216—217). Thus, relating to Augustine does not mean believing that each new beginning leads to an improvement; rather it leads to a difference that can be taken up for better or worse.

plurality—into the world. In both concepts—natality and action—inheres a beginning in the world that is constitutive of relationality and plurality in the public political space (see Schües 2019). This possibility is inherent in natality because it enables a beginning—a beginning of acting and speaking in the political world. This particular feature is not only fundamental to Arendt's work in general but, furthermore, contains a promise that gives rise to optimism concerning historical crisis and political conduct.

Birth as beginning realizes plurality because someone new comes like a »miracle« into the world; such a beginning realizes plurality first by making people appear in their relationships not only in the sense of what (e.g. a woman, a professional) they are but of who they are and, secondly, by bringing something new into the world. Arendt assumes a structural parallelism of existential natality and political natality, where the former brings into the world a new beginning, i.e. a newborn, while the latter initiates a new beginning by way of political action and public speech. Thus, the basis of natality is the capacity to begin new action and speech and to take the initiative to create new relationships with other people and, thereby, a new political space between human beings. Both existential and political natality can be understood as introducing a »new world« into the world.[8] Regardless of what may transpire, a relationship is a beginning, even if it is broken off or becomes a matter of indifference. The beginning is rooted in this relation (see Cavarero 1997, 212; Schües 2008, chapter VI).

Arendt would agree that all beginnings—of action or birth—are based on accidental conditions and, because of the introduction of the new, they contain »a measure of complete arbitrariness« (Arendt 1990, 206). Certainly, the relationships with our parents, grandparents, or other relatives are contingent. But more importantly for Arendt, the contingency and »the obvious danger of arbitrariness« are the prices we pay for being free and for having gained the experience of freedom by beginning with other people (Arendt 2003, 168). In analogy, by responding to one's own birth, the practice of acting and speaking is world-opening and is bound to the relationships with others who respond to the one who began to act. If nobody were to connect to the beginning of someone else, then it simply would not become a begin-

8 Arendt does not suggest that the new is always necessarily good. The new that came with totalitarianism suffocated the relationships between human beings and annihilated the pluralism among them. In *The Crisis in Education* she wrote: »But the world, too, needs protection to keep it from being overrun and destroyed by the onslaught of the new that bursts upon it with each new generation« (Arendt 1961, 186).

ning. Therefore, »[t]his character of startling unexpectedness is inherent in all beginnings and in all origins« (Arendt 1958, 178).

Therefore, »[p]hilosophically speaking, to act is the human answer to the condition of natality. Since we all come into the world by virtue of birth, as newcomers and beginnings, we are able to start something new« (Arendt 1970, 82). In this quote, Arendt very clearly suggests that *structurally* the first birth, the birth to the world, resembles the second birth, the beginning of acting in the world. For whoever acknowledges the fact that human beings are born in their concrete uniqueness will also have to confirm the plurality and relatedness of human beings—regardless of how they live. This confirmation can be taken as a response by which human beings refer to their own birth: »With word and deed we insert ourselves into the human world, and this insertion is like a second birth, in which we confirm and take upon ourselves the naked fact of our original physical appearance« (Arendt 1958, 176—177). Thus, if the plurality and relationality of human beings are initiated again and again by birth, and if these are the human conditions—*conditio humana*—of human beings, then by our political action we respond to the relationality and plurality that were initiated at the time of our own birth. By affirming the fact of being born and by responding to this structural situatedness, we are drawn into responsibility for ourselves and for the very concrete structure of beginning. Responsibility therefore means renewing the world in response to, in recognition of and with care for the world, i.e., a world in which plurality and successful interpersonal relationships are recognized and sought after. Arendt elevates natality to the condition of action and speech, and thus to the condition of responsibility in the world and for its constitution and re-constitution. Ideally, the world itself contains the conditions of appearance and possibility for the realization of natality. Thus, care for natality would be both a political and an ethical matter for the *conditio mundana*, the constitution of the world itself.

A further characteristic of natality is bound to understanding: the world in which someone is born is an alien one (*Fremdwelt*) that needs to be learned and understood. Everyone is born as a stranger into an alien world and lives in it from then on. Being alive is not, however, understood in a reductionist sense but in a specifically human way, which is its way of understanding:

> It is the specifically human way of being alive; for every single person needs to be reconciled to a world into which he was born a stranger and in which, to the extent of his distinct uniqueness, he always remains a stranger. Understanding begins with birth and ends with death (Arendt 1994, 308).

Since human beings are born as newcomers and strangers, understanding begins with their birth: »Each new generation, every human being, as he becomes conscious of being inserted between an infinite past and an infinite future, must discover and ploddingly pave anew the path of thought« (Arendt 1981a, 210). By inhabiting the world and by finding new paths for thinking, reconciliation with a world that has been broken down may begin. Thus, Arendt even draws an analogy between the understanding and reconciliation with the world that happens with birth or being a newcomer in a strange world, and the strangeness and unworldliness of a world's crisis or collapse. It is due to the enabling of these three dimensions of beginning—freedom of will, acting, and understanding—that a promise is inherent in natality.[9]

2. What Sort of Promise Is Inherent in Natality?

Arendt acknowledges that, in the history of philosophy, the promise is a central concept of the moral and the contract a central concept of the political (see Arendt 2016, I, 135). Examples of different ideas of promise can be found in the Roman legal system and its agreements and treaties (*pacta sunt servanda*) or, with reference to Abraham, the founding legends (*Gründungslegenden*) and the eventual conquest (*Eroberung*) of a promised land (»And the LORD appeared unto Abram, and said, Unto thy seed will I give this land«; Gen. 12:7). Different sorts of promises inhere in these references to contracts, legends or foundations. Basically, three notions of promise can be distinguished:

9 Yet, the strangeness that surrounds every newcomer upon his entry into the world may be one that goes hand in hand with a basic trust in the world. It is a world that is unknown but still one in which a newcomer can grow up, which in its immediate connection with natality brings a newcomer or a beginner to appear, and which appears through newcomers. But it may also be a world that is impregnated with danger, broken relationships, and loss; the intentional turning towards the world in wonder and curiosity may then become unbearable. Arendt wrote in a time of totalitarian government and she tried to understand this central event of our world: »[T]o understand totalitarianism is not to condone anything, but to reconcile ourselves to a world in which such things are possible at all« (Arendt 1994, 308). However, drawing Arendt's account a bit further, it is not only the understanding that might begin with a birth, but also a reconciliation with a world whose relationships have been broken and which needs a new beginning.

First, a promise can be understood in the sense of a pledge (*Gelöbnis*), e.g. the promised land, or as a promise to a third instance, such as God, a state, a government, or one's conscience. Its direction is futural yet infinite. Second, promise can be understood in the sense of fate, spirituality, or prophecy (*Verheißung*). Its temporal sense is infinite. And third, a promise can concern matters between two persons, in which case its temporal sense is futural and finite because it is redeemed (or broken) by the promised action or replaced by a contract. Below, I will focus on the third concept of a promise; however, by considering the interrelation between natality and promise, it can be shown that a promise, in its second sense (prophecy), might also be involved.

The promise, particularly the keeping of a promise, has been at the center of political and moral philosophy throughout modernity. Niccolò Machiavelli saw the promise as a mere tactic to gain an advantage; Thomas Hobbes understood it as a kind of pre-contract giving the binding force within a relationship and for the future. Promises are given to other persons who (ideally) believe in the given promise. Thus, people are bound into the contract and the promise expires. Friedrich Nietzsche referred to the faculty of promising in *On the Genealogy of Morality* as »the will's memory« (Nietzsche 2007, 35). He claims that the capacity to promise gives the human self its superiority because it privileges him over animals and gives him a particular responsibility in connection to his pride and superiority. Thus, it functions as an empowering of the will. Yet as Nietzsche claims in *Human, All Too Human*, we cannot promise everything. We can promise actions but not sensations. Thus, we cannot, for instance, promise love (Nietzsche 1996, 42).

Arendt was particularly influenced by Hobbes and Nietzsche; she emphasizes that a promise gives some security for the future but that its binding force rests on the morality of the one who gives the promise and the belief of the one to whom it is given. As Arendt says in *The Human Condition*:

> The moment promises lose their character as isolated islands of certainty in an ocean of uncertainty, that is, when this faculty is misused to cover the whole ground of the future and to map out a path secured in all directions, they lose their binding power and the whole enterprise becomes self-defeating (Arendt 1958, 244).

For Arendt, »all morality can effectively be reduced to promises and the keeping of what is promised. This has nothing at all to do with the concrete question of right or wrong on the one side and the ›Ten Commandments‹ on the other« (Arendt 2016, I, 54; my transl.).[10] Promises and the acts of keeping them show that morality takes place between people and thus they constitute a strong moral and social bond between them. More concretely, in order to understand why there is a promise already embedded in existential natality and how this can be the foundational structure of political natality, two dimensions of natality's promise must be distinguished. One has to do with the notion of trust. In order to explain the relation between promise and trust, we will have to go beyond her text. The other dimension can be brought out through Arendt's references to tradition and reliance on religion, which are expressed by the vocabulary of miracle, hope, and faith.

In natality inheres (a) a promise to the child that, if given, relies on trust and is given in the face of the world because of *amor mundi*, and (b) a promise to the world on behalf of the world.

(a) The relationship between promise and trust is based on different aspects. Children are born with a basic trust in the world and their dependence manifests itself in boundless trust. Enacting parenthood means responding to the newborn's basic trust with a promise. However, this promise is not an act of speech, but a moral and a bodily parental promise, which *is* the mother as mother and the father as father, thus, a promise with a double sense; one lies in the presence of a person herself and her performance as mother or father, and the other responds to the newcomer with recognition of him or her as a human person with dignity (see Schües 2008, 468). Thus, I agree with Arendt that with the birth of a child, new trust comes into the world. The promise is »induced by a trust granted, which uses the one to whom the child is entrusted as the one who will justify this trust. Every child gives birth to a new trust, which others can prove worthy of without having earned it beforehand« (Liebsch 1996, 339). From this idea, we can conclude that the only way to answer to this trust lies in the promise! This promise, the correlate of which is trust, has a binding force that is not grounded on reciprocity (for otherwise the child would not be free) and that cannot (or should not) be expressed in the language of rights, planning or administration, means or ends. The threat of betraying the child always lurks in this promise.[11] In this parent-child relationship, the children are dependent on the promise for

10 The original German is as follows: »Alle Moral lässt sich wirklich auf Versprechen und Halten des Versprochenen reduzieren. Dies hat nichts zu tun mit der konkreten Frage von Recht und Unrecht einerseits und den ›Zehn Geboten‹ anderseits.«

11 Compare this to the betrayal regarding fidelity: Marcel 1949, 97; Liebsch 1996, 343. Arendt does not follow up this line of thinking.

their further way of inhabiting the world.[12] The promise is not simply a reaction to the children's dependency and their being exposed to someone's mercy (*Ausgeliefertsein*). If the level of the child's dependence were to be used as the sole basis of the promise, the child's exposure would be reduced to the level of survival. Rather, a promise is given, as Emmanuel Levinas would claim, in the face of the newborn child, and thereby *to* society as well, emphatically speaking, to the world and its »social ties« (Bedorf and Herrmann 2016).

(b) A promise is not just initiated between the parents and a child. Bringing Arendt's approach to natality closer to her political intention, a promise of natality is one that the parents of a child give to the *world*. The openness and willingness to conceive and give birth to a child implies an affirmation of the world, which Arendt describes emphatically with the expression *amor mundi*—as love or care for the world.[13] Thus, the parents are bound to a promise to the world in the face of the child, because they have brought a child into the world. But they are also held responsible because of gratitude for everything they have received. Arendt is ambivalent as to whether love is there only for »the love of persons« (Arendt 2007, 467),[14] yet in a letter to Jaspers in 1955 she wrote: »I've begun so late […] to truly love the world […]. Out of gratitude, I want to call my book on political theories *Amor Mundi*« (Arendt and Jaspers 1992, 264).

A promise is not just given; it always carries the possibility of being kept. The promise that the parents give to the newborn and thereby, in the name of *amor mundi*, to the world, includes recognizing the child as the beginner and as the beginning in the world. Thus, birth and caring for the newborn can be understood as the *performance of a promise*: the way a child is loved and cared for. The contents of the promise include taking care of this beginning (the child) in such a way that

> we love our children enough not to expel them from our world and leave them to their own devices, nor to strike from their hands their chance of undertaking something new, something unforeseen by us, but to prepare them in advance for the task of renewing a common world (Arendt 1961, 196).

12 They are initially oblivious to the meaning of their surrounding world; they have to get used to the world as new for them and, at the same time, as a new beginning; and because of their uniqueness (plurality), they can insert new ways of understanding, new voices, and new paths of thinking into the world (see Arendt 1981a, 210).

13 Accidental conceptions or violent acts like rape are not considered by Arendt.

14 Hannah Arendt to Gershom Scholem, July 24th, 1963.

Violence, oppressive discipline and education, all relying on the reproduction of a certain function in society, would not live up to this promise. Thus, the promise inherent in natality is oriented towards the child and the world, namely to help shape the world, i.e., the relationships and plurality between people, in such a way that it is also a world for the children to come.

A child cannot grow up without a world; likewise, the world cannot be shaped without newcomers. This non-reciprocal double-sidedness that is performed by a promise for the world and in interpersonal relationships, grounds relational trust, individual hope, and invocation.

3. Which Element of Arendt's Philosophy of Natality is Based on Religion or Reference to the Bible?: Promise as Hope and Invocation

It can be said that a promise has two positional sides: the person who promises and the one to whom something is promised. The one who makes a promise is supposed to keep it[15]; by promising something, she »appeals« to the other: »believe me!« The promise thus possesses an element of a calling that can be linguistically framed as »vocative.«[16] The promise of natality also contains an element of invocation, but it is an *implicit invocative element* when it comes to the theme of being able to begin. In this context, Arendt refers to Augustine's thesis: »that there be a beginning, man was created« (*initium ergo ut esset, creatus est homo*) (Arendt 1958, 177). This reference brings the promise to a metaphysical level that lets the element of invocation resemble magic more than an argumentative language of testing and proof.[17] Remaining on a metaphysical level, Arendt writes in her thought diary: »Every new birth is like a guarantee of healing [*Heilen*] in the world, like a promise of salvation of those who no longer are a beginning« (Arendt 2016, I, 208).[18] In this entry, she opens up an analogy between birth as a guarantee of healing and promise as the salvation of persons. In *The Origins of Totalitarianism*,

15 In reality, people sometimes use the language of a promise in order to cheat, take advantage of, or manipulate other people. Such promises are not given with the intention of keeping them. Ethically speaking, such »promises« are actually not promises at all.

16 The vocative is the element of a promise that is lost when it is transformed into a contract.

17 For the term »magic,« see Foucault 2017.

18 See also the endnote on page 972, and footnote 20 below.

Arendt proclaims that the »beginning is guaranteed by each new birth; it is indeed in every man« (Arendt 1979, 479). Although a guarantee is not just a promise, I believe that this parallel setting is the impulse of »an immanent invocation« that reaches out into the future (Trawny 2005, 141; my transl.). More concretely, invocation stands for a commitment to care for or to love which is felt rather than rationally understood. Yet, even though it is rooted in a pre-reflexive level of our consciousness, it needs the activity of acting and thinking in order to shape our life and relationships.

Arendt explains that »[t]he new always happens against the overwhelming odds of statistical laws and their probability, which for all practical, everyday purposes amounts to certainty; the new therefore always appears in the guise of a miracle« (Arendt 1958, 178). Because of the unpredictability of each beginning, i.e., each interruption of a process, it is necessary to act and speak in freedom and plurality for the world-constitution that takes place in shared practices; and yet we fear its uncertainty and the impossibility of predicting the consequences for the community as well as the unreliability of the actors themselves, who can never guarantee whether what they do today will also hold tomorrow. The price paid for freedom is »[m]an's inability to rely upon himself or to have complete faith in himself (which is the same thing)« (ibid., 244).

If the faculty to begin and to make promises is truly human, then, Arendt asks, in what sense is »miracle-working« also truly human? Her literary source is Jesus of Nazareth, who is the »discoverer of the role of forgiveness in the realm of human affairs« (ibid., 238). In *The Human Condition*, Arendt cites passages from the New Testament (Luke 17:4): »And if he trespass against thee seven times a day, and seven times in a day turn again to thee, saying, I repent; thou shalt forgive him« (Arendt 1958, 239—240).[19] A footnote explains that, in the New Testament, the Greek words *aphienai* (dismiss, release, rather than forgive), *metanoein* (change of mind, return, sin no more = opposite of doing penance), and *hamartanein* (trespassing, fail, to miss) all carry connotations that have eluded translation in both the English and the German version of the gospels. Thus, the re-translation by Arendt: »And if he *trespass* against thee [...] and [...] turn again to thee saying, *I changed my mind*; thou shalt *release* him« (ibid., 240). Similarly, in order to understand the constellation of releasing someone from being guilty and enabling her to begin anew, Arendt refers to the following saying by Jesus in her thought

19 καὶ ἐὰν ἑπτάκις τῆς ἡμέρας *ἁμάρτη* εἰς σὲ καὶ ἑπτάκις τῆς ἡμέρας ἐπιστρέψῃ πρὸς σὲ λέγων, *μετανοῶ*, *ἀφήσεις* αὐτῷ (source: https://biblehub.com/text/luke/17-4.htm; emphasis mine).

diary: »And forgive us our debts, as we forgive our debtors« (Matt. 6:12) (see Arendt 2016, I, 69; April 1951).

But »[t]he fact that [...] [Jesus] made this discovery in a religious context and articulated it in religious language is no reason to take it any less seriously in a strictly secular sense« (Arendt 1958, 238). This quote shows that Arendt is not shy about referring to literary or religious sources that might form the history of ideas and human conduct. However, she does not use such texts as a religious source but rather in a secular sense of human life (and not with regard to man's relationship with God). For Arendt, the lessons of Jesus of Nazareth, who was actually talking about affairs with Israel's bureaucrats, were instructive. For he compares the power of performing miracles to the power to forgive: they are both »on the same level and within the reach of man« (ibid., 247). Both rest on faith. Faith and hope—faith in the world and hope for the world—these are the elements of promises. Then she writes the words of the message of Christmas: »A child has been born unto us« and this child is born to act (ibid., 247). Thus, a new beginning has been born unto us.[20]

The point here is that concern for the world that exists between people does not lie in the weighty notion of »forgiving« a person but in the rather secular idea—even though it is taken from the Bible—that by performing a release (by forgiving), the other person can react, act again, or begin again in the realm of human affairs and within the web of relationships. Thus, the release is meant for him or her personally out of respect (political friendship as elaborated by Aristotle). It has a structural force for the world and in the world. And as such, by grounding hope and faith, it opens up new beginnings in the world. It is a release for the world (just like a birth is also a release, *Ent-*

20 A letter exchange between Hannah Arendt and her husband Heinrich Blücher shows her casualness, reflexivity, and openness to her emotions: having heard Händel's *Messiah* with the Munich Philharmonic, Arendt is very touched by the music and the words. »The Hallelujah is still in my ears and in my limbs. For the first time it became clear to me how great it is: A child is born to us. Christianity was not so bad« (Arendt and Blücher 1996, 270; May 18th, 1952). Blücher, being close to her, had also just come across Händel. He noticed that with Händel one could form the idea that »the good news had been metaphysical.« He added: »The mystery was only the idea of the real miracle.« For Blücher the »eternal reality of the immaculate conception« can be proven as »the metaphysical possibility of every birth« (ibid., 279; May 29th, 1952). In his answer Blücher takes Arendt's sentiments further and even introduces the religious elements of Jesus' birth. Most importantly, he also puts forward the notion of »miracle« that was already part of the vocabulary of the notion of birth in *The Human Condition*. These sentiments acknowledge that it is a human being's birth, rather than her death, that became a fundamental metaphysical concept in Arendt's work. (My transl.)

bindung, by a mother of a child) that can be upheld only by a political practice of those who act together for a common world. It is a salvation or a healing of the web of relationships that is the world. Here, too, we find an element of invocation (petitionary prayer, appeal to the court, conjuration (*Beschwörung*), appeal, call) for the world.

Amor mundi—love of the world—Arendt is secularizing a reference to the Augustinian *amor Dei*, which she originally considered using as the title of what became *The Human Condition*. By introducing *amor mundi*, Arendt does not dismiss »the love of God«; rather, she directs the focus of the reader towards the world that has been destroyed and lost in-between us. One might consider Arendt's move of secularization to be eclectic or syncretic thinking; I consider it to be, however, the bringing of human relationships back to human responsibility. Arendt shifts the attention from searching for God's love to a search for the love of the world between us, and that very shift initiates her phenomenological inquiry.

The expression *amor mundi* contains a double meaning, depending whether it is read as genitive or locative: on the one hand, *amor mundi* can be interpreted as love *for* the world, as care for and responsibility for the world in the face of the child and the reconciliation with the world in »coming to terms with what has been done« (Arendt 2016, I, 4). On the other hand, love *in* the world refers to the intermediate world, the networks of relationships in which we live, act, and experience the responsibility and actions of others. Therefore, the invocation of *amor mundi* is accompanied by a feeling of gratitude. Thus, the performance of action is not only directed towards the release of the new and the newcomer who »suffers« the actions and their consequences, but—perhaps—continues to bring to light such actions (Arendt 1958, 190). In this interplay lies the promise of natality—existentially and politically. Arendt assembles literary, political, and religious sources of all sorts and introduces them into the realm of human affairs. The truth of new beginnings, to which Arendt refers to at the end of *The Origins of Totalitarianism*, is not found in religion but is a truth that can actually be observed in daily life. The responsibility for the world is not religiously but »ontologically rooted« in »the miracle that saves the world« (ibid., 247), namely, natality. Yet, the possibility of a new beginning can also be ruined through evil doing or senseless routines.

Works Cited

Arendt, Hannah (1948). *Sechs Essays*. Schriften der Wandlung 3. Heidelberg: Schneider.

Arendt, Hannah (1958). *The Human Condition*. Chicago/London: University of Chicago Press.

Arendt, Hannah (1961). The Crisis in Education. In Hannah Arendt. *Between Past and Future: Six Exercises in Political Thought*. New York: The Viking Press.

Arendt, Hannah (1970). *On Violence*. New York: Harcourt, Brace & World.

Arendt, Hannah (1979). *The Origins of Totalitarianism*. San Diego/New York/London: Harcourt Brace Jovanovich.

Arendt, Hannah (1981a). *Thinking*. In Hannah Arendt. *The Life of the Mind*. Ed. Mary McCarthy. San Diego/New York/London: Harcourt Brace Jovanovich.

Arendt, Hannah (1981b). *Willing*. In Hannah Arendt. *The Life of the Mind*. Ed. Mary McCarthy. San Diego/New York/London: Harcourt Brace Jovanovich.

Arendt, Hannah, and Karl Jaspers (1985). *Briefwechsel 1926—1969*. Herausgegeben von Lotte Köhler und Hans Saner. München: Piper.

Arendt, Hannah (1990). *On Revolution*. London/New York: Penguin Books.

Arendt, Hannah, and Karl Jaspers (1992). *Correspondence, 1926—1969*. Ed. Lotte Kohler and Hans Saner. Transl. Robert and Rita Kimber. New York: Harcourt Brace Jovanovich.

Arendt, Hannah (1994). Understanding and Politics. In Hannah Arendt. *Essays in Understanding, 1930—1954*, 307—327. Ed. Jerome Kohn. New York: Harcourt, Brace & Co.

Arendt, Hannah, and Heinrich Blücher (1996). *Briefe 1936—1968*. Herausgegeben und mit einer Einführung von Lotte Köhler. München: Piper.

Arendt, Hannah (2003). Thinking and Moral Considerations. In Hannah Arendt. *Responsibility and Judgment*, 159—189. Ed. and introduction Jerome Kohn. New York: Schocken Books.

Arendt, Hannah (2007). The Eichmann Controversy: A Letter to Gershom Scholem. In Hannah Arendt. *The Jewish Writings*. Ed. Jerome Kohn and Ron H. Feldman. New York: Schocken Books.

Arendt, Hannah (2016). *Denktagebuch 1950—1973*. Zwei Bände. Ed. Ursula Ludz and Ingeborg Nordmann. München: Piper Verlag.

Bedorf, Thomas and Steffen Herrmann (eds.). (2016). *Das soziale Band: Geschichte und Gegenwart eines sozialtheoretischen Grundbegriffs*. Frankfurt/New York: Campus Verlag.

Cavarero, Adriana (1997). Schauplätze der Einzigartigkeit. In Silvia Stoller and Helmuth Vetter (eds.). *Phänomenologie und Geschlechterdifferenz*, 207—226. Wien: WUV-Universitätsverlag.

Foucault, Michel (2017). La magie—Le fait social total. *Zilsel*, 2(2), 305—326.

Liebsch, Burkhard (1996). *Geschichte im Zeichen des Abschieds*. München: Fink.

Marcel, Gabriel (1949). *Being and Having*. Transl. Katharine Farrer. Westminster: Dacre Press.

Nietzsche, Friedrich (1996). *Human, All Too Human*. Transl. R.J. Hollingdale. Introduction Richard Schacht. Cambridge/New York: Cambridge University Press.

Nietzsche, Friedrich (2007). *On the Genealogy of Morality*. Transl. Carol Diethe. Ed. Keith Ansell-Pearson. Cambridge/New York: Cambridge University Press.

Schües, Christina (2008). *Philosophie des Geborenseins*. Freiburg/München: Alber.

Schües, Christina (2019). Hannah Arendt—Philosophie der Praxis als Welteröffnung. In Thomas Bedorf and Selin Gerlek (eds.). *Philosophien der Praxis: Ein Handbuch*, 179—209. Stuttgart: Mohr Siebeck.

Trawny, Peter (2005). *Denkbarer Holocaust: Die politische Ethik Hannah Arendts*. Würzburg: Königshausen & Neumann.

Part IV: Politics Without the Absolute

Actions That Deserve to Be Remembered: Transcendence and Immortality in a Secular World

Roger Berkowitz

> Without this transcendence into a potential earthly immortality, no politics, strictly speaking, no common world and no public realm, is possible.
>
> *(Hannah Arendt, The Human Condition, p. 55)*

The crisis in politics today is that we live at a moment when, as W.B. Yeats said, »things fall apart; the center cannot hold.« The very idea of a meaningful political community is questionable. We live amidst what Carol Becker calls the »agitated now,« a time where the narrative that binds the past to the present is broken. Not only in the din of war or in the chaos of catastrophe, but also in everyday life, there is an ever-present feeling

> that our lives are discontinuous, that we have lost the sense of home that once anchored us to the physical world, that we have disrupted the continuity of generations (families are dispersed across the nation and the world, trying to stay connected), and that we cannot envision a path to the future (Becker 2018).

Geographically dispersed, spiritually isolated, and above all lonely and purposeless, we are adrift and abandoned. Hannah Arendt's name for the »agitated now« is the »break in our tradition« (Arendt 1961c, 26). The break begins with the French Revolution:

> [E]ver since the great failure of the French Revolution people have repeatedly re-erected the old pillars which were then overthrown, only again and again to see them first quivering, then collapsing anew. The most frightful errors have replaced the »best-known truths,« and the error of these doctrines constitutes no proof, no new pillar for the old truths (Arendt 1968, 11).

With every new or failed attempt to restore or establish new pillars of tradition, its loss becomes ever more apparent. At some point we know that the tradition is lost even if we are too scared to accept it: »ultimately the public order is based on people's holding as self-evident precisely those ›best-known truths‹ which secretly scarcely anyone still believes in« (ibid., 11).

The break in our tradition »is now an accomplished fact« (Arendt 1961c, 26). What broke the tradition was »neither the twentieth-century aftermath nor the nineteenth-century rebellion against tradition« (ibid., 26). Instead, what finally broke the tradition of the West was »a chaos of mass-perplexities on the political scene and of mass-opinions in the spiritual sphere which the totalitarian movements, through terror and ideology, crystallized into a new form of government and domination« (ibid., 26). It was the fact of totalitarianism—which was unprecedented and which brought with it unprecedented crimes—that »has broken the continuity of Occidental history« (ibid., 26). Amidst the broken pillars of the old truth there can be nothing but a chaos of opposing opinions. Our »tradition has worn thinner and thinner as the modern age progressed« and »the thread of tradition finally broke« (Arendt 1961a, 14). To call upon moral, political, or religious standards is futile.

The fact of the break in the tradition leaves what Arendt calls a »gap between past and future.« It is in this gap—this space where traditions can no longer offer the answers to fundamental moral and political questions—that we live today. To live in this gap is to be thrown back on ourselves without a meaningful past to guide our present and our future. »The crisis of the present world,« Arendt writes, »consists primarily in the decline of the Roman trinity of religion, tradition, and authority, with the concomitant undermining of the specifically Roman foundations of the political realm« (Arendt 1961d, 140). Absent religion, tradition, and authority, we have to think for ourselves; we have to engage in »thinking without a banister,« to use another of Arendt's metaphors.

The basic experience of being abandoned by tradition and left to ourselves is one that Arendt calls loneliness. While loneliness has always existed, it is for most of human history confined to the extremities of the public world. The elderly are often alone as they are left behind by the forward motion of the young. And certain outcasts or pariahs may feel totally abandoned by society. But the break of tradition thrusts loneliness to the center of human experience so that for the masses today there is a pervasive feeling of abandonment and meaninglessness.

It was always the case that the few, the thinkers, could question customs and think outside of the tradition. But for most people, the tradition provided moral and political boundaries. Amidst the rubble of the break in our tradition, the masses of humanity are left rudderless. The challenge today is to learn again to think politically and freely without being propped up by the banisters and pillars of a tradition.

Arendt finds both danger and freedom in the break of the tradition. The loss of authority, once broken, is unlikely to be reestablished. With the »loss of the groundwork for the world,« it is true that »we have ceased to live in a common world where the words we have in common possess an unquestionable meaningfulness« (ibid., 95). The loss of tradition is the loss of a »thread which safely guided us through the vast realms of the past« (ibid., 94). Amidst the break of tradition, politics still happens, but it is negatively focused. We can fight against tyranny or anarchy. But there is an »ominous silence that still answers us whenever we dare to ask, not ›What are we fighting *against*‹ but ›What are we fighting *for*?‹« (Arendt 1961c, 27). What is lost in the modern age is the actuality of a shared common world. The political fight *for* a positive and inspiring political ideal is no longer conceivable except as a dangerous exercise in authoritarian nostalgia.

Arendt saw clearly that totalitarianism is a response to mass loneliness. What totalitarianism offers lonely people is a coherent fiction that promises to make our insignificant lives meaningful. Such fictions, as fictions, can only be held together by the terror of totalitarian states. But amidst the loneliness and abandonment of the agitated now there is also an opportunity to build a new common world. Arendt's optimism comes from her undaunted belief in the possibility of human freedom and spontaneity, the ability of mankind to work together to build meaningful and lasting public worlds. The task of politics today is to articulate if not a new ideal, at least some immanent transcendent togetherness that would provide new pillars of political togetherness.

The kind of imminent transcendence Arendt has in mind comes from the practice and activity of living together with others and not from abstract ideals. In attending to others, hearing them, and understanding them, one reaches outside one's own limited perspective and opens oneself to the connections that can build a common world. Only in this kind of transcendence from within can we confront anew »the elementary problems of human living-together« without a religious trust in »self-evident standards of behavior« (Arendt 1961d, 141). The challenge of politics in the modern age is to build from within the shared world a meaningful center around which the many can gather without falling prey to the totalitarian temptation to create a coherent ideological fantasy that will need to be enforced with terror.

The question of how to formulate a common center is and long has been *the* question of politics. In *Concerning the Polis*, usually translated as *The Republic*, Plato named politics the practice of bringing the many under a single common truth and collective way of seeing. Aristotle countered that Plato's desire for unity overlooked a fundamental premise of politics, namely, that the unity of a multitude must nevertheless respect an underlying plurality. It is this challenge, to find what is common amongst a plurality while maintaining the fundamental multiplicity of a community of unique human persons, which defines the task of politics.

The question I ask in this essay is: what is needed to build a shared world, a common world, after the pillars of the old world have been shattered? Absent god, absent living traditions, and thus absent a public world, how do we build a human and meaningful world? While political unity is needed to build a common world, the question is, how can we build unity in a homeless and rootless world without imposing a tyrannical unity on a plural people? In other words, we need to address head-on the question Arendt asks in her *Denktagebuch*, a question she characterizes as the guiding thread of her thinking: »Is there a way of thinking which is not tyrannical?« (Arendt 2016, I, 45; December 1950). As my colleague Thomas Wild writes, »[t]he question of the relationship between tyranny and thought is a political and theoretical one« (Wild 2017, 52). It requires that we articulate theoretically a political ideal that can unite a plurality without resorting to tyranny, ideology, and terror.

In what follows I explore Arendt's argument that to unify a plurality involves two linked ideas that are frequently overlooked and yet are central to her political thinking: transcendence and immortality. Arendt condenses her thinking about the political importance of transcendence and immortality into a single sentence that has always struck me as a central thought in *The Human Condition*: »Without this transcendence into a potential earthly immortality, no politics, strictly speaking, no common world and no public realm, is possible« (Arendt 1958, 55).

Part One explores Arendt's insistence that politics requires transcendence, and thus the need for what is often called a political theology. Part Two takes seriously Arendt's claim that any transcendental politics must, of necessity, engage with the question of immortality, specifically what she calls an earthly immortality. In Part Three, I argue that political transcendence into an earthly immortality demands courageous action that gives meaning and purpose to the being of human beings. Finally, in Part Four,

I ask how, at a time when transcendence and immortality are being lost as public goods, can we imagine institutions and persons who can do the unifying work of transcendence required by politics.

I. Transcendence

Deep within Arendt's political thinking is a recognition of the need for transcendence, a conviction that the political project of unifying a plurality requires a trans-individual sanction. In a religious world, religion and tradition can serve to authorize and define a common world that we can share together. Amidst the break in tradition, however, we no longer live in a religious world. Secularization means, above all, »the separation of religion and politics« (Arendt 1961b, 69). It is a fact, Arendt writes, that »the separation of church and state occurred, eliminating religion from public life, removing all religious sanctions from politics« (ibid., 70).

Arendt's use of transcendence differs from its traditional religious and philosophical sense. Both religion and philosophy aim to rule over the plurality of the political world by erecting a universal and true standard. Plato's theory of the Ideas, for example, while not originally a political conception, was mobilized by Plato and later political philosophers to create »standards« and »units of measurement« that stand above and rule over the plurality of the real world. It is not Plato's ideas themselves, »but the non-religious concept of transcendence in philosophy [that] is political in origin.« In other words, Arendt sees in philosophy and religion a demand for universal standards that would rule over the »relativity of human affairs« (Arendt 2018b, 501).

Against the religious and philosophical transcendence into universal standards, Arendt imagines another form of political unity based in those »activities in which men are related and communicate with each other, that is *lexis*, speech, and *praxis*, action« (ibid., 501). While the universal standards of religion and philosophy are unspeakable and found in »the truest solitude and ultimately in speechlessness,« the togetherness of politics on earth means »being caught in the web of relationships and interdependencies of human affairs through speaking and acting« (ibid., 502). For Arendt, politics depends on transcendence; but positioned against the Western philosophical tradition that seeks transcendence through universals, Arendt imagines an immanent transcendence founded in human relations that could bring about a common world. What is needed in the post-religious and post-metaphysical age is »to discover in the secular realm an independent, immanent meaning which even God could not alter« (Arendt 1961b, 70).

Being mortal, individuals are fleeting and without lasting significance. There is nothing that binds them to a larger meaningful community. Religion is one way of making human life meaningful as a creation of God and as part of an ethical whole. And politics, for Arendt, is another way of binding man to a meaningfully transcendent whole. There must be something that allows individuals to »overcome the mortality of human life and the futility of human deeds« (Arendt 1958, 71).

Thus, there is, for Arendt, no politics without some kind of transcendence. To transcend, which literally means »to step over« in its Latin root form, is for Arendt a stepping over from our mortal lifespan to an »earthly immortality.« And this transcendence into an immortal world is at the very heart of what it means to live politically, that is, to live in a public and common world. While transcendence into religiously or philosophically determined universal rules is politically dangerous, an immanent transcendence through the acting and speaking together of a plurality is the necessary precondition for a common world.

The context for Arendt's discussion of transcendence in *The Human Condition* is her inquiry into the nature of the public. For her, the public is, first and foremost, that which appears and what we can see: »everything that appears in public can be seen and heard by everybody« (ibid., 50). Second, the public »signifies the world itself, in so far as it is common to all of us and distinguished from our privately owned place in it« (ibid., 52). The world is comprised of lasting and durable things that we all share and that relate us and bind us to a common reality. The example Arendt offers is that of a table we sit around; if the table magically disappears, we are suddenly deprived of that which gathered us in a common endeavor (ibid., 52—53). The common world we share is like the table that holds us in common; it is that which we stand upon and live within and which keeps a community of people together. The public world—as a world common to all—must not be my own personal fantasy.

That the world transcends my limited perspective does not mean it is objective. The requirement for the common world is not objectivity but impartiality. Impartiality has its model in Homer's decision to »sing the deeds of the Trojans no less than those of the Achaeans, and to praise the glory of Hector no less than the greatness of Achilles« (Arendt 1961b, 51). It is an openness to an »infinite number of different standpoints, to which correspond the most diverse points of view« that allows one to »look upon the same world from one another's standpoint, to see the same in very different and frequently opposing aspects« (ibid., 51). Arendt argues that the public world, being impartial, »relies on the simultaneous presence of innumerable perspectives and aspects in which the common world presents itself and for which no common measurement or denominator can ever be devised« (Arendt 1958, 57). The true difference between private and public life is that, in private life one lives by one's own perspective, whereas in public life »being seen and being heard by others derive their significance from the fact that everybody sees and hears from a different position« (ibid., 57).

Politics guarantees a common reality by creating a common sense, the conditions for an impartiality that allows all citizens to be »always concerned with the same object« (ibid., 58). Politics requires a collective space of appearance where speaking and acting citizens relate and engage with one another and, in doing so, they step over from their independent selves to a common world. Politics, thus, depends on transcendence, the emergence of a common sense »that fits into reality as a whole our five strictly individual senses« (ibid., 208). Common sense is what discloses the real world and thus allows for a world to exist impartially amongst a plurality of individuals. To the extent that political impartiality is lost and we are left to live in a world visible only from our own perspective, we experience the »end of the common world« (ibid., 58), alienation from the world, and the death of politics.

If the task of politics is to find amidst our plurality that which gathers us together as one while also respecting our plurality, Arendt teaches that politics is not possible without a concern for immortality, which is the condition for transcendence. The standing out in the world that is transcendence means that the common world must endure beyond our personal perspectives and also beyond our mortal lifespans. To be seen as common to all, it must transcend the interests and lifespans of individuals. The question before us today is how, in the modern age—the age of the death of God and the break of the tradition—we can strive for an immortal world that would be worthy of preserving. This striving for immortality, Arendt argues, is the task of politics.

II. Earthly Immortality

Arendtian politics demands transcendence into a common world that is, in Arendt's words, »a potential earthly immortality« (ibid., 55). Transcendence is not to a universal philosophical or religious ideal, but to an »earthly« unity. But what does the idiosyncratic phrase »earthly immortality« mean?

Arendt speaks of earthliness in the sense that humans are both earthly and worldly. To be humanly conditioned includes the fact that we are born and live on this earth. As earthly creatures, we exist on a planet that we did not create and in a form and universe that precedes us. As are all other earthly beings, we are subject to fate and live and die in accord with laws and the rules of fortune that are beyond our control. It is in this sense that »[t]he earth is the very quintessence of the human condition« (ibid., 2). At the same time, we humans are different from animals insofar as we transcend our earthly existence. She writes, »[t]he human artifice of the world separates human existence from all mere animal environment« (ibid., 2). As worldly beings, we humans can escape our earthly fortune and, through artifice, reimagine and remake the world in which we live. This means that while we live on the earth and are of the earth, we can make and remake our earthly habitat into a human world.

As both earthly and worldly beings, we humans can bring forth cities, temples, and works of art. Above all, we can tell stories that build a web of relations that emerges as an »altogether different in-between which consists of deeds and words and owes its origin exclusively to men's acting and speaking directly *to* one another« (ibid., 183). It is from the condition of our divided earthly and worldly humanity that we develop those »human« capacities that include laboring, preserving life, working, creating a durable world, and action, all in order to express our freedom. Labor, work, and action as the faculties of the human condition are all inscribed in the human effort to grant everlastingness and permanence to the human world. It is our human ability to build a lasting and even immortal world on earth that is the source of our earthly immortality. But what is immortality?

For Arendt, immortality means »endurance in time, deathless life on this earth and in this world as it was given, according to Greek understanding, to nature and the Olympian gods« (ibid., 18). In the Greek firmament, gods and nature as such were everlasting and immortal; only man was mortal. The cosmos and the gods were enduring and unchanging. And even animals, as members of species, reproduced and lasted. Both gods and animals were part of the cycle of life. But only man was the individuated being who had a unique birth and death that defined his mortality. The »rectilinear course« of human life contrasts with the »circular movement of biological life« (ibid., 19). »Imbedded in a cosmos where everything was immortal, mortality became the hallmark of human existence« (ibid., 18). For mortals within such an immortal world, the task of human life is to act and speak in ways that they become immortal. This is the great task of politics.

The central aim of Greek life was *eudaimonia*, the blessedness of the *daimōn* »who accompanies each man throughout life, who is his distinct identity, but appears and is visible only to others« (ibid., 193). *Eudaimonia* is not »a passing mood« (ibid., 193). Arendt cites the »ancient saying that nobody can be called *eudaimōn* before he is dead« and adds that »*eudaimonia*, like life itself, is a lasting state of being which is neither subject to change nor capable of effecting change« (ibid., 192, 193). To have *eudaimonia* is to manifest publicly and to others a fundamental character that is visible and lasting; it is to possess a spirit that is lasting and thus to achieve a kind of immortality.

Arendt opposes immortality to the search for the eternal associated with the life of the mind. When Socrates and Plato left the life of the *polis* for the quiet groves of the Academy, they shifted their attention from immortality to eternity. The very fact that Socrates »never cared to write down his thoughts« (ibid., 20) is evidence of his lack of concern for his earthly immortality. Instead, the philosophers sought to catch sight of the »experience of the eternal, which to Plato was *arrhēton* (›unspeakable‹), and to Aristotle *aneu logou* (›without word‹), and which later was conceptualized in the paradoxical *nunc stans* (›the standing now‹)« (ibid., 20). Such an unsayable and wordless eternal present »can occur only outside the realm of human affairs and outside the plurality of men« (ibid., 20). The »decisive« experience of the eternal over and against the immortal is that it »cannot be transformed into any activity whatsoever, since even the activity of thought, which goes on within one's self by means of words, is obviously not only inadequate to render it but would interrupt and ruin the experience itself« (ibid., 20). The philosophical focus on the eternal is thus a kind of political death, a retreat from the messy, chaotic, and untrue world of humankind into the universal realm of eternal truth.

The distinction of immortality against eternity is that immortality is of this earth and is the political goal of earthly human beings. Politics, the activity of acting in and through a common world, aims at immortality. That is why Arendt writes that »the drive toward immortality should lie at the foundation of political communities« (Arendt 1961b, 71—72). When she writes of political immortality, Arendt does not mean the eternal verities of religion or philosophy. She means, instead, the worldly stories that re-make the earthly foundation on which we humans live and act in common. It is in and through stories that we tell amongst ourselves that we build a human world that can be a lasting and durable home for a people. Only in nurturing a home can we lend purpose and meaning to our world and thereby combat the loneliness of modern life.

III. Immortality and Human Meaningfulness

What still needs to be understood is why such an earthly immortality is so important to politics? Arendt's answer is that immortality is what gives meaning to human lives. As mortal beings whose death is a final end, the problem for mankind is: What is the meaning of human life? After we die, why does our having lived matter? Why should we suffer through the outrageous fortunes of a painful existence if it is all for naught? How are we to guarantee meaning to the limited life of mortal beings?

To be meaningful, to matter, is the core of what it is to be human for Arendt. To live a meaningful life is to have said and done things that are remembered, made into stories, and preserved after one has died. What distinguishes humans in their humanity is the capacity to act meaningfully and achieve a certain immortality.

This connection between human meaningfulness and immortality is already nascent in *The Origins of Totalitarianism* where Arendt argues that the only true human right is the right to speak and act in public in ways that matter. »The fundamental deprivation of human rights,« Arendt argues, »is manifested first and above all in the deprivation of a place in the world which makes opinions significant and actions effective« (Arendt 1979, 296). Above all to be human is to have the right to be seen and to be heard; to be taken seriously; to be significant; and to matter. To matter is to be seen and heard in a way that one's actions are worthy of being noticed and remembered.

Distinguishing between poverty and misery in her book *On Revolution*, Arendt argues that only the miserable are truly excluded from a political and thus a human community. It is the miserable, because they are forced to spend all their time and energy simply to stay alive, who have no possibility of appearing in public and thus mattering in the world. The poor, in contrast, can still speak and act in ways that matter; they can, she argues, have dignity as people whose opinions are significant and whose actions are effective.

The standard against which human life is measured is »the things that are forever« (Arendt 1961b, 45). Human deeds, however, are fleeting. As soon as one acts, the deed is lost, so that human action is one of »the most futile and least lasting activities of men« (ibid., 46). »[G]reatness was understood in terms of permanence« (ibid., 46), something that was never guaranteed to result from human action. To be human is to build things that last, tell stories that immortalize our deeds, and create political communities that carry a humanly created world into the future. What this means is that it is human to strive for great deeds that make an enduring and even immortal mark upon the world. There is in every human being a need to matter and a drive to do things that will bring about a lastingness and thus a kind of immortality.

> The task and potential greatness of mortals lie in their ability to produce things—works and deeds and words—which would deserve to be and, at least to a degree, are at home in everlastingness, so that through them mortals could find their place in a cosmos where everything is immortal except themselves (Arendt 1958, 19).

All of us want to matter and to endure beyond our human lives. But only some of us are willing to take the risk of acting and speaking in public that can lead to immortal fame. Action that can lead to immortality is dangerous because the actor acts in ways that are original and spontaneous and such action will be noticed by the public. The spectators who witness an action are struck by the act and can either recoil in the face of such unprecedented criminality or be transformed by an action that shows them a new truth that had previously been hidden. In either case, the actor must take the risk of coming out of his or her private life and entering into the tumultuous realm of public censure.

»It requires courage,« Arendt writes, »to leave the protective security of our four walls and enter the public realm« (Arendt 1961e, 156). When one acts, the danger one faces is not the specific prospect of arrest, mockery, or death. The real danger is to one's very existence and the public realm can only be entered by those who have ceased to be concerned for their lives. The actor puts the collective world above his or her private self-interest. »Courage is indispensable« for the actor »because in politics not life but the world is at stake« (Arendt 1961e, 156). The very distinction between human and animal, Arendt writes, is that humans can, in the words of Heraclitus, »»prefer immortal fame to mortal things‹« (Arendt 1958, 19)[1] and thus can build a world that lasts and that deserves to last. This means, for Arendt, that those of us who pursue immortality act more in line with our humanity than others.

The distinction between man and animal runs right through the human species itself: only the best (*aristoi*), who constantly prove themselves to be the best (*aristeuein*, a verb for which there is no equivalent in any other language) and who »prefer immortal fame to mortal things,« are really human; the others, content with whatever pleasures nature will yield them, live and die like animals (ibid., 19).

That only some of us will consciously strive for public immortality, that even fewer of us will do deeds that inscribe us in an immortal world, and that most of us will live and die like animals, is not a problem for Arendt. She takes it as simply a fact of human life that most people, most of the time, do not strive to do great deeds and live freely. Arendt's elitism is not an elitism of birth or substance. The elite for Arendt is an elite that rises from the bottom up based on courage, talent, and a love for action. What is more, elitism serves an essential role in a republican democracy. For even if it is only a few people who think and act in public, they provide an example of action that keeps alive the idea of freedom and the aspiration to immortality.

IV. The Loss of Immortality, Meaning, and Politics

The connection between meaningfulness and immortality was explicit for the ancient Greeks and the human pursuit of immortality was taken for granted. The Greek way to achieve immortality is first and foremost through the public life of the *polis*. The *polis*, and here Arendt recalls Pericles famous funeral oration recorded by Thucydides, »gives a guaranty that those who forced every sea and land to become the scene of their daring will not remain without witness and will need neither Homer nor anyone else who knows how to turn words to praise them« (ibid., 197). In acting greatly in the *polis*

1 Citing Heraclitus, fragment B29, which in Hermann Diels *Die Fragmente der Vorsokratiker* (Berlin: Weidmannsche Büchhandlung, 1912) is given in German as »Eine gibt es, was die Besten allem anderen vorziehen: den Ruhm den ewigen den vergänglichen Dingen. Die Meisten freilich liegen da vollgefressen wie das liebe Vieh.« (The best of humanity choose one thing rather than all else: everlasting fame among mortals. The majority are satisfied, like well-fed cattle.) (Mark Farrier's translation).

where their deeds will be seen, talked about, and remembered, those who act were assured that their fleeting and least tangible actions »would become imperishable« (ibid., 198). Pericles' oration found »the glory of Athens in having left behind ›everywhere everlasting remembrance (*mnēmeia aidia*) of their good and their evil deeds‹« (ibid., 206). In politics, happiness is a product of »what is great and radiant« and the *polis* is there to »inspire men to dare the extraordinary« (ibid., 206). Because the *polis* promises to remember those great deeds that stand out, the *polis* ensures that greatness will earn *eudaimonia* and immortal fame.

But even great actions in the *polis* will be forgotten if they are not immortalized in poetry or history. Poetry bestows immortal fame on fleeting human actions, which is why poetic and also historical memorializing are central activities of the polis. History brings the world as it is and as it was to presence so that we remember it in its beauty and its pain. Both poetry and history elevate singular deeds to greatness and secure their immortality. Poetry and history are important because of »the immortal fame which the poets could bestow upon word and deed to make them outlast not only the futile moment of speech and action but even the mortal life of their agent« (Arendt 1961b, 46).

The need for immortality to grant meaning to human and mortal existence was also true for the Romans. If the Greeks saw action as an exceptional heroic deed that »serves as a kind of yardstick with which to measure one's own capacities for greatness,« the Romans saw human deeds as comprising a »storehouse of examples« (ibid., 67, 66). From each event the Romans took for granted its meaning or its lesson; each happening that is taken up into the story of the Roman republic exemplifies »what tradition, the authority of ancestors, demanded from each generation and what the past had accumulated for the benefit of the present« (ibid., 64—65). All events are exemplary and repeat themselves and thus there emerged an »ancient trust in the world's being more permanent than individual men and in political structures as a guarantee of earthly survival after death« (ibid., 74). For the Romans, as for the Greeks, »the foundation of a body politic was brought about by man's need to overcome the mortality of human life and the futility of human deeds« (ibid., 71).

What unites the Greek and Roman understanding of immortality is the conviction that certain individual actions are politically meaningful in themselves. The great deeds that were to be immortalized were obvious to common sense; the ancients simply accepted as fact that some actions and some words deserved to be remembered. »Praise, from which came glory and eventually everlasting fame, could be bestowed only upon things already ›great,‹ that is, things that possessed an emerging, shining quality which distinguished them from all others and made glory possible« (ibid., 47). Greatness, if not natural, was at least obvious and it was the talent of the poet simply to elevate what was great but fleeting to its rightful place in the pantheon of everlasting immorality. »The great was that which deserved immortality, that which should be admitted to the company of things that lasted forever« (ibid., 47). The poet and the historian elevate the already great to their everlasting fame so that, in spite of their mortality, they »may remain in the company of the things that last forever« (ibid., 48).

It is precisely this clarity regarding the belief in great deeds that Arendt sees separating the ancient and modern worlds. The Greeks and Romans both could make poetry and tell history because they knew what was »worthy of immortalizing praise« (ibid., 51). Homer knew that both Achilles and Hector were great and could »sing the deeds of the Trojans no less than those of the Achaeans, and to praise the glory of Hector no less than the greatness of Achilles« (ibid., 51).

Impartial judgment about greatness is not scientific. It emerges out of a rich public life, a life where people in their plurality meet and talk in the agora and the public square. In talking with others, »the Greeks discovered that the world we have in common is usually regarded from an infinite number of different standpoints, to which correspond the most diverse points of view« (ibid., 51). For the ancients, »[g]reatness was easily recognizable as that which by itself aspired to immortality—that is, negatively speaking, as a heroic contempt for all that merely comes and passes away, for all individual life, one's own included« (ibid., 52).

In the modern age, however, the loss of immortality is entwined with the loss of impartiality. Without the ability to see impartially, to »look upon the same world from one another's standpoint« (ibid., 51) there is no common and durable world that exceeds our individual and partial perspectives. In the absence of a durable and immortal world, there is no impartial agreement on what acts are great and deserving of immortality. Thus, Arendt argues that the idea of greatness is trebly out of joint in the modern world.

First, most Christians deny the idea of an earthly immortality altogether. Christianity focuses our attention on the life and soul of an individual person, not on the world we share. This world is not immortal; it is sinful and will pass away. For Christians, »mankind has a beginning and an end« (ibid.,

67). Man is simply a »pilgrim on earth« (ibid., 66). Christians depoliticized the world and made meaning and immortality a question of the individual soul. The true world is the eternal and divine world, the one we can attain as individuals.

Second, modernity is utilitarian and rejects the pursuit of immortality because it valorizes the individual pursuit of self-interest that sees life as the supreme good. »Since we have made life our supreme and foremost concern, we have no room left for an activity based on contempt for one's own life-interest« (ibid., 52—53). There is no place in the modern conception of self-interested politics for the heroic contempt for life that can give birth to the immortal. Great deeds are thus seen as foolish rather than inspiring.

The third reason for the loss of earthly and worldly immortality today is the rise of science and the consequent emergence of world alienation. In the modern age, world alienation is the »basic condition of our whole life« (ibid., 53). World alienation is rooted in the essential drive of the scientific worldview to seek causes and explanations for everything. Science follows the axiom *nihil est sine ratione* (»nothing is without reason«).[2] But if everything that is has a reason, then nothing exists without a reason given for it, which means that existence depends upon our giving reasons. The tree does not exist unless we rationalize it, set it within a humanly understood world. Even laws of justice, for Leibniz and subsequent legal thinkers, only exist and operate insofar as they are meaningful and have a rational purpose given by man. In the age of scientific reason, all things—from a tree falling in the forest to justice—come to be knowable only by the human mind. As Arendt writes, science brings about the »dissolution of objective reality into the subjective states of mind or, rather, into subjective mental processes« (Arendt 1958, 282). Science is both a cause and an effect of our transformed understanding of the modern world, one in which the once-external and once-objective world is increasingly internalized.

Arendt's worry about the modern retreat from transcendence and immortality stems from her insight that the political importance of human immortality is imperiled in the modern world that has lost the belief in and capacity for immortality. For us moderns, Arendt writes, »concern with immortality is not a matter of course, and Herodotus, since this was a matter of course to him, does not tell us much about it« (Arendt 1961b, 41). For the Greeks and other ancient civilizations, immortality was a common sense re-

2 This is the thesis of my book, *The Gift of Science: Leibniz and the Modern Legal Tradition* (Berkowitz 2005).

ality. This is no longer the case. And with the loss of the concern for immortality comes, as well, the loss of the transcendence to an earthly immortality that is at the heart of politics.

Arendt offers a poem by Rainer Maria Rilke as a simple example to illustrate »quickly and with some measure of clarity how far we today are removed« (ibid., 43—44) from the Greek understanding of a natural immortality. The poem, which she insists defies translation, reads:

Berge ruhn, von Sternen überprächtigt;
aber auch in ihnen flimmert Zeit.
Ach, in meinem wilden Herzen nächtigt
obdachlos die Unvergänglichkeit.

Rilke's poem speaks of the mountains and the stars—the greatest symbols of immortal nature—and says that even these most enduring of natural wonders flicker with time. In Rilke's poem, mountains will crumble and stars will burn out; nature is made mortal. But even if nature will fade, there is in the wild heart of man, naked and homeless, something eternal that will never decay. In the modern world that Rilke represents, »everything has become perishable, except perhaps the human heart« (ibid., 44). In the modern age, immortal beings and immortal acts »have lost their home in the world« (ibid., 44) and reside, now, only inside the immortal soul of a naked, homeless, and ultimately worldless human being.

Conclusion

In the same section of *The Human Condition* where Arendt writes about necessity of transcendence and immortality for politics, she adds: »There is perhaps no clearer testimony to the loss of the public realm in the modern age than the almost complete loss of authentic concern with immortality« (Arendt 1958, 55). Our age is one in which »the illusion of immortality has collapsed« (Luban 1994, 195). We no longer believe in the immortality of gods. Nor do we believe in eternal truths. Nature—the sky and the earth—the most immortal of things, have come to be scientifically manipulable by and subject to human engineering. And most importantly, we no longer believe in the greatness of human deeds.

The challenge posed by the modern break of the tradition is to confront the meaninglessness of the world, our homelessness, and thus the loss of transcendence. Without transcendence, politics and political unity is fragile, something to be attained only through human action. And if we do not find a way to reconcile with the sense of meaninglessness that pervades modern life once the threat of tradition is broken, our politics is susceptible to ideological movements like Nazism and Bolshevism that breed resentment and promise to bring meaning and purpose to our lives. In a world deprived of immortality, the danger is that human beings seek to stabilize the world in other dangerous ways.

If Arendt has an alternative way to build a meaningful, transcendent, and immortal world it is through the human capacity to speak and act. Arendt holds a fundamental belief in the power of talking. She writes: »we become more just and more pious by thinking and talking about justice and piety« (Arendt 2018a, 331). Why does Arendt believe this? First, in talking about the world, we make the world visible in its complexity. The world contains the plurality of its opinions, the infinity of its facts, and the unpredictability of its actions. Arendt likes to cite Pierre-Joseph Proudhon to make her point that the human drive to master the world falters: »The fecundity of the unexpected far exceeds the statesman's prudence.« We confront a world that defies rational deduction.

In talking about the world, we also make judgments and decisions about the world. Those decisions, Arendt admits, »may one day prove wholly inadequate« (Arendt 2018a, 331). But even absent agreements on the nature of a crisis and how to solve it, the act of speaking with one another about the crises of our times will, she argues, »eventually lay the groundwork for new agreements between ourselves as well as between the nations of the earth, which then might become customs, rules, [and] standards that again will be frozen into what is called morality« (ibid., 331).

Her point is that by talking with one another, we create the kinds of shared experiences and common points of connection that might, over time, become the building blocks of a new shared world that can give birth to new traditions and thus a new moral order. Arendt sees this potential rebirth of a new common ethical world as not only possible, but likely: »I personally do not doubt that from the turmoil of being confronted with reality without the help of precedent, that is, of tradition and authority, there will finally arise some new code of conduct« (ibid., 330). The only way to constructively engage the crisis of our time, Arendt argues, is to confront the reality »that we do indeed live in a situation of crisis« (ibid., 331) and talk honestly about it with others.

Works Cited

Arendt, Hannah (1958). *The Human Condition*. Chicago/London: University of Chicago Press.

Arendt, Hannah (1961a). Preface: The Gap Between Past and Future. In Hannah Arendt. *Between Past and Future: Six Exercises in Political Thought*. New York: The Viking Press.

Arendt, Hannah (1961b). The Concept of History: Ancient and Modern. In Hannah Arendt. *Between Past and Future: Six Exercises in Political Thought*. New York: The Viking Press.

Arendt, Hannah (1961c). Tradition and the Modern Age. In Hannah Arendt. *Between Past and Future: Six Exercises in Political Thought*. New York: The Viking Press.

Arendt, Hannah (1961d). What Is Authority?. In Hannah Arendt. *Between Past and Future: Six Exercises in Political Thought*. New York: The Viking Press.

Arendt, Hannah (1961e). What Is Freedom?. In Hannah Arendt. *Between Past and Future: Six Exercises in Political Thought*. New York: The Viking Press.

Arendt, Hannah (1968). On Humanity in Dark Times. In Hannah Arendt. *Men in Dark Times*. New York: Harcourt, Brace & World.

Arendt, Hannah (1979). *The Origins of Totalitarianism*. New edition with added prefaces. San Diego/New York/London: Harcourt Brace Jovanovich.

Arendt, Hannah (2016). *Denktagebuch 1950 bis 1973*. 2 Bände. Herausgegeben von Ursula Ludz und Ingeborg Nordmann, in Zusammenarbeit mit dem Hannah-Arendt-Institut, Dresden. München/Berlin/Zürich: Piper.

Arendt, Hannah (2018a). The Crisis Character of Modern Society. In Hannah Arendt. *Thinking Without a Banister: Essays in Understanding, 1953—1975*. Ed. and introduction Jerome Kohn. New York: Schocken Books.

Arendt, Hannah (2018b). Tradition and the Modern Age. In Hannah Arendt. *The Modern Challenge to Tradition: Fragmente eines Buchs*. Herausgegeben von Barbara Hahn und James McFarland, unter Mitarbeit von Ingo Kieslich und Ingeborg Nordmann. Göttingen: Wallstein Verlag.

Becker, Carol (2018). The Agitated Now: Perceptions of Time and the Contemplative Space of Art. Paper presented as the 23rd Annual Kimon Friar Lecture at the American College of Greece in June 2018.

Berkowitz, Roger (2005). *The Gift of Science: Leibniz and the Modern Legal Tradition*. Cambridge, Mass.: Harvard University Press.

Luban, David (1994). Hannah Arendt and the Primacy of Narrative. In David Luban. *Legal Modernism*. Ann Arbor: University of Michigan Press.

Wild, Thomas (2017). »By Relating It«: On Modes of Writing and Judgment in the *Denktagebuch*. In Roger Berkowitz and Ian Storey (eds.). *Artifacts of Thinking: Reading Hannah Arendt's Denktagebuch*, 51—72. New York: Fordham University Press.

Absolute Goodness, the Banality of Evil, and the Wickedness Beyond Vice

Milan Hanyš

Hannah Arendt is an author who devoted enormous effort to exploring the structures of the interpersonal world and defending its autonomy, contingency, and independence from rational constructs and metaphysical or theological projects. Spontaneity at the individual level, which she associates with freedom, means, at the political level, the acceptance of contingency and plurality. In Arendt's view, totalitarian regimes have sought to eliminate spontaneity and thereby reduce the contingency that otherwise accompanies human affairs. It is less known that the tendency to eliminate spontaneity is also characteristic of bureaucracy as a government of nobody (Arendt 2006b, 289). This is not to say that bureaucracy is an expression of totalitarianism, but that the tendency to reduce plurality is dangerous if it becomes a dominant feature of the policies of modern states with their technological apparatus of surveillance and coercion. A kind of unifying motif in Arendt's rich thought, then, is the critique and defense of the world against any attempt to dehumanize humans by disregarding or eliminating plurality or contingency, and in so doing, to apply absolute criteria to the realm of contingency. This manifests itself in a series of texts ranging from *The Origins of Totalitarianism* to *The Human Condition* to texts from the late 1960s and early 1970s such as the essay »Civil Disobedience.« The objective of this chapter is to discuss the theme of good and evil in this context and the tensions between secularity and the absolute; plurality and unification; and between perfection and contingency.

In *On Revolution*, Arendt makes a claim that »absolute goodness is hardly any less dangerous than absolute evil, that it does not consist in selflessness« (Arendt 1990, 82). By this, she did not make a theological statement, but rather she dealt with the political consequences of certain convictions about human nature, e.g. the Rousseauian belief that human nature originally leans towards good and only the pollution of culture and inter-subjective influence might lead to a disaster for politics and the human world. She supported the claim by her interpretation of literary works by Herman

Melville and Fyodor Dostoyevsky, for »[i]f we want to know what absolute goodness would signify for the course of human affairs (as distinguished from the course of divine matters), we had better turn to the poets« (ibid., 82).

In her interpretation of the novelists' works, she argues that both Dostoyevsky and Melville depict peculiar examples of absolute goodness on earth in some of their characters. Such literary examples reveal not just the frailty and vulnerability of absolute goodness in the world but even its destructive character. Melville's *Billy Budd* novel evokes the situation in which a sinless Christ-like figure would reappear in the world inhabited by humans in the personality of a young sailor. The consequences would be tragic and disastrous. After Billy Budd is confronted with an unjust accusation by his fellow-sailor Claggart, he is unable to speak a single word and only stammers. Instead of acting in the manner of speech, he hits his adversary and causes his sudden death. Billy Budd is then judged by captain Vere who is torn by, on the one hand, the demands of his professional responsibility to the English throne that urge him to have Budd be executed and, on the other, the demands of justice which surpass the mundane rules.

It is not difficult to guess what attracted Arendt to Dostoyevsky and Melville's novels. They both confront a conflict of conscience and justice with the demands of political responsibility, a theme that is found in many of her texts (see, e.g., Arendt 1972a, 60—61). Arendt often characterized this topic with the old Latin saying *fiat iustitia, et pereat mundus* (»Let justice be done though the world may perish«), which allowed her to ask: »Should justice be done if the world's survival is at stake?« (Arendt 2006a, 224). Her answer to this is definitely no. While it is not worth living in a world entirely deprived of justice, responsibility for the existence and maintenance of the political sphere clearly precedes moral concerns. The other way to approach this is the famous maxim of Machiavelli from his letter to Francesco Vettori where he wrote »I love my native city more than my own soul.« Strange as it may seem, it encapsulates the crucial conflict of the two different approaches to ethical conduct.[1] While the one subordinates political action to morality and the demands of the sacred, the other prioritizes earthly political commitments over individual moral purity and salvation.

1 A similar approach with reference to Machiavelli can be found in Max Weber's distinction of two ideal types of approaches to politics that he termed the »ethics of conviction« and the »ethics of responsibility« (Weber 2004, 83—84).

Besides that, there is another thing that attracted her attention: the ability to speak and act, and by doing so, to change the course of human affairs. While violence is mute and destroys the political sphere (i.e. power and the mutual trust necessary for acting), speech is an essential tool in the creation of a common world and for the maintaining of its character as a space for action (Arendt 1972b, 134—155). Budd is unable to speak because he is, in his heavenly goodness and purity, not prepared to confront the false accusation of the earthly villain Claggart. As shocking as it may seem, we can say that Budd lacks the same capability as Adolf Eichmann, namely, neither of them can think from the perspective of the other and imagine that someone else might not share their convictions and perception of the world. That naivety ended in a disaster for Budd. Since viciousness is so alien even to his imagination, he is thoroughly unprepared to face the wicked accusation, remains silent, and then does nothing else but strike as a punishing Angel who acts not from deliberation but from a passionate feeling evoked by a perceived injustice. In short, Melville, in Arendt's reading, revealed that »goodness beyond virtue« (Arendt 1990, 83) has a destructive potential to the political community as such.

The destructive character of absolute goodness or the goodness beyond virtue can be observed in Dostoyevsky's *Brothers Karamazov* as well. In the famous parable of the Grand Inquisitor, the middle brother, Ivan Karamazov, vividly depicts that if Christ had reappeared in sixteenth century Seville, he would have been put into jail and would be in real danger of being burned at stake as a heretic. Rather than a harsh critique of only the Catholic worldview (which the parable indeed is), many of its readers are tempted to understand the parable of the Grand Inquisitor as a critique of Christianity in general. What Arendt might have liked about the story is the argument of the Inquisitor who considered the Second Coming of Christ as a threat to the institutional order as well as to human freedom. If there were an absolute Goodness present on Earth, then humans would have no freedom, and no free pursuit of happiness (Dostoevsky 1992, 212—213). When the Inquisitor confronts Christ with the critique of his acts, he remains quiet. Then he kisses him without a word. The same motive of silence and speechlessness thus appears in both the novels through which Arendt chose to show that absolute Goodness would be, in its consequences, disastrous if it were to appear in the human world. Both Dostoyevsky's Christ and Melville's Billy Budd are literary figures incapable of words when confronted by evil; they do not defend themselves and thus do not add anything positive for establishing and maintaining justice in the world. They represent the politically dangerous type of goodness beyond virtue. Furthermore, both Budd and Christ do not create and maintain the distance necessary to preserve political plurality: the former hits and kills the accuser while the latter kisses them. Both physical acts, which exceed the boundaries of personal intimacy, are completely alien to politics as understood by Arendt. In short, the absolute goodness embodied in the two literary figures would destroy the distance indispensable for the political sphere.

What is politically destructive, however, is not just the epiphany of the absolute good, but the human striving towards it in the sphere of politics. In *On Revolution*, Arendt convincingly shows the political consequences of the efforts to realize the absolute good in people and society during the French Revolution. Moral concepts such as compassion or guilt, which are of indispensable importance in individual moral reflection, become perverse and destructive when they are socially demanded and publicly displayed.[2] Similarly, love has a meaning in the private sphere, but its demand or extension into the collective is something Arendt considered potentially threatening (see Arendt 2007, 467). We can see from this that, to Arendt, the boundaries between the private and the public have a similar significance to the boundaries between the absolute good and the political good.

However, it is not only absolute goodness or the goodness beyond virtue that constitutes a grave danger to the world. Arendt compares the consequences of absolute Goodness to that of absolute Evil. She wrote that »absolute goodness is hardly any less dangerous than absolute evil [...] it does not consist in selflessness« (Arendt 1990, 82). Even though such a claim is highly problematic theologically (what theologian would say that Christ's and the Devil's revelation would have the same consequences on Earth?), it is thoroughly compatible with her emphasis on the world having been created by and for free-acting humans.

The use of the term »absolute evil« in the book *On Revolution* evokes her earlier considerations of radical Evil in *The Origins of Totalitarianism* published a dozen years earlier. Other than the extensive scholarly research done on the topic of evil and its development in Arendt's thought,[3] it is a well-acknowledged fact that the important discussions concerning evil took place already in the private letter exchange between Hannah Arendt and Karl Jaspers, her former teacher and life-long friend. After Jaspers obtained a copy of *The Ori-*

2 See especially Arendt 1990, 88 ff; as well as Arendt 2003.

3 See particularly Villa 1999, 11—60; and Bernstein 2002.

gins of Totalitarianism in 1951 and read its first excerpts, he posed a rather peculiar question to her: »Hasn't Jahwe faded too far out of sight?« (Arendt and Jaspers 1992, 165).[4] Arendt's response to Jaspers provides us with a self-reflection on her religious stance at the time:

On the personal level, I make my way through life with a kind of (childish? because unquestioned) trust in God (as distinguished from faith, which always thinks it knows and therefore has to cope with doubts and paradoxes). There's nothing much you can make of that, of course, except be happy. All traditional religion as such, whether Jewish or Christian, holds nothing whatsoever for me anymore. I don't think, either, that it can anywhere or in any way provide a basis for something so clearly political as laws. Evil has proved to be more radical than expected. In objective terms, modern crimes are not provided for in the Ten Commandments. Or: the Western tradition is suffering from the preconception that the most evil things human beings can do arise from the vice of selfishness. Yet we know that the greatest evils or radical evil has nothing to do anymore with such humanly understandable, sinful motives (ibid., 165—166).

By her confession, she has *trust in God* (*Gottesvertrauen*) but not faith (*Glauben*); she posits herself explicitly outside of any set of religious contents and prescriptions. The radical evil which appears in the modern totalitarian regimes cannot be overcome by a return to the traditional religious norms and answers. The reason for this lies in the unique and unprecedented character of the evil of the twentieth century. From her above-quoted statements it may seem to some readers that she thought of evil as something existing per se. She admits that she does not have a clear answer to the question of what is radical evil. Instead, in the following lines of the same letter, she argues that the totalitarian evil was radical because it made »human beings as human beings superfluous« (ibid., 166). It is not just a reduction of humans to »means« for some end, but it involves, as it were, treating humans as useless waste. Arendt already realized at that time that such an attitude towards a human is not only a characteristic result of totalitarian domination but also an inherent structural danger of modernity as such. She suggested such an idea in *The Origins* (Arendt 1973, 267—302) and developed it more comprehensively in *Eichmann in Jerusalem* (Arendt 2006b, 253—279). Thus, making human beings as human beings superfluous is not caused by an intentional demonic power underlying totalitarianism but instead is something enacted by ordinary people like Eichmann and enabled by the coincidental conjunction of diverse aspects of modernity, particularly a novel political organization of nation-states, growing state bureaucracy accompanied by technolog-

4 Jaspers to Arendt, February 15th, 1951.

ical progress and automatization which makes human strength more or less useless. That led to a novel situation in history which resulted in a danger that a vast number of people need not belong to political, social and economic systems, not even as exploited slaves (Arendt 1973, 297).

In the introduction to *The Origins*, Arendt characterized radical evil as an equivalent to the absolute:

> And if it is true that in the final stages of totalitarianism an absolute evil appears (absolute because it can no longer be deduced from humanly comprehensible motives), it is also true that without it we might never have known the truly radical nature of Evil (ibid., viii—ix).

That word-choice, however, puts her dangerously close to theology and metaphysics. While the concept of radical evil goes back to Immanuel Kant and does not necessarily bear a theological meaning, this cannot be said about the term »absolute evil,« which carries on its back a heavy load of theological connotations.

Unlike Kant,[5] Arendt uses the concept of radical evil deliberately to indicate that in extreme cases of totalitarian domination one faces an evil beyond any motivation that can be understood, not even a sadistic one. Only in the totalitarian regimes did a radical nature of evil, which Kant had only conceptualized, come to its full realization in a way which our forerunners had not expected. The difference between murder and the organized genocide of totalitarianism is not just a difference regarding the number of victims. The difference is qualitative, and Arendt uses the term radical evil or absolute evil to underscore it. The Nazis did not just commit crimes. The factory system of the production of corpses, organized oblivion and the de-humanization make it impossible to conceive of those deeds as mere crimes. It is something that exceeds the ideas of crime, guilt or the traditional notion of evil. Therefore, Arendt writes, in *The Origins*, about the chasm between our situation and the considerations of Evil contained in the religious and philosophical tradition:

5 Kant in his *Religion Within the Boundaries of Mere Reason* distinguishes three degrees of evil in human character and behavior. Firstly, some evil deeds result from the frailty of human nature. Although there is a good intention, a person fails to pursue good since they are weak. Secondly, evils result from the *impurity* of human volitions that is from *mixing immoral and moral motivating causes*. Thirdly, there is the *wickedness* or *pervertedness* of the human heart. This is a *conscious adoption of evil maxims or motivations* (*perversion of will*) that includes, for instance, a sadistic person who finds pleasure in observing human suffering. Although this is perverted, it is still comprehensible as a vicious desire for pleasure. For a very good summary of Kant's conception and its comparison to Arendt's, see: Bernstein 2002, 220.

> It is inherent in our entire philosophical tradition that we cannot conceive of a »radical evil,« and this is true both for Christian theology, which conceded even to the Devil himself a celestial origin, as well as for Kant, the only philosopher who, in the word he coined for it, at least must have suspected the existence of this evil even though he immediately rationalized it in the concept of a »perverted ill will« that could be explained by comprehensible motives. Therefore, we actually have nothing to fall back on in order to understand a phenomenon that nevertheless confronts us with its overpowering reality and breaks down all standards we know. There is only one thing that seems to be discernible: we may say that radical evil has emerged in connection with a system in which all men have become equally superfluous (Arendt 1973, 459).

When speaking about the theological implications and various intersections of religion and her considerations of evil, another thing might be essential to consider: throughout Western intellectual history, we can see the quasi-Gnostic assumption that to achieve something good one has to undergo a path through evil. It is the idea that good and evil are somehow mutually interrelated or that to be initiated into the good one has to experience the evil. Arendt in her book on totalitarianism refuses those peculiar dialectic and denies that one can get something positive, in the political and moral sense, from the experience of the total domination in concentration camps. Goodness does not arise from any entanglement with evil. Evil does not come from a fallen Angel—a fallen one but still an angel who might return to the right path empowered by the fall. Evil is not a deviation from the good; it is not a temporary stopover on the overall path towards good. She makes her refusal of the dialectic very clear in one passage of *The Origins*:

> Just as the horror, or the dwelling on it, cannot affect a change of character in him [in Lazarus, *Muselmann*, survivor of the camp—MH], cannot make men better or worse, thus it cannot become the basis of a political community or party in a narrower sense. The attempts to build up a European elite with a program of intra-European understanding based on the common European experience of the concentration camps have foundered in much the same manner as the attempts following the First World War to draw political conclusions from the international experience of the front generation. In both cases it turned out that the experiences themselves can communicate no more than nihilistic banalities (ibid., 441—442).

Dialectic of a Hegelian or Christian type is not a feasible way out of the horrible events and the post-war conditions. According to Arendt, we are still all based (or were at the time when she wrote it) »on the superstition that something good might result from evil« (ibid., 442). She warns in *The Origins* as well as much later in *Eichmann in Jerusalem* about the attempts to build a political society on something purely *negative*.[6] The experience of a radical evil is a denial of all politics since people in camps were isolated, deprived of the world and politics as it were. The establishment of a political community requires the opposite experience: an abundance of trust in the world and other people, rather than the horrible incommunicable experience.

Banality of Evil or the Wickedness Beyond Vice

In her reply to Gershom Scholem, Arendt, however, distanced herself from the term »radical« in relation to the totalitarian horrors:

> It is indeed my opinion now that evil is never »radical,« that it is only extreme, and that it possesses neither depth nor any demonic dimension. It can overgrow and lay waste the whole world precisely because it spreads like a fungus on the surface. It is »thought-defying,« as I said, because thought tries to reach some depth, to go to the roots, and the moment it concerns itself with evil, it is frustrated because there is nothing. That is its »banality.« Only the good has depth and can be radical (Arendt 2007, 471).

Evil is, according to Arendt's new understanding, never *radical*, and it does not possess a *radix*, it is not deeply rooted; it is only shallow. There are reasons to agree with Richard J. Bernstein's claim that such a change of terminology does not necessarily mean that she abandoned the idea that totalitarian regimes have radically challenged the prevalent notions of human nature (Bernstein 2002, 218). The evil of total domination and the making superfluous of humans is still incomprehensible but not because of some depth in the motivation of the perpetrators but because thinking about this problem encounters only nothingness. There is only a sheer banality of the perpetrator, i.e. a lack of reflexivity, a thoughtlessness.

Dana R. Villa argued that she later abandoned the concept of radical evil because she realized that she had essentialized the evil and implied its »Faustian grandeur« (Villa 1999, 57—58). However, Arendt did not change her mind about the crimes of the totalitarian regimes being different from crimes we know from the past. That difference does not imply that the horrible and unprecedented crimes of the twentieth century can be ascribed to a certain metaphysical or demonic intentional power underlying modernity or even

6 Such a conviction underlies her critique of David Ben-Gurion and the prosecutor, Gideon Hausner, during the Eichmann trial (see Arendt 1963, 3—20).

to the loss of religious faith.[7] She knew that objection as early as 1946 and it was again Jaspers who raised it in their private correspondence. In the letter, he gave a notable argument that firstly involves the notion of the banality of the Nazi perpetrators.[8] Arendt partially accepted the critique and explicitly rejected the idea of the satanic greatness of evil while insisting on the novel and peculiar character of the Nazi mass murders that cannot be adequately understood by contemporary ethics and law. She replied to him:

> I found what you say about my thoughts on »beyond crime and innocence« in what the Nazis did half convincing; that is, I realize completely that in the way I've expressed this up to now I come dangerously close to that »satanic greatness« that I, like you, totally reject. But still, there is a difference between a man who sets out to murder his old aunt and people who without considering the economic usefulness of their actions at all (the deportations were very damaging to the war effort) built factories to produce corpses. One thing is certain: We have to combat all impulses to mythologize the horrible, and to the extent that I can't avoid such formulations, I haven't understood what actually went on. Perhaps what is behind it all is only that individual human beings did not kill other individual human beings for human reasons, but that an organized attempt was made to eradicate the concept of the human being (Arendt and Jaspers 1992, 69).[9]

Thus, in the correspondence, we first see that Arendt rejects the idea of a theological and metaphysical load of her description of totalitarian evils. Secondly, she tries to maintain her long-lasting belief that Nazi crimes were not just crimes but also some kind of horrible experiment on the human condition and that through such a horrible experiment people might even lose their characteristic human features. Thirdly, we see that it was not Arendt, but Jaspers who spoke about the banality and triviality of the perpetrators of the horrible deeds, and they discussed the idea already in 1946 almost twenty years before the Eichmann controversy.

If the change in terminology she undertook in the 1960s did not mean a fundamental revision of the metaphysical or religious content of her conception of evil, why did she place such an emphasis on this change? The difference between the concepts of radical and banal evil thus lies rather in a change of perspective. While *The Origins of Totalitarianism* was a descriptive analysis of the rise of extreme political evil and its sources, in *Eichmann in Jerusalem* it is more about the motivational and personal assumptions of those

7 Arendt refused Eric Voegelin's early theory of political religions as a substitute for genuine spirituality. See her exchange of opinions with him: Baehr 2012.

8 Jaspers to Arendt, October 19th, 1946.

9 Arendt to Jaspers, December 17th, 1946.

who perpetrate such evil. Both perspectives are complementary to some extent. The horror of the evil described in *The Origins* is not diminished by the fact that the motivations of the actors can be quite banal and need not be monstrous in any way. The notion of radical evil was abandoned because it might have suggested the existence of some depth. Evil is only banal, nevertheless, it resists thought, defies it, escapes it into the void of non-thought and empty platitudes.

At the same time that she published her reports from the Eichmann trial, she was also preparing the book *On Revolution*. Actually, both books were published in 1963. The thematic connection between the two books has, to my knowledge, so far eluded interpreters, although Arendt draws attention to it in her letter to Scholem (Arendt 2007, 467—468). In *On Revolution* she mentions the concepts of radical evil and absolute goodness and quotes them in one remarkable sentence: »Neither Rousseau nor Robespierre was capable of dreaming of a goodness beyond virtue, just as they were unable to imagine that radical evil would ›partake nothing of the sordid or sensual‹ (Melville), that there could be wickedness beyond vice« (Arendt 1990, 82). It is striking that Arendt remarked in the letter that she abandoned the idea of radical evil, while she had used the phrase in a different context in *On Revolution*. Such a coincidence may prove the idea of a continuity of her thought in which the change of terminology testifies to a change of perspective rather than to a substantial reconsideration of the question of evil. The conundrum can be further disentangled if we consider what a »wickedness beyond vice« might be. Regarding that, Arendt mentions the literary figure of Dostoyevsky's Grand Inquisitor:

> The sin of the Grand Inquisitor was that he, like Robespierre, was »attracted toward *les hommes faibles*,« not only because such attraction was indistinguishable from lust for power, but also because he had depersonalized the sufferers, lumped them together into an aggregate—the people *toujours malheureux*, the suffering masses, et cetera (ibid., 85).

The inquisitor is not greedy, nor does he show any kind of vice. However, he lacks any kind of compassion for a singular person. He shows general pity but cannot have compassion for a suffering individual. In that, he represents a wickedness beyond vice. At the same time, when Arendt wrote about the wickedness beyond vice and goodness beyond virtue, she was referring to Eichmann's personality. In her famous report, she described him as someone average, a normal person with a lack of reflexivity:

> Except for an extraordinary diligence in looking out for his personal advancement, he had no motives at all. [...] He merely, to put the matter colloquially, never realized what he was doing. It was precisely this lack of imagination which enabled him to sit for months on end facing a German Jew who was conducting the police interrogation, pouring out his heart to the man and explaining again and again how it was that he reached only the rank of lieutenant colonel in the S.S. and that it had not been his fault that he was not promoted (Arendt 2006b, 287).

Such a lack of ability, compassion, and empathy is what Arendt described as thoughtlessness, something which exactly »predisposed him to become one of the greatest criminals of that period« (ibid., 265). Instead of paying attention to individual suffering, Eichmann is the one who followed abstract principles and noble but plain phrases, which in his mouth turned into banalities. It is precisely this remoteness from concrete reality and »thoughtlessness« that can be understood as the wickedness beyond vice. This does not mean that the evil that it causes is not extreme or that the term banality describes not the deed but the shallow depth of the motifs of the perpetrator. Since a modern evil is more often than not accompanied by thoughtlessness, lack of reflexivity, lack of imagination, inability or an unwillingness to think from the perspective of others, the adequate response to this kind of modern evil is very traditional: self-examination or thinking in a Socratic way cultivated by arts and philosophy.

However, it is not only Socrates to whom Arendt could appeal in her late considerations of the importance of thinking and judging in practical matters but also to the sacred texts of the Torah and the Gospels. Even though I would not go so far as to speak about an implicit theology in her case, her statements about evil are thoroughly compatible with the Jewish-Christian moral tradition. In the Torah, it is said: »Thou shalt not follow a multitude to do evil« (Ex. 23:2). While in the New Testament there appears the Golden Rule: »Therefore all things whatsoever ye would that men should do to you, do ye even so to them: for this is the law and the prophets« (Matt. 7:12). Those quotes indicate that even the two biblical religions involve inner plurality and their moral message cannot be simply reduced to the Decalogue. Both of the above-mentioned quotes require from an acting person not just obedience to any prescribed set of norms and rules but also, in the latter case, obedience to the imagination, the ability to imagine the perspective of the other or, to put it more simply, the ability to think and judge.

Conclusion

In this study, we have examined the political implications of the concept of the absolute good as analyzed by Arendt. It has been shown that the absolute good, in the form of, for example, unconditional love and compassion, may have its place in relations to particular people, but when these phenomena are brought into the public sphere, they can become destructive. Compassion, for example, destroys the distance between actors that is necessary for the maintenance of the public sphere. When a purely good person who is incapable of reflexivity is confronted with evil, they react in a politically dangerous way. Turning the other cheek or reacting affectively is not an adequate response, which would consist rather in the formulation of general principles such as solidarity, appeal to the law and worldly, if imperfect, justice. Thus, it turns out that for Arendt it is extremely important to maintain the disjunction between the private and public spheres as well as the disjunction between the religious quest for perfect moral purity and the world of politics.

The change in terminology concerning evil that Arendt then undertook in the 1960s was not related to her fundamental change of mind about the specific nature of modern evil—an evil made possible by technological advances and the bureaucratization of life—but rather arose from a focus on the motivations of one of its greatest perpetrators. She found his motivations neither profound nor radical, but banal. Rather, she located the personality prerequisites for his involvement in monstrous crimes in his inability to think from the position of the other, his lack of imagination and empathy. If one reads *On Revolution* and *Eichmann in Jerusalem* in parallel, it becomes clear that what unites the two books, apart from the date of publication, is the theme of evil, the roots of which lie not in selfishness and vice, but precisely in the inability to judge and relate in thought to concrete facts and the concrete suffering of individuals. In other words, Adolf Eichmann and the Grand Inquisitor share the same extremely dangerous feature of what might be called a wickedness beyond vice. And it is equally important to see that an absolute goodness unaccompanied by virtue, exemplified by Billy Budd or a Christ figure, can be as dangerous in its consequences as a wickedness beyond vice. In a contingent world, all attempts to transcend the plurality of people, to reduce randomness or to impose absolute standards and demands on oneself and others is a dangerous betrayal of the human condition.

Works Cited

Arendt, Hannah (1972a). Civil Disobedience. In Hannah Arendt. *Crises of the Republic*. New York: Harcourt Brace Jovanovich.

Arendt, Hannah (1972b). On Violence. In Hannah Arendt. *Crises of the Republic*. New York: Harcourt Brace Jovanovich.

Arendt, Hannah (1973). *The Origins of Totalitarianism*. New ed. with added prefaces. New York: Harcourt Brace Jovanovich.

Arendt, Hannah (1990). *On Revolution*. London/New York: Penguin Books.

Arendt, Hannah, and Karl Jaspers (1992). *Correspondence, 1926—1969*. Ed. Lotte Kohler and Hans Saner. Transl. Robert and Rita Kimber. New York: Harcourt Brace Jovanovich.

Arendt, Hannah (2003). Personal Responsibility Under Dictatorship. In Hannah Arendt. *Responsibility and Judgment*, 17—48. Ed. and introduction Jerome Kohn. New York: Schocken Books.

Arendt, Hannah (2006a). *Between Past and Future: Eight Exercises in Political Thought*. Introduction Jerome Kohn. New York: Penguin Books.

Arendt, Hannah (2006b). *Eichmann in Jerusalem: A Report on the Banality of Evil*. Introduction Amos Elon. New York, N.Y.: Pinguin Books.

Arendt, Hannah (2007). The Eichmann Controversy: A Letter to Gershom Scholem. In Hannah Arendt. *The Jewish Writings*. Ed. Jerome Kohn and Ron H. Feldman. New York: Schocken Books.

Baehr, Peter (2012). Debating Totalitarianism: An Exchange of Letters Between Hannah Arendt and Eric Voegelin. Ed. and introduction Peter Baehr. Transl. Gordon C. Wells. *History and Theory*, 51, 364—380.

Bernstein, Richard J. (2002). *Radical Evil: A Philosophical Interrogation*. Cambridge, UK/Malden, MA: Polity Press.

Dostoevsky, Fyodor (1992). *The Brothers Karamazov*. Transl. Richard Pevear and Larissa Volokhonsky. Introduction Malcolm V. Jones. New York: Knopf.

Villa, Dana R. (1999). *Politics, Philosophy, Terror: Essays on the Thought of Hannah Arendt*. Princeton, N.J.: Princeton University Press.

Weber, Max (2004). *Vocation Lectures*. Ed. and introduction David Owen and Tracy B. Strong. Transl. Rodney Livingstone. Indianapolis: Hackett Pub.

A Jurisprudence of Neglect: Arendt, Ambedkar, and the Logic of Political Cruelty

Aishwary Kumar

»The Hindu would prefer to be inhuman rather than touch the untouchable.«

»But God knows, they had learned how to resist temptation.«
(Bhimrao Ambedkar, Waiting for a Visa – Hannah Arendt, Eichmann in Jerusalem)

No two thinkers of the human condition attached the seeming passivity of human neglect to the willful, active disposal—and disposability—of human beings with as much clarity as did Hannah Arendt (1906—1975) and Bhimrao Ambedkar (1891—1956). Pariahs in the lands of their birth, active witnesses to the morphing of democratic societies into tyrannical majorities, remorselessly skeptical of grand claims of civilizational glory made by champions of empire and nationalism alike, as doggedly unmoved by theological delusions—»the devil makes a good theologian,« Arendt would write in »Some Questions of Moral Philosophy« (Arendt 2003b, 69)—as they were repelled by secularist vanities of the modern liberal, Arendt and Ambedkar nonetheless remained resolutely bound to their own faith in revolutionary miracles: miracles with the power to produce durable political forms anchored in the equal sharing of human freedom. If these two thinkers seem joined together today by the shortest line on our political horizon, it is not only because of their commitment to understanding the insoluble relationship between violence and identity, between expulsion and rights, but also because of their ceaseless pursuit of the desires and fantasies—the specter of the unsaid and the unsayable—that underlie the theological and juridical dimensions of modern homelessness.

More than a brute material fact, this homelessness is, for both Arendt and Ambedkar, an almost transcendental condition. For it is not simply one physical home among others that is lost to the politics of abandonment, normalized by the modern regime of rights and reinforced by archaic notions of authority alike. Instead, the earth itself has been opened to the delusional,

»cruel majesty« of the law, which has become but one instrument for speeding up human alienation—and human flight—from its very ground.[1] And all this has transpired right in the middle of the age of peace, so to speak, at the peak of international institutionalism and declarations of human rights, with the law's majesty frequently mutating into a compulsive jurisprudence of neglect, its apparatuses not merely destroying worlds but decomposing the idea of the human itself.[2]

For Arendt, sovereignty was the fulcrum of these cruel delusions of the law, one that appeared in the world not as a will to transcendence but as a desire for omnipotence, now imploding into tyranny—rule of one over many—and now into ochlocracy—rule of many over one. For Ambedkar, in contrast, a world without sovereignty and its legal guarantees—if not moral certainties—would be even more arbitrary in its neglect and segregation of the world's most vulnerable, and politics would be even less secure against the vigilantism of armed factions whose religious pathologies simmered right underneath the democratic surface, even as they increasingly spoke in the language of modern jurisprudence, constitutionalism even. Yet, few postwar thinkers matched Arendt more powerfully than Ambedkar in linking humanity's perverse temptation to sovereignty with its inverse temptation to inaction and indifference—the decision to do nothing—in the face of its own evil. The encounter between Arendt and Ambedkar occurs on the theologico-political firmament of this cruelty, sprawled between sovereignty and neglect, temptation and abandonment. »God knows,« Arendt would write of this indifferent humanity in the searing final sentence of the eighth chapter of *Eichmann in Jerusalem*, »they had learnt how to resist temptation.«

Who is Arendt's God? Or better yet, where is he when human beings hesitate to respond to evil? Therein lies the whole history of Arendt's turbulent faith in the actions of human beings freed from the authority and constraints

1 On this expression, see Arendt 1979, 269.

2 It is on the dilemmas unleashed upon the moral claims of nationalist politics by the tragedy of twentieth-century statelessness worldwide, which had already by the end of the First World War led to the creation of vast minority populations hurtling towards superfluity, that the first convergences between Arendt and Ambedkar begin to appear. Their major works on the limits of international institutionalism—of which the Minority Treaties formed the spine—were bookended, on the one hand, by the period of fascist assaults on the liberal imperial system and, on the other, by the eventual liquidation of that system during the first wave of decolonization in Asia and Africa in the 1940s and 1950s. For a fragment of the archive of this missed encounter, see especially Ambedkar, *Thoughts on Pakistan* (1940), its second, enlarged edition published as *Pakistan, on the Partition of India* (Ambedkar 1945) and Arendt, *The Origins of Totalitarianism*.

of tradition, in their miraculous ability to find freedom by beginning things anew even in »the epochs of petrification and foreordained gloom« (Arendt 1961b, 169). Therein also lies her baffled frustration with their willingness to destroy this freedom as quickly, in a thoughtless combination of barbarism and indifference. Freedom and barbarity have often hidden each other in their very hearts, after all, and under suitable conditions, even intensified each other.

For both Arendt and Ambedkar, it was the »contagion« of faithlessness—the infection of the public realm by distrust and mendacity—that was at work beneath the moral negligence and misanthropic irresponsibility of modern political life. For both, this faithlessness had spiraled out not from the vanity of the atheists—who, shorn of any fear of divine judgment, were infinitely more susceptible to being corrupt in their fidelity to the oath—but from the monotheistic vision of government instead, at whose center was the omnipotent sovereignty of one God alone. Both were determined in their mining of the secrecies and mystery—*arcana imperii*—that crippled the powers of truthful self-government every time human compulsions were given the language of sacred, untouchable laws. If Ambedkar decried the monotheistic zeal of political Hinduism that was masked by its rhetoric of plurality—its punitive sanctions and obligations scaffolded by the untranslatable, civil subterfuge of the word *dharma*—Arendt sought in political plurality an escape from the fantasies of a sovereignty harbored by the same monotheistic zealots whom Ambedkar deplored for pretending they were compelled by anything but their will to absolute domination over minorities, their fantasies couched in secularist invocations of plurality. In moments of counterintuitive, even paradoxical convergences like these, Arendt and Ambedkar seem to be joined in their search for a non-sovereign freedom not by a straight line but an elusive curve. And at the center of this curve is the history of use and abuse of plurality for politics.

Making Inequality Hurt

The nearly half a dozen passages of Arendt's most trenchant indictment of what we might today call, following Charles Taylor, »democratic degeneration,« appear in *The Human Condition* right after she has posited polytheism—the plurality of gods—as the theologico-political counterpoint to the trouble that human freedom has always faced in the form of monotheism's will to sovereignty. In fact, Arendt posits polytheism as nothing short of an exit from the fantasy of omnipotence itself, into a realm of plural freedom. »Omnipotence [...] is never an attribute of gods in polytheism, no matter how superior the strength of the gods may be to the forces of men« (Arendt 1958, 202), she writes in the first of two instances, positing a somewhat strange equivalence between the heavenly plurality of gods and the worldly plurality of human beings, using one as the analogue of the other. »Conversely,« she adds, »aspiration toward omnipotence always implies—apart from its utopian *hubris*—the destruction of plurality« (ibid., 202). Arendt returns to the formula later in the text, this time even more directly siding with polytheism. »In polytheist systems, [...] even a god, no matter how powerful, cannot be sovereign; only under the assumption of one god (›One is one and all alone and evermore shall be so‹) can sovereignty and freedom be the same« (ibid., 234—235).

Do people in polytheistic societies always reflect the plurality of their gods, and, in doing so, really privilege freedom over sovereignty? What of the gods themselves, their thousand resentments and rage, their petty quarrels and pernicious jealousies, which so frequently, in more than one Indian epic (but not Indian only), lay the world of human beings itself to ruin? What if, under polytheism, sovereignty was not expelled from the world of the free but instead—to use Ambedkar's term—»graded« like an uneven topography of fratricidal *ressentiment* and pathological megalomania? What if plurality was polytheism's political ruse, a monotheistic drive for mastery that is diverse only in how many ways it seeks to punish the mortal subject?

By way of probing Arendt's and Ambedkar's central theses on polytheism—its closest Indian signifier might be *dharma*—I want to outline in this chapter one critical element of what we might call a Southern theory of political freedom. At the heart of this theory of freedom, I argue, must be a new critique of violence (and thus, of *nonviolence*): a critique that excavates the organized, archaic brutalism of liberal democratic life, on the one hand, and the systemic, unexamined inequality lodged at its seemingly passive, civil, and negligent center, on the other, as two dimensions of the same moral and political affliction; a critique that, at the same time, remains undeterred by the civilizational (and always theologico-political) claim of plurality and self-determination that underwrites the legitimacy of the idea of government in the Global South. And this in order precisely to highlight the consequences of the fundamental claim that remains underdeveloped in both Arendt and

Ambedkar: that the threat to constitutional democracy—especially in polytheistic societies but not only in them—might come not from sovereignty and its monotheistic perversions (if there is such a thing), but from the majority's ability to do exactly the opposite: be plural.

It is after all undeniable that some polytheistic societies—even and especially when they define themselves by their plurality—deface as many gods as they consecrate, and this idolatrous strife invariably unleashes an enigmatic tussle—while, at the same time, forging a perilous bond—between plurality and cruelty, between faith and fratricide. Far from having freed freedom from the temptation to sovereignty, violence in polytheistic societies might simply disappear behind the idolatry of a thousand deities, their mortal followers on earth only replicating the fetishistic compulsions and mean snobberies of their gods whose actions are sometimes designed to do nothing more than to »make inequality hurt« (Shklar 1984, 87). As Judith Shklar points out in this stunning definition of snobbery, such a practice of moral cruelty by reinforcement of inequality does not hurt just the body, for after all physical pain is the material fact of inequality. Rather, snobbery—which reeks of the resentment of the affluent for the destitute and the rage of the delusional toward the vulnerable—damages the moral psychological supports of life itself.

For all the theatrics of civility and self-knowledge in which it couches itself, snobbery, Shklar writes, is »a very destructive vice.« And a cruel, self-destructive one. It hurts the very joy of being alive among human beings who, despite political divisions and social inequities, might have still been capable of loving one another. This capacity to love in the face of mutually inflicted pain is the hurting soul of the democratic covenant, one that must be underwritten by the unconditional humility of the majority no less than it is by the minority's rebellious faith in the world that hostilely surrounds it. For all its tragic and unequal violence, this act of faith is what makes the modern social contract—and constitutional concord—possible.

Snobbery, with its repeated assault on personhood by insult, destroys this faith. It kills trust not only among unequals but the ability of the self to trust itself. And it always sets up a very worldly theater, an intensely democratic dramaturgy that is at once fierce in its sacrificial energy and wholly devoid of emancipatory passion. Overseen by idolatries of all sorts, including constitutional idolatry—whose jurisprudential guise we call »originalism«—this dramaturgy is nontheological only in name. Underneath it is a search for absolute mastery, fueled by a lethal disdain for the unequal and an insatiable, snobbish desire for height, whose origins, even legitimacy, is sought in the ancient constitution.

The descent of sovereignty from its perch, in other words, is by itself no guarantee of freedom. On the contrary, it might be a function of its pernicious counterpart: the degeneration of democratic majesty—popular sovereignty—into liberal snobbery and resentments, aided not by the humbling of the high-born but instead by the intensification of behaviors endemic to political liberalism and its privileging of civic surfaces (or performative civility) over material truths. It is this descent of sovereignty and its corresponding escalation of violence through the all too ordinary means of hypocrisy, lying, and indifference that Arendt calls »cruel majesty.«

Such a depreciation of sovereignty in the earthly world of power play is bound neither to make inequality necessarily more unequal nor make violence more violent. But it does make the neglect of the vulnerable a common fact, and sometimes, even elevates it to a common purpose. Which is to say, it makes active neglect unpunishable by the law, lending it a legal and ritual credence—*sanction*—that allows, in plain sight, the abandonment of entire swathes of human beings. It is an abandonment that might go socially unnoticed and even considered morally permissible, because there is no one center to account for this neglect. Or better still, the center itself is empty, a sovereign void. Even if she barely touches upon this vacillating border between polytheism and peace, between the plurality of gods and the indiscriminate, extraconstitutional, and unaccountable zeal of those who follow their many gods, Arendt—as her work *On Revolution* (1963) would testify—never took lightly the risk of their lethal metamorphoses under the stress of majoritarian deliriums.[3]

Does political freedom really stand a better chance in those polytheistic societies that are seemingly free from the monotheistic sovereignty of

3 This hardly sounds alarmist anymore. The majority's will to biologically and politically »liquidate« minorities does not require, for its realization, a total overthrow of the constitutional order of things. If anything, the fantastic drive to exterminate the poor and the minor—or make human beings entirely disappear from politics—is immanent to the democratic principle of the »majority-decision« itself, which can quickly degenerate into a zeal for »majority-rule« (Arendt 1963, 155—56). In such moments, as Ambedkar warns in the 1940s, a people does not have to necessarily declare itself as belonging to one whole, ruled by one God, aligned against a single enemy. Instead, it is precisely its heterogeneity—with an absent or empty center—that rips political society open to multiple wounds inflicted by multiple means on newer human targets in the name of multiple gods, dissolving the very border between monotheistic hubris and pluralist humanism. As a theory of government, liberalism has historically been the art and politics of this border; Hindutva is its murderous intensification to the point of official barbarity.

one God? Is plurality (even of the gods) a truly resilient bulwark against either oligarchy (the theft and concentration of power by a few) or tyranny (the rule over many by one) in the liberal age? Or has plurality itself degenerated into a constitutionally calibrated compromise of the democratic promise and twisted the resplendence of its political faith into a cruel normalcy, a law of neglect?

What I call »the neodemocratic condition« is the normalization, even legalization, of this combustible, extrajudicial bond between constitution and cruelty, between civilizational hubris and extrajudicial war, cultured inside the petri dish of liberal democracy. I believe democracy is not simply in the throes of a reactionary upsurge of extreme nationalism worldwide (which is of course obvious); it is also at the threshold of a setting in of a new, self-lacerating political form that feeds on the suicidal intensification of the most fragile elements of democracy: the *making majoritarian of its political faith*.

As Arendt never fails to remind us, the bond between concord and cruelty goes deep into the heart of the western tradition. But not only of the western tradition. Rather, this bond compresses the history of authority in every tradition theological and political, western and southern, in which sovereignty—and the mortal subject's subservience to it—never wholly dissociated itself from its roots in mystical foundations, drawing its legitimacy from the enchanting powers of the law to create conditions of generalized, voluntary servitude. The most devastating articulation of this formula appears in the last paragraph of the eighth chapter of Arendt's *Eichmann in Jerusalem*, hauntingly entitled »Duties of a Law-Abiding Citizen«:

> And just as the law in civilized countries assumes that the voice of conscience tells everybody »Thou shalt not kill,« even though man's natural desires and inclinations may at times be murderous, so the law of Hitler's land demanded that the voice of conscience tell everybody: »Thou shalt kill,« although the organizers of the massacres knew full well that murder is against the normal desires and inclinations of most people. Evil in the Third Reich had lost the quality by which most people recognize it—the quality of temptation. Many Germans and many Nazis, probably an overwhelming majority of them, must have been tempted *not* to murder, *not* to rob, *not* to let their neighbors go off to their doom [...] not to become accomplices in all these crimes by benefiting from them. But God knows, they had learned how to resist temptation (Arendt 2006, 150).

It is not merely obedience to a sovereign authority but rather sovereignty's strategic indifference, its tactical unraveling, which sends democracies spiraling toward degeneration. After all, a government can be said to have become properly majoritarian—or tyrannical—only when the border between criminal and political violence has dissolved and assaults on the government's political opponents begin to be delegated, tacitly or directly, to organized bands of armed men out on a legally immune politico-criminal enterprise, as if they had been granted a preemptive pardon, even parole (as some indicted among the Hindu nationalist leadership in India today are, and to whose politics Ambedkar had already in the 1940s given the name »gangsterism«).[4] Attacks on the police, whose constabulary might be drawn from among the poor and who are almost always inadequately trained and equipped, are no longer uncommon. As society's most vulnerable and most derelict, they are given uniforms colored to this day in colonial khaki, armed with batons even more archaic in their bluntness, and sent out to crush the population from which they are themselves drawn, only to be turned into—or left to become—targets of neofascist paramilitary factions that have immunity even higher than that of the police (if that were imaginable), as soon as the police display so much as a trace of independent, neutral power on the streets.

This is the one suicidal dimension of late modern populism that is least spoken of: the voluntary loosening of popular sovereignty—that is, the dissolution of the democratic will and constitutionally legitimate authority over means of violence—in the very name of the people; the tactical withdrawal of police and other judicial-civil institutions in the face of the brute strength of numbers; and, as political faithlessness sets in, the making legitimate (in its stead) of a self-lacerating violence by a people against itself.

The police in Hindutva's ochlocracy—rule by mob—is made into one more component of *kar seva* or religious service, its forces turned into the leading edge of a poor population pushed into war with itself, sometimes summoned to destroy mosques and dig up medieval tombs; sometimes to haplessly guard the subcontinent's riverine sweeps of land during waterborne festivals where millions pack in and pray in the midst of a raging pandemic, their holy dips accountable to nobody but their gods; and, most often, to attack and maim their own during operations of blunt repression of the citizenry. No attempt to grasp the core of Hindutva's gurgling appetite for violence can do without taking into account its calibrated hatred of the poor, Muslim or Brahmin, Christian or Dalit, uniformed or civilian: the poor whom, beyond all the known limits of psychopathology, it displays as proof of India's plurality, their tragic attempts at survival serving as evidence of

4 On this moment, see Kumar 2015.

a religious populations' ascetic prowess, their famished resilience a site of nationalistic display of a plural society's monastic heroism in the face of brutal adversity and hunger.

This institutionalized hatred of the poor, backed by a perverse, ritualistic celebration of the destitute—its liturgical roots go deep into the Indian epic tradition—and a »police power« that is soaked in the disciplinary logic of caste, does not replace the political will to create permanent minorities, however. Nor does the will to punish them for the originary crime of being born a minority—or outcaste—cease to be the Hindutva's sovereign drive. Instead, poverty and plurality merge in a new majoritarian technique of rule in which one legitimizes the other. Destitution is justified in the name of pluralism of castes—some of whom must by birth still have ritually polluting occupations—while plurality becomes the value worth defending because it legitimizes, precisely within the framework of liberal civility, a barbaric inequality among the constituents of an idolatrous, liturgical universe where the duty and work of each is laid out in scrupulous detail. Only now, the majority does not simply obey the law; it unforgivingly enforces it upon itself and its own. The brutalism of the neodemocratic condition—the removal of forgiveness from it, Arendt might say—cannot be grasped without this destructive mutation in the structure of the modern political majority from whose good faith democracy once drew hope. Far beyond its numbers, the majority is now a self-lacerating technique of making inequality hurt.

Sacrifice Without a Future

Of India, the world's most populous and precarious democracy, this must be even more explicitly asked: how do decisive shifts in the logic of government towards a regime of cruelty come to be written off under the sign of a history of nonviolence with which a society has somehow come to be associated with as if by a lethal lie? What is the name one gives to this historically *violent nonviolence*, this barbaric civility and indifference now feeding a new, destructive *violence of violence*, this violence that brutalizes not always by spilling blood but by inscribing neglect itself into the law? What if we were to suggest, in the wake of Ambedkar, that this jurisprudence of neglect is yet another, even more modern specter of caste? In its »mechanism« if not its face, in its »obdurate logic« if not in its name, what if this jurisprudence—with its elaborate grammar and liturgy of »sanctions«—marks the making majoritarian of caste itself, only now not as a moving front of social violence against the minority or as calibrated, »graded inequality« of the outcaste alone, as Ambedkar calls it, but as the political apotheosis of inequality as such, normalized by the metastasis of an old, barbaric refusal to touch and elevating that archaic social strategy of abandoning entire populations to the status of a legitimate principle of democratic government itself?

There is both a dreadful repetition and a catastrophic difference in the malice of these masters who see their power unconstrained by any sort of authority whatsoever, constitutional or moral. Indeed, there is a name for this punitive structure of extrajudicial repetition and difference: *caste*, that apparatus of tenacious belief systems and tendentious relationship to facts in which truth is merely a moral flutter, and truthfulness but a brief temptation to break the shackles of dharmic constraint and do the right thing before the most human of all temptations—the temptation to do right by those who share one's world—is swallowed by the law. »God knows,« to again recall Arendt's disturbing diagnosis, India might have lost that temptation to respond to evil entirely. And all this not because to *not* kill, to *not* murder, to *not* let neighbors go to their doom entirely would be morally difficult—their caste after all gives them immunity when they decide to do the right thing—but precisely because it is by deciding to *not* do any of these right things can they convince themselves that they have obeyed the law of *dharma* to its spirit and letter.

In his revolutionary manifesto, *Annihilation of Caste* (1936), Ambedkar, who rarely ever found himself attracted to Indian tropes of secularity, calls this exemplary, violent conjunction between lying, cruelty, and government—a conjunction whose ghost might never cease to haunt the scene of democratic politics—the state of India's »armed neutrality,« a precarious truce in hostilities that simply continues the polity's factional, civil war by other means. It is less a war on civil society than it is a war waged by civil society upon itself in a manner that inscribes violence at the heart of civility, beyond all normative exchanges of fire between violence and counterviolence. In fact, one symptom of cruelty made political is the remorseless disabling of all resistance by counterpowers. There might not even be two sides in this war that a society wages against itself; there might be no desire in its heart for an end or ends, only a sacrificial zeal let loose in a lethal anomie, which only confirms Ambedkar's suspicion: caste, like death, leaves the earth parched and worldless in the very middle of its festivity. And its weapon is no more an iron rod than it is moral hesitation.

In that indeterminate zone between homicidal hesitation and murderous cruelty lies a lie, a perjury, which sometimes begins a lethal rumor that then sparks a cruel, targeted wave of vigilante violence, one that is not itself free of an institutional—or systemic—dimension. It is to Ambedkar, arguably along with James Baldwin, one of the greatest moral chroniclers of the infinite human capacity to lie in the face of cruelty, that we owe the singular insight that rumor is possibly India's most lethal weapon, one that can keep the majority tranquilized into subservience; that can have the minority eliminated and disappeared, or perhaps worse, kept frozen or fossilized in place; that there is something systemic about rumormongering in societies where people have been turned into animate vehicles of resentment and lying; that rumor, above all, is the perversely beating heart of a *stasis*: a technique or maneuver in the machine of a ceaseless autocratic attempt deployed not just to intimidate and incarcerate but to systemically immobilize a people in time by sheer indifference to their want and plight. To reverse Ambedkar's formula, would political cruelty—that is, the generalized destruction of and indifference toward the very idea of the human, elevated to the principle of civic rule—be possible in a society that did not already have at its heart an active, archaic *jurisprudence of neglect*?

By jurisprudence of neglect, I mean the laws—moral, religious, and positive—made to rule over those who are left most derelict in society by hunger but who have at the same time lost all their appetite, except the one for survival. Deprived of personhood, let alone livelihood, right under the stern eye of the law, they can barely swallow. It is the sort of lawmaking that pulls the poor into cycles of migration without mobility, hurling them across space but freezing them in time. Unable and unwilling to feed them, the purveyors and jurists of neglect force them to swallow their dignity instead, adding more than just moral insult to their injury. Even the feeblest complaint is deemed evidence of their criminality, their fearless dissent a proof of seditious intent deserving infinite, languishing incarceration without trial, sometimes unto death. Numbering millions, they become, not surprisingly, in Ambedkar's searing formula, a famished, outnumbered fraction of themselves.

Neglect is not simply a function of official dereliction of duty, an effect of bureaucratic inaction, or a consequence of governmental inertia, all of which have come to be organized under the rubric of impersonal, »systemic violence.« Instead, neglect elevated to a jurisprudential art—and theater—is part of the social and moral imaginary of mastery itself, scaffolded by elaborate liturgies of power and its theatrical display (of which snobbery is one, albeit most viciously personal, part). We must approach this neodemocratic jurisprudence as a locus of social and legislative practices and tactical, paramilitary maneuvers at the same time, designed to dominate the vulnerable not in a world where norms of civic care or legislations on social welfare are entirely absent but precisely where they are meticulously defined and ritualistically followed, obedience now deemed the only admissible evidence of propriety and personhood as such. Neglect belongs not to a world where juridical—and judicial—abandonment thrives in the absent-minded negligence or thoughtless distractions of law-abiding bureaucrats (as sometimes the word »neglect« can come to mean); instead, it thrives in a world of unforgiving adherence to the laws made with the sole intent of transforming brutalism into a political instrument, one where cruelty takes the form of slow lacerations of delay and individual hesitation as often as it does of fetishistic spurts of extreme violence. There is, as Arendt writes, even if all too obliquely for her own good, in *Eichmann in Jerusalem*, no such thing as a truly thoughtless bureaucrat, except the one who blindly obeys the law of extermination, making even killing his moral law, unconstrained by any faith in transcendence and any fear that the future might judge him.

More is lost in this faithlessness than just the sacral element that was once attached to commitments of oath and office and that bound the political actor to truthfulness in the conduct of his duty. Futurity itself—faith in the world of equals still to come—is swamped by the *making majoritarian of democracy*, which is now unconstrained by any fear other than its perverse fear of the minority, and which therefore seeks refuge not in transcendence but, absent any rigorous commitment to truth, in political mendacity instead. This loss of authority (and thus of futurity), for Arendt, is the one irreversibly crippling effect of a disenchanted world that has lost all sense of the religious sanction:

> [T]he loss of belief in future states is politically, though certainly not spiritually, the most significant distinction between our present period and the centuries before. And this loss is definite. For no matter how religious our world may turn again, or how much authentic faith still exists in it, or how deeply our moral values may be rooted in our religious systems, the fear of hell is no longer among the motives which would prevent or stimulate the actions of a majority. This seems inevitable if secularity of the world involves separation of the religious and political realms of life; under these circumstances religion was bound

to lose its political element, just as public life was bound to lose the religious sanction of transcendent authority (Arendt 1961a, 135).

This, then, is where the most political, most worldly element of Hindutva—the word that comes closest in Indian parlance to fascism—appears; on a planet enchanted by sacrifice but utterly emptied out of transcendence. To amplify the point I am making, nothing passive remains of neglect when something perniciously sacrificial and intensely personal—narcissistic—is inserted into it. To the contrary, there is an injurious doubling of the self against itself (and thus against the other), or starker yet, a violence of violence. Onto the systemic brutalism of neglect of the vulnerable is now grafted a regime of faithless sacrifice by the vulnerable of their own and of themselves.

It is at the point of this grafting that Ambedkar's »communal majority« appears. And this sacrificial will of the communal majority becomes the norm, even a fetishistic drive, as the bureaucracy makes active brutalization of populations—permanent minorities among them—its governing principle, a matter of fidelity to its electoral mandate, a silent sanction purportedly backed by the majority that seeks authenticity in rituals of purification, training violence upon itself and its own (which it calls sacrifice, asceticism even).[5] No place is less sovereign than a country that feeds its poor this diet of strategic neglect and legalized disregard; no violence more brutal, more wrong, Ambedkar writes, than the violence perpetrated by a society's willful abandonment of its most injurable. Political cruelty is the braiding of these two poles of civic violence (or violent civility): the hostile brutalism of the majority's self-lacerating pain, on the one hand, and the homicidal effects of its resentful, extrajudicial abandonment on those closest to itself, on the other.

5 Arendt's remarks in *The Human Condition* on this suicidal streak in majoritarian violence remain instructive. »The will to power, as the modern age from Hobbes to Nietzsche understood it in glorification or denunciation,« she writes, »far from being characteristic of the strong, is, like envy and greed, among the vices of the weak, and possibly even their most dangerous one« (Arendt 1958, 203).

Liquid Majority

What I have called the neodemocratic condition is this swerving, bipolar order of violence, one in which a democratically legitimate government is as likely to not participate as it is to not interfere at all. Neither the compulsion to participate in violence nor the desire to sometimes abide by the moral norm of interfering in it in order to prevent it—*rajadharma*—is ever gone entirely missing from the scaffolds of governmental reason and reasoning. If anything, bureaucratic psychology has always tended to oscillate between participating, interfering in, and even preventing some violence, thereby exactly mirroring the pathology of the indifferent majority whose false sense of agency it harnesses for its own ends. This counterfeit agency explains the tragic confusion of majoritarian cruelty with popular action and the willful conflation of misanthropic indifference with civic fairness, moral judgement even.

The paradoxical point is that cruelty becomes truly political not in the dissolution of the democratic pact but in the intensification of its covenant to its depoliticizing extremities. It becomes politically deployable not just because large numbers succumb to its pleasure but because the unresolved relationship between a people's bristling sense of dignity (or worse, entitlement) and their unbridled resentment, the irresolvable conflict between the sovereignty of One—including the people as One—and the rights of many is let to metastasize into a theater of sacrificial action where nothing but extreme violence and extreme neglect has any currency.

In this theater of cruelty, the majority is not simply a calculable number. It must be approached at once as a liquid, communal form and as a hard, political *calculus*; as a deployable technique, a mode of violence already so degenerate and disgraced that any form of counterviolence can only worsen it. Which it paradoxically does itself—that is, it worsens its own violence even without the provocation of a resisting counterviolence—through an active abuse and abolition of democratic norms and moral constraints, on the one hand, and, on the other, by a boundless intensification of democratic strategies put in place by the very liberal democratic order it now accuses of cowardice, hypocrisy, and downright alienation from the plight of the people, trading those vices with its claims of authenticity and purity, dignity even. Nothing feeds the neodemocratic majority's delirium of power more than its utterly powerless, loveless, and faithless gambit against the poor who constitute the people in the first place and in whose name it speaks. As Arendt recalls in a dramatic passage in *The Origins of Totalitarianism*:

> [T]his kind of factual propaganda worked better than Goebbels' rhetoric, not only because it established the Jews as scum of the earth, but also because the incredible plight of an ever-increasing group of innocent people was like a practical demonstration of the totalitarian movements' cynical claims that no such thing as inalienable human rights existed and that the affirmations of the democracies to the contrary were mere prejudice, hypocrisy, and cowardice in the face of the cruel majesty of a new world. The very phrase »human rights« became for all concerned—victims, persecutors, and onlookers alike—the evidence of hopeless idealism or fumbling feeble-minded hypocrisy (Arendt 1979, 269).

What better way might there be for reveling in the delirium of un-alienated authenticity than treating a swathe of adjacent humanity as the »scum of the earth« by actively reducing them to »scum of the earth« and thereby proving every claim of rights to be a mere artifact of liberal, globalist hypocrisy? What saves democracy from this barbarism masquerading as authenticity? Not the inexhaustible surfeit of laws for sure, insofar as the rule of law is the very scaffold of political cruelty. Nor the omnipotence of a state that promises to eradicate all injustice, insofar as such a promise would be theology by yet another name. What saves democracy instead is the moral intelligence of the citizen. »In Kant's own words,« Arendt quotes from *Perpetual Peace*,

> »The problem of organizing a state, however hard as it may seem, can be solved even for a race of devils, if only they are intelligent.« In a similar spirit, it has been said that the devil makes a good theologian. In the political order, as in the religious framework, obedience may have its place, and just as this obedience is enforced in institutionalized religion by the threat of future punishments, so the legal order exists only to the extent of the existence of sanctions. What cannot be punished is permitted (Arendt 2003b, 69).

And therein lies the insoluble bond between permission and punishment, between power and pain, which is to also say, between liberty and the law, upon which rests the entire burden of the theologico-political entanglement in modern democratic thought. It is hard to overstate how devastating the effects of mechanical habits of political and social, even paternal obedience are on the moral intelligence of the citizen upon whose faith democracy rests. And this is not only because the citizen obeys the law purely out of his fear of God or gods at large—as if the law were a divine command—but also because anything that now happens in the world becomes a testament to the gods' unquestionable will. Any evil of which the law does not explicitly speak, any action that the law does not explicitly bar, now becomes permissible. The greater the number of gods, the better for the cruel malcontent seeking legitimacy for his actions in their tacit approval. One or the other god, no less misanthropic than the devotee, invariably comes through.

Even when it leaves unspeakable pain in its wake, this sort of cruelty—which rides on plurality—remains impossible to police: not because the law ever explicitly condones it but precisely because the law meets it only with a tacit silence. To be politically cruel might not be legal but, by its very name, it is not illegal either. In fact, it is difficult to even think of *politicized* cruelty and of the utterly faithless world that brings it to pass without grasping the power of the unsaid and the unsayable; which is to say, the mystical power of that which is left tactically unsaid, precisely because cruelty can hide behind its own unspeakable effects.[6] Cruelty's sanction—and it will always be, as Arendt never fails to repeat, for all its faithlessness, a »religious sanction«—comes from the silence of the law, not its absence; it comes from originalist mystifications of the constitution (as if the spirit and letter of the constitution ever had sacred, transhuman origins), not from an open, fearless argument about constitutionality; it comes from a jurisprudence of mystery, not the principled, anarchic freedom of *isonomy*. A world that has lost its fear of God, after all, is also the world that can invoke the mysterious will of God for—and demand obedience to—any law. To modulate Derrida's formula of this theologico-political (or theologico-juridical) nexus, »no cruelty without some obedience, no obedience without some cruelty.«

This condition, where whatever is not punishable is considered permitted and whatever is not explicitly barred is deemed legitimate, undoes the fundamental premises of the border between tyranny and democracy. Constitutionality is not an antithesis but central to this undoing; in fact, to be constitutionally cruel might be the sovereign mark of the neodemocratic condition.[7] What decomposes under its shadows, where cruelty and constitu-

6 On the fascinating itinerary of the »sanction« in Arendt, see Moyn 2008.

7 In June 2021, the Supreme Court of the United States—the country on whose »revolutionary treasure« Arendt (1963) had pegged so much of her own political faith—upheld a slew of voting restrictions passed by the state legislature of Arizona and signed into law by the state's Republican governor. In weeks leading up to the judgment, lawmakers in more than one state had conceded more than once, tacitly and sometimes directly, that such restrictions were devised in effect to disenfranchise people of color by making it difficult for them to vote. Arizona is not alone in this antidemocratic endeavor to curtail the Black vote, which has a long racial history in the American South. But the Supreme Court deemed the new laws constitutionally valid simply because they were not definitively unlawful, and because the disproportionate »inconvenience« they might bring upon racial minorities and the urban poor in America's largest cities furnished—to the majority of the Court's conservative bench—no proof that such inconvenience could be shown, be-

tion come together in a perilous and volatile bond, is not simply the citizen's capacity for moral judgment—the faculty that, according to Arendt, tempts him to rise to the moment and become or at the very least steadfastly remain a human, despite the absence of just guiding laws—but the moral guardrails of entire societies and their political majorities (although not the majorities alone). Oscillations between moral seizure (the refusal or inability to act beyond the law) and fetishistic will (that deforms the other even as the act decomposes the self in a barbaric breach of all known laws) is the sovereign mark of the neodemocratic condition.

Neodemocracy appears in the world today as this cellular degeneration of the modern political self into an animate, deployable instrument of political cruelty, its resentments and hostilities now made willingly ready to use and abuse for governmental ends. In a tragic sense, this is an intensification and not the death of the political form that moderns call democracy. And this, to use the term Derrida uses for the structure of the religious, is »the worst,« precisely because it is not merely a symptom of democracy's sacrificial, zealous autoimmunity; it is the worst of the autoimmune seizure of the system itself, which I call above »the violence of violence.« Not only because this doubling makes inequality hurt the body but because, by closing off any alternative vision of time—and thus dignity—through its occupation of both extremities and poles of the political realm (brutalism *and* civility), this majestic cruelty is able to graft with a new panache the vicarious delirium of modern life onto the archaic structure of an old, a very old, absolutism.

---

yond reasonable doubt, to be the result of a legislative intent rooted in racial animus. Nor could it be deemed an extraconstitutional overreach by the state legislature against the rights enshrined in the Civil Rights Acts of the 1960s. Race here becomes, yet again, the pernicious unsaid of American jurisprudence because racist intent—much like the intent to *not* touch someone—remains so hard to prove. In fact, untouchability is a cruelty that never occurs; it becomes visible in law only upon its abolition. Its evidence, by the very nature of the crime, simply does not appear. It is just such a trumping of truth by procedure, upon which is built an active *jurisprudence of disregard*—the disregard, by the highest court of the land, not only of the country's obdurate racial inequality that still insidiously shapes its laws, but also of the conditions of the nation's founding pact forged in enduring silence around slavery—that puts Arendt's constitutional theory to its severest test. Indeed, there is very little in Arendt's entire oeuvre that matches her silence on something as if it were not more foundational to America's history than the Declaration of Independence: its Civil War. Effects of this silence shape, most notoriously, her »Reflections on Little Rock« (Arendt 2003a), parts of which she eventually—and thoughtfully—stepped back from.

An Indifferent War

Enchanted by the first »earth-born object made by man« propelled into space, from where it could, for the first time, relay back to earth the image of the planet in full, the human mind might have been forever ensnared in the delusion of its infinite capacity to lord over the universe. And while it sometimes believes it has supplanted, or perhaps destroyed the power of the gods, this alienated mind, even in full flight away from its finite, terrestrial world, might never cease to desire that its transcendental flight path have it be »admitted tentatively to their sublime company« (Arendt 1958, 1). The desire to be way more than human, be an equal among the gods (if not altogether God), after all, has always been the primary drive of modern humanism (and the site of its incurable alienation). Neither Arendt nor Ambedkar—both of whom were planning book-length studies on Marx—wholly distance themselves from Marx in their belief that religion is indeed the site of this originary alienation, its fetishistic urges morphing under capitalism into a fantastic drive for commodities or heavenly bodies still to be found. And yet, both also discern in alienation a more ambiguous force, which opens both to dimensions of political violence in a manner that Marx perhaps never was.

In alienation, Arendt and Ambedkar see not only the moral and material estrangement of workers from value that underwrites their oppression and creates enemies out of classes; they also discern underneath it a more paradoxical will that compels human beings towards subservience and transcendence at one and the same time, towards obedience and majesty (or lordship) at one and the same time. Cruelty becomes a politically legible and juridically unpunishable exercise of power only in the shadows of this paradoxical, delirious will lurching between fantastic sovereignty and voluntary servitude. For Ambedkar, the will to punish, whose apotheosis is the death penalty and to which he returns in several works, including in his manuscripts on Marx, remains the sovereign example of this collective delirium. For no other institution replicates more perfectly, more cruelly, the *dispositif* of height that caste exemplifies than the social and mechanical contraption of capital punishment.

As a function of sovereignty—or brutal asymmetry of height—cruelty is not one among other elements in an economy of violence. It is not a clash of violence against violence, a fraternal dispute of the home (*oikos*). It is instead violence for more violence. There is no fratricidal conflict of motivations in cruelty; there are no degrees or measures in it. It does not leave a home untouched or a world intact, not even of its victors and executioners. And yet, while cruelty reaches its crescendo in death, its sense of security comes not from blood but from its punitive appetite for security, one that retains no distinction between neighbor and enemy. »Death is no longer torture,« Foucault writes in an unflinching passage on this remorseless, indiscriminate, society-wide will to punish; instead, »it is definitive closure, absolute security« (Foucault 2015, 11). And security not of the borders, which have anyway ceased to hold any line between country and city, war and peace, but rather the security of the familiar, proprietorial, snobbish, urbane civility guarded by the lethal force of the police: the kind of security that Marx calls, in his critique of property, »the supreme social concept of civil society, the concept of the *police*«; the security that allows a society to look away, so long as its property is intact, even if homes around it succumb to a dreary, cruel, disembodied wordlessness (Marx 1994, 46).

Nothing expresses the delusional, alienated heart of tyranny more devastatingly than a people's generalized indifference, locked in place by its faithless disenchantment with the world and its pervasive disinterest in distinction, in excellence, in rigor, in thought. And with the dissolution of those passions also dies that most human of desires, the desire to live with others, to contemplate and compete with them, to find glory or even immortality together. As Arendt writes in her letter to Gershom Scholem, countering his misreading of *Eichmann in Jerusalem*:

> It is indeed my opinion now that evil is never »radical,« that it is only extreme, and that it possesses neither depth nor any demonic dimension. It can overgrow and lay waste the whole world precisely because it spreads like a fungus on the surface. It is »thought-defying,« as I said, because thought tries to reach some depth, to go to the roots, and the moment it concerns itself with evil, it is frustrated because there is nothing. That is its »banality« (Arendt 2007, 471).

It is my sense that we need to supplement Arendt's archaeology of evil and renew, for the times, Ambedkar's critique of violence and his passionate critique of the violence of this violence, whose regimes of bodies—a regime neither of the people nor of the masses but of bodies—he calls the »communal majority.« This majority is communal because, before everything, it affords the oppressor an anomic anonymity, even illegibility, in its encounter with law. Thus, Ambedkar's deconstruction of caste as a *dispositif* of height, or gloomier still, a topography of graded sovereignties, one that never fails to seduce its subject with an almost irreproducible sense of liberty, insofar that it frees up time for excellence for those even slightly higher up than the most decrepit bottom, even if this time is stolen from someone else, someone below, someone minor. In even the gravest, most injurable scene of subjection, the caste subject finds liberty, a chance for mastery even, through his domination of some other (subject) immediately below and under him. That every subject feels touched by a trace of liberty at least once within this systemic logic—so much so that they are willing to kill for it or, worse, look away when someone else kills in its name—is perhaps the system's greatest stroke of genius, even if such mastery, drenched in a fetishistic will to power—or the will to punish—has no freedom in it.

If there is a visible trace of Stoicism in the caste system's oppressor and its oppressed alike, it is because of this alienated belief—delusion—pervasive in caste society that everyone in it is a master, even if nobody is not a slave. There is every counterrevolutionary liberty in caste except, as Arendt might say, »the freedom to be free«; there is every inalienable, natural right in it—there is tragically only natural right given by birth in it—except the »right to have rights,« which for Arendt, let us recall, is simply the right to live in a community of equals: a community in which the self always yields to the other and where the self's dwelling is no more inviolable than the other's home (Arendt 1979, 296—297). This moral ability to make room, to forge political trust and solidarity across communal schisms and silences, is what Ambedkar calls *fraternity*. More than once, in his later writings, moving beyond the masculine air that the notion of fraternity sometimes carries, he calls it the politics of friendship or *maitri*, the only moral foundation of a society that would otherwise find itself repeatedly facing the hostile unraveling of its social bond, assailed from within in the very name of its constitution, even liberty.

If Kant is right about virtue—anyone who has lived only with rascals will never know virtue—then it is clear what caste truly destroys: not simply virtue, but the ability to cultivate a moral knowledge that is the ground of freedom itself. Caste isolates, quarantines, and segregates not simply one's body and thinking, it disables fraternity itself, and therefore, cripples the only true freedom of equals: a freedom free of resentment towards others. This extraction of all traces of the other from the self—and of the self from the other—goes to the heart of the jurisprudence of purity that structures caste time: freely used and abused by those who will never return this time because it is a theft that came before all law and which in fact founded all law. In effect, this theft is illegible to the law. Which is to say, the law does not even recognize this originary theft of time as theft. To be born in the shadow of caste is to already be a subject of—and subjected to—this theft that shall never be restituted. And thus, to grasp the »mechanism of caste«—that is, its fetishistically guarded secret—is to grasp this *conversion* of theft to mastery, of appropriation to property, of violence to nonviolence, of interest to indifference. It is a system that puts the unbearable burden of all on some in order to emancipate an indifferent few from the necessities of life so that they can pursue happiness, perfection, glory, and even heroism. Slowly but steadily, the complexity of this monastic, sacrificial man—the masculine, misogynistic, paranoid *purusha*—swallows the rights of the citizen.

The destructive effect of something as seemingly passive as indifference is thus hard to overestimate. Perhaps it has been from the very beginning an extremely thin, wavering line that has separated the majority's resentment against the history of theft that has constituted it and its hostile, active indifference towards those who are that history's true—and truthful—heroes. It is along such vacillations that the uneasy truce of caste life exists in its nonpartisan civility and armed neutrality. A socially complex and morally disturbing recognition lies compressed behind Ambedkar's phrase »armed neutrality,« which appears only once in his entire oeuvre. What Ambedkar means by it, if I read him correctly, is a state where the greatest cruelty comes to reside—or is perfected—not in the spilling of blood but in the abandonment of bodies; not in active, murderous assaults on the vulnerable but in the practiced passivity—which is to say, deliberate, scrupulous, and active passivity—of hesitation in the face of truth (Ambedkar 1968).

In *Waiting for a Visa*, his unfinished autobiography, Ambedkar writes unflinchingly of this human, all too human coldness that lets the flesh of another human being become meat right in front of its eyes. A caste Hindu, he recalls, would »prefer to be inhuman rather than touch the untouchable.« What is devastating in the bluntness of Ambedkar's sentence, which is written to describe the rootless actions of a doctor who chooses to let an ill outcaste woman die rather than examining (and thus, touching) her, is not that it is constructed to shock liberal consciousness. Instead, it is that Ambedkar's sentence cuts the bare logic of caste off at the point of its most frigid, systemic, and biting coldness. It is an attribute—a combination of physical coldness and analytical cruelty—that India's classical epistemology ratifies and which its modern economy of ordinary vices executes. What dissolves in this epistemology is not simply agency but will itself; what is left cold, or rather deformed, is not the only self but its very freedom (which can truly ensue only ever from the freedom of others).

Cruelty is a specific mode of violence—distinct from, say, murder—because it uproots, devastates, and deforms not only the victim; it decomposes the perpetrator himself, his act depositing his soulless existence beyond the limits of the forgivable. Cruelty is always cruelty of the other, as Derrida notes. It is always a barbarity of the other lodged in one's own self even when it is directed towards the other outside (if there is ever a pure outside), its violence so unbearable that the border between the self and other itself ceases to hold. Perhaps this is why, possessed with the singular illumination that caste—with its logic of hostile intimacy between self and the other—gives him, Ambedkar goes further than both Arendt and Shklar in placing moral cruelty before the systemic one, insofar as he sees the cruelty of ordinary vices not simply as a betrayal of promise intrinsic to human nature—betrayal, no matter how morally ambiguous or politically unavoidable, after all, is always a decision—but as a primary effect of exactly its opposite: a willful, sanctioned nonchalance not only toward one's own world and toward the world of the other but toward the idea of worldliness as such; an active hesitation in making room in the political realm for the incurable finitude of those who inhabit it closest to oneself, at the risk of imperiling one's own freedom, indeed will, itself.

For Kant, let us recall, freedom is the expression of a will free of external coercions, free from those tempting inclinations whose sources lie outside of oneself. Such freedom, in Kant's view, grounds itself in the self-legislations of the moral law alone. It is the nature of human freedom conceived in this fashion from which Ambedkar breaks. What if cruelty thrives precisely in this seizure of the will by inwardness, that is, by a solipsistic vanity of a self that only ever speaks to its own commandments? What else is caste if not this hardening of self-legislated hesitation into mechanical habit?

For Ambedkar, the coercive effect of outward temptation—which for Kant might mark the end of freedom—is replaced in caste by the turning inward (and then, inversion) of free will into its wholly other, that is, into an absolute subservience to rules of ascetic withdrawal from the world of others. Free of any external compulsions, exactly as Kant would have liked, the self is instead hamstrung by a web of juridical hesitations and moral indecisions, unable to break free of the law it has given itself. *Dharma* is the web—*dispositif*—of this radical indecision. Which explains, as Ambedkar writes in *Revolution and Counterrevolution in Ancient India*, why so many warrior heroes of the Indian epic tradition are all made to surrender, momentarily or otherwise, to their own crippling, desolate hesitation in the face of evil. And those among them that are not felled entirely by their righteous self-despair—or somehow recover from it—rarely ever show a trace of self-contempt for their fateful indecision. Cruelty becomes political in exactly such a world: a world rife with disdain but stripped of self-contempt; a world in which even perjury, let alone hypocrisy, has ceased to be a moral failing and morphed into an unforgiving technique of domination.

Purity and the Unforgivable

Excessive without being gratuitous, precise without exhibiting any sense of measure, anchored in a mythic past that has no faith in the future, intense in its purposefulness yet marked by extreme indifference, political cruelty has a troubling kinship with the history and theology of purity within which its compulsions are located. And while the fetishistic will to purity among its executioners is distinct from the purity of »divine violence« that figures like Benjamin attach to the general strike, what should not be lost sight of is the sacrificial structure that scaffolds both these notions and histories of purity and which both notions of purity cannot but share (Benjamin 1978, 277—300). There is some religion, some desire for the incorruptible and the transcendent, the sacred even, in both the mystical revolutionary and the counterrevolutionary zealot. And yet, political cruelty is distinct from the »pure violence« of Benjamin's revolutionary proletariat—or from the absolutely »rational revolt« of Fanon's colonized—in that it becomes political not only because it has freed itself from all instrumentality or ends (exactly like the revolutionary will to emancipation and decolonization) but because this cruelty—this will to purity—has at its lethal center the desire for an *absolute violence*: the reproduction of violence by means of no external temptation other than more violence, committed to an unforgiving dehumanization and destruction of the political itself.

It is not that, when Narendra Modi rose to power in New Delhi in 2014 on the back of a massive democratic mandate, he could not have been forgiven for his tacit crimes committed in Gujarat just over a decade earlier. If anything, liberals, having by then depleted any theoretical arsenal they had possessed against Hindutva, were all too quick to do so. And this even though

Modi, displaying all through his national campaign a disturbing lack of repentance (and thus an utter disinterest in memory), had compared the killing of Muslims during the Gujarat pogrom to dogs who might sometimes run right in front of a speeding vehicle for no reason and accidentally die. How is such a meaningless death of the animal, Modi had half-jokingly asked, to be blamed on the driver? And this when Hindutva is perfectly willing to kill human beings in the uncontrolled rage of its zoophilia, for its love precisely of the animal.

The question is not *if* but *how* to forgive a crime that, even in the bloodshot eyes of the murderer, simply did not occur? How does one circumscribe the boundaries of a crime so groundless that even the perpetrator, who might at least be suspected of harboring—like any legal or moral person—some conviction behind his act, has no person at its center at all? But then, that is the very point of violence driven by an unforgiving purity of intent. It is a crime that seeks to brutalize not the body but memory, so that there is not only nobody left but there is also nothing—not a thing, or perhaps better, only a thing left—to forgive. Worse, there is no moral person seeking forgiveness. »To put it another way,« writes Arendt, »in granting pardon, it is the person and not the crime that is forgiven; in rootless evil there is no person left whom one could ever forgive« (Arendt 2003b, 95).

And yet, for all its moral complexity, political cruelty—rootless evil turned into governmental technique—is no less lucid in its practice. It is rooted not only in unforgivable crimes that decompose the perpetrator; it also becomes political by the very fact of active abrogation of responsibility by entire majorities and social assemblages, stemming from their ordinary, misanthropic compulsions. And its fatal consequence arrives often in a sequence: first, as hostile distrust of the poor, the migrant, and the outcaste; then, as willful destruction of institutions that enfranchise them; and finally, as the setting in of collective disdain for their presence and existence itself. Among all the powers and privileges of the majority, it is its power to not do anything about the oppression closest to it that proves most destructive. It is a theology of the nothing that culminates in an epistemology of non-doing, and eventually, in *political undoing*. This is perhaps why Ambedkar often laments not the coming loss of civil liberties alone, which is but a function of a deeper, more crippling loss; he laments instead the fate of freedom as such in caste society, whose bonds, sometimes out of ascetic withdrawal and sometimes out of sheer fear, are reduced to a system of voluntary obedience by that society's founding logic—the very »genesis«—in a »cruel wrong.«

Wrong: someone has willed this catastrophe, even if only by looking away from it. Such indifference is not only a function of social withdrawal or isolation, if it is that at all. It is instead a function of a contagious depoliticization of the city on a political scale, one that empties out the gravity of democratic faith at its very core, towards anti-political ends. Hindutva uses the structure of caste in this very precise fashion, for this very specific purpose: to deliver a deployable indifference of India's urban majority, not to destroy the human, but, in Étienne Balibar's evocative expression, to »capture the political« (Balibar 2015, 141). By its very nature, caste has that viral, infectious, and suicidal sweep—it is an »infection« for a reason, if we follow Ambedkar's necromancy—reproducing itself through endless improvisations in techniques of giving death and disposing of bodies under different conditions. »Like weed on the surface of a pond,« a young Ambedkar writes in his 1916 essay, »Castes in India,« »it just hangs there to this day without support,« with no moral gravity, and yet, with the fullest, tacit force of law behind it.

Caste is not one wrong among others; it is the purest wrong—the *exemplary wrong of purity*—in the annals of human servitude, a wrong whose entire weight hinges on its economy of making the dead and the living seem equally impure and disposable, sometimes cremated, sometimes let to float away on water. Thus, that striking moment in *Annihilation of Caste*, where, speaking of the highest form of cruelty known to jurisprudence—capital punishment—Ambedkar declares not just limitless vengeance to be the heart of caste; he calls the frequent measure of delivering »penalty by death« to be its unforgiving, categorical imperative. »Forgiveness,« which Arendt describes as »the exact opposite of vengeance,« does not exist in caste (Arendt 1958, 240). What does, at best, is pure neglect, which is the silent counterpart to pure rage, one frequently tipping over on to the other.

The politics of purity that Hindutva has historically deployed and which it now seeks to perfect as a technique of government is hinged upon exactly such an unrelenting concentration of purity to its lethal absolute, spinning outward in concentric circles rather than on a search for social equality or expansion of Hinduism's ritualistic core, which its purported anti-Brahminism can sometimes suggest. True, Hindutva is a very modern absolutism, insofar as it might genuinely seek to dismantle the Brahminic dream of preserving the restricted, measured purity of the scriptural tradition. Already, in the late 1940s, for example, the opening lines of the assassin Nathuram Godse's confession *Why I Killed Mahatma Gandhi?* declare without any irony, in a tone only slightly less deranged than modern day Hindutva, the Brahmin Godse's unequivocal hatred of untouchability. This is a politics that intensifies the murderous struggles, even endemic strife, over surfaces and things, spaces and sites, then, not so much for a Brahminic restoration of the pure life—although asceticism is an unambiguous part of its universe—as much as it seeks, in the slow simmer of history, to establish the majority's absolute right to destroy the inherited, historical forms and norms of purity (including the Brahminic liturgies of untouchability).

All this is done, however, not to discard the concept of purity but to intensify it in a paradoxical, delirious frenzy. So that while being blatantly prepared—and armed—for the legal elimination of permanent minorities, this majoritarianism thrives in its production of displaced populations upon whom rage can be projected psychically when it is not expended physically. Its fantasy of expulsion and extermination works as much by morally concentrated cruelty—pure, psychic violence—as it does by physical violence, leaving minorities desolate rather than dead. This desolation, the minority's worldlessness, is perhaps the greatest barbarism there is. Arendt writes of this worldlessness in *The Origins of Totalitarianism*:

> The calamity of the rightless is not that they are deprived of life, liberty, and the pursuit of happiness, or of equality before the law and freedom of opinion [...] but that they no longer belong to any community whatsoever. [...] Only in the last stage of a rather lengthy process is their right to live threatened; only if they remain perfectly »superfluous,« if nobody can be found to »claim« them, may their lives be in danger. [...] The point is that a condition of complete rightlessness was created before the right to live was challenged (Arendt 1979, 295—296).

By the time Arendt had finished assembling her reports for what would become in the early 1960s *Eichmann in Jerusalem*, it was clear that the age of humility among postwar democratic majorities worldwide was all but over (and not only in Israel). In India, the world's most populous democracy (with the world's largest Muslim minority), that humility, which Ambedkar never stopped looking for, was slowly but steadily taken over by a nationalistic hubris obsessed with restoration of civilizational purity. Part technocratic in its zeal to transform the natural world in order to eradicate social destitution, it was in equal part a fantasy waiting to maraud the pluralist landscape of a country in search of a civilization. It did not take long for the colonized to turn their inconsolable rage against their own (or themselves). A people bound by love in its struggle against colonial power was transformed, haltingly but inevitably, into a passionless, and sometimes, insidious majority in search of the enemy within, gnawingly creating the preconditions of rightlessness well before it had begun to physically violate democracy's moral limits. And all this while the loudest in the majority—often liberal and urbane, civil but dogmatic—continued to tout its civilizational love of nonviolence.

What prevents such purported love of nonviolence from becoming an entitlement, a monopoly of sorts? What does such a claim of having mastered nonviolence, of knowing and loving it like none in the world, truly mask? Uncannily, as she writes to Baldwin in response to his November 1962 »Letter from a Region in my Mind« published in *The New Yorker*, a year before she would publish *Eichmann in Jerusalem* herself, Arendt's issue with making love political is not that it is inauthentic but that in politics it flatters only to deceive. No sooner had the oppressed wrested their freedom back from their masters than the bonds of love—which have always, beyond doubt, been the legitimate province of the oppressed—were turned into a system of organized, self-lacerating hatred. As political passions, Arendt writes, »[h]atred and love belong together, and they are both destructive; you can afford them only in the private and, as a people, only so long as you are not free.« For Ambedkar, the struggle against colonial barbarity—and India's miraculous success in pitching its resistance as an exemplary nonviolent mobilization against empire—had the insidious effect of solidifying an archaic hatred of democracy, a love of mastery upon which the »Indian political« was founded and which it had always sought to conceal. If the brutalism of Hindutva's political logic is today a testament to anything more fundamental than the logic of caste that it has twisted for its own ends, it is a testament to this dark, autocratic, and loveless streak of anticolonial politics and its long, cold shadow now sharpening its edges.

It is not that Hindutva's crimes, let alone its mendacity, are not transparent in their effects; it is that caste has required the majority to let its temptation to *not* steal from the poor, to *not* murder the minority, to *not* look away from that murder, dissolve in the power that comes from indifference (and is in turn manifested in it). Hindutva's brutalism is not insurmountable; it has simply become unpunishable. Its majoritarian pact is forged not out of an authentic force—which is an attribute only of those who fearlessly resist tyranny—but out of a depraved disdain for the poor, the woman, the minority *sans papier*. Its greatest cruelty comes not from the preparedness among its converts to spill blood but from their impotent faithlessness and inaction itself, from their lack of willing anything new in the world. Worldlessness, af-

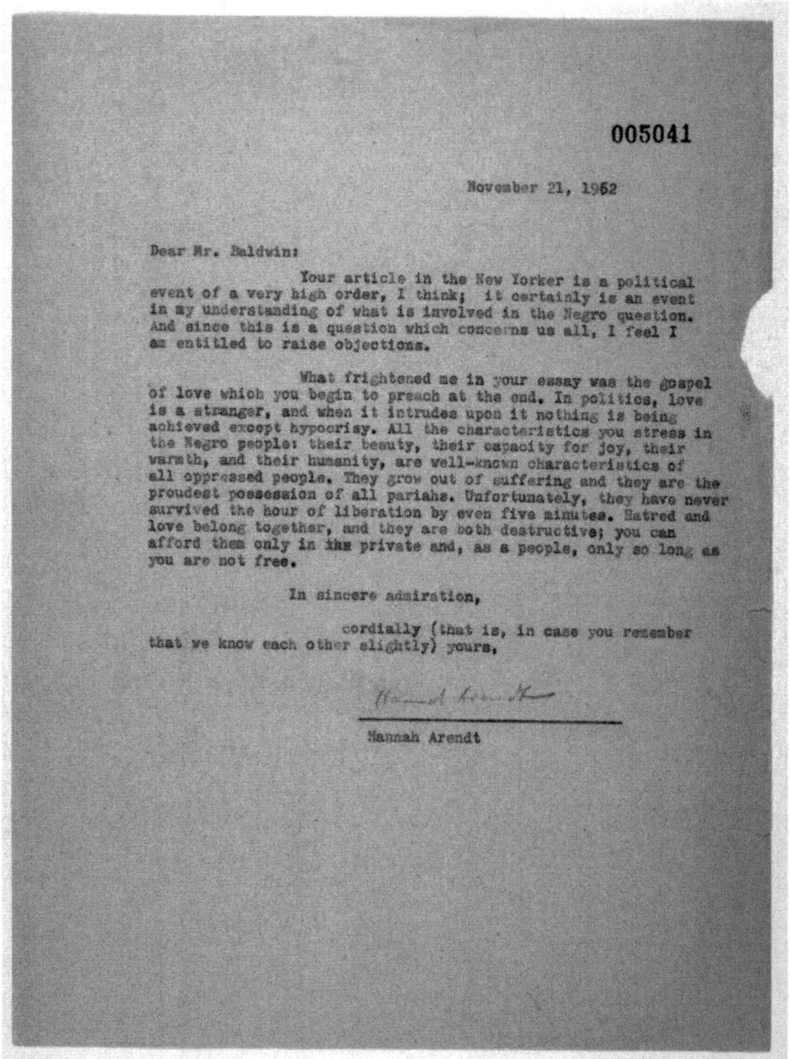

005041

November 21, 1962

Dear Mr. Baldwin:

Your article in the New Yorker is a political event of a very high order, I think; it certainly is an event in my understanding of what is involved in the Negro question. And since this is a question which concerns us all, I feel I am entitled to raise objections.

What frightened me in your essay was the gospel of love which you begin to preach at the end. In politics, love is a stranger, and when it intrudes upon it nothing is being achieved except hypocrisy. All the characteristics you stress in the Negro people: their beauty, their capacity for joy, their warmth, and their humanity, are well-known characteristics of all oppressed people. They grow out of suffering and they are the proudest possession of all pariahs. Unfortunately, they have never survived the hour of liberation by even five minutes. Hatred and love belong together, and they are both destructive; you can afford them only in the private and, as a people, only so long as you are not free.

In sincere admiration,

cordially (that is, in case you remember that we know each other slightly) yours,

Hannah Arendt

A letter to James Baldwin, 21 November 1962.
Courtesy of the Hannah Arendt Bluecher Literary Trust.

ter all, stems not simply from the denial of one person's right to have rights. It stems from the experience of losing entire cities to cellular degeneration: neighborhoods turned into camps, violence cut to the bone, fabric of souls woven together for generations torn, a boy made to disappear in one state, a girl murdered by the police in another faraway one, an octogenarian dissenter left to die in a prison cell without trial, the judiciary becoming another cog in the government's massive acquittal machine letting murderers get away with impunity.

The only antidote to this conquest of power by strength is force, Arendt writes in a decisive passage in *The Human Condition* (Arendt 1958, 201—202). For force is the potentiality nobody can monopolize and even the weakest never exhaust (this inexhaustibility of the weakest Ambedkar calls »weak force«). From which ensues the irreducible risk inherent in force itself. For like courage, force is a complex, equivocal attribute. A virtue of the unequal and the vulnerable, it turns barbaric the moment it changes hands and moves to the side of power. The moment it is robbed of the gift it carries in itself—the capacity for action, the promise of creativity, the faith to begin something new out of the debris of heroic resistance—force exhausts its transformative, emancipatory promise and degenerates into an instrument of tyranny in the hands of the hopeless and the hubristic alike. Neodemocracy is this tragic exhaustion of our times, the catastrophic combination of power and faithlessness, the suicidal conceit of a people's cruel majesty bent on leaving an entire swathe of its own species worldless.

Works Cited

Ambedkar, Bhimrao Ramji (1945). *Pakistan or the Partition of India*. 2nd ed. Bombay: Thacker and Company.

Ambedkar, Bhimrao Ramji (1968). *Annihilation of Caste: With a Reply to Mahatma Gandhi*; and, *Castes in India: Their Mechanism, Genesis and Development*. 3rd ed. Jullundur, Punjab: Bheem Patrika Publications.

Arendt, Hannah (1958). *The Human Condition*. Chicago/London: University of Chicago Press.

Arendt, Hannah (1961a). What Is Authority?. In Hannah Arendt. *Between Past and Future: Six Exercises in Political Thought*. New York: The Viking Press.

Arendt, Hannah (1961b). What Is Freedom?. In Hannah Arendt. *Between Past and Future: Six Exercises in Political Thought*. New York: The Viking Press.

Arendt, Hannah (1963). *On Revolution*. New York: Viking Press.

Arendt, Hannah (1979). *The Origins of Totalitarianism*. San Diego/New York/London: Harcourt Brace Jovanovich.

Arendt, Hannah (2003a). Reflections on Little Rock. In Hannah Arendt. *Responsibility and Judgment*. Ed. and introduction Jerome Kohn. New York: Schocken Books.

Arendt, Hannah (2003b). Some Questions of Moral Philosophy. In Hannah Arendt. *Responsibility and Judgment*. Ed. and introduction Jerome Kohn. New York: Schocken Books.

Arendt, Hannah (2006). *Eichmann in Jerusalem: A Report on the Banality of Evil*. Introduction Amos Elon. New York: Penguin Books.

Arendt, Hannah (2007). The Eichmann Controversy: A Letter to Gershom Scholem. In Hannah Arendt. *The Jewish Writings*. Ed. Jerome Kohn and Ron H. Feldman. New York: Schocken Books.

Balibar, Étienne (2015). *Violence and Civility: On the Limits of Political Philosophy*. Transl. G.M. Goshgarian. New York: Columbia University Press.

Benjamin, Walter (1978). Critique of Violence. In Walter Benjamin. *Reflections: Essays, Aphorisms, Autobiographical Writings*. Transl. Edmund Jephcott. Ed. and introduction Peter Demetz. New York: Harcourt Brace Jovanovich.

Foucault, Michel (2015). *The Punitive Society: Lectures at the Collège de France 1972—1973*. Ed. Bernard E. Harcourt. Transl. Graham Burchell. New York: Palgrave Macmillan.

Kumar, Aishwary (2015). *Radical Equality: Ambedkar, Gandhi, and the Risk of Democracy*. Stanford: Stanford University Press.

Marx, Karl (1994). On the Jewish Question. In Karl Marx. *Marx: Early Political Writings*. Ed. and transl. Joseph O'Malley with Richard A. Davis. Cambridge/New York: Cambridge University Press.

Moyn, Samuel (2008). Hannah Arendt on the Secular. *New German Critique*, 35(3), 71—96.

Shklar, Judith N. (1984). *Ordinary Vices*. Cambridge, Mass.: Belknap Press of Harvard University Press.

Epilogue: Abraham's Agency

Vivian Liska

Hannah Arendt's life-long striving for a purely secular politics makes the endeavor of this book, the exploration of her work from a (crypto-)theological perspective, all the more exciting: tracing and recovering the scattered and often submerged theological elements in Hannah Arendt's thinking did not lead the authors to deny her secularism but rather to uncover its specific theological underpinnings. Tracking down these sources in a variety of different facets of her work discloses Hannah Arendt's political theology that insistently rejects the mythological elements of religion while saving religion's transcendence in the figure of freedom. The contributions united in this book explore her theological imagination as a driving force underlying the pillars of her thought: from natality's singularity to political pluralism; from *amor mundi* to *inter-esse*; religious, mystical or scriptural figures and motifs that help her articulate the imperative of human empowerment come to light. It is, for instance, the mystical idea of Adamite origin that nurtures Arendt's insistence in human plurality, and the shift from God to the world prefigured in Lurianic Kabbalah that preceded her philosophical turn from mortality to the singularity of natality. A non-absolute conception of God found in heterodox religious streams grounds the faith in one's phenomenal existence as strong and thus guarantees the limitation of political sovereignty within the body politic. The authors of this book inspect Arendt's pronounced insistence in a worldly politics, in human agency and in ethical responsibility for their heterodox theological, pro-cosmic thoughts. These thoughts, hidden in Arendt's writings, are in each case, embedded, transposed or even translated into a secular, philosophical and/or political framework and constitute an important dimension of Arendt's continued relevance in times of growing resistance to the flattening effects of nihilism, materialism and posthumanism.

What emerges from a focus on this dimension of her work are the residues of a religious tradition that survived the rupture caused by modernity and that fundamentally impacts the presumed radical secularity of

Arendt's thought. This survival can be seen in the context of a cryptotheological »immigration into the profane« practiced by some of her German-Jewish contemporaries such as Theodor W. Adorno, Walter Benjamin, Gershom Scholem or Franz Kafka. Linking this perspective with some of the strands developed in this book, an association of Arendt's presumably most secular critique of the discourse on Human Rights with the Bible and of this ostensibly political discourse with the literary work of Franz Kafka can yield an afterthought that points to the ubiquitous theological bedrock subtending the most resilient aspects of Arendt's oeuvre.

In *Placeless People* (2018), a literary history of modern statelessness, Lindsay Stonebridge states that Arendt's »critique of human rights was forged, at least in part, from her reading of fiction and, in particular, from the work she did on Kafka in the mid-1940s.« Stonebridge refers to Arendt's essays from 1944, »The Jew as Pariah« and »Franz Kafka: A Revaluation.« These two texts approach the Prague author in the context of exile, homelessness, and the vulnerability of the stranger, a situation Arendt herself faced in those years. These essays prefigure the critique of Human Rights that Arendt would formulate a few years later in »The Decline of the Nation State, and the End of the Rights of Man« (Arendt 2004). There she points to the feebleness of Human Rights when and where they are needed most: dependent for their implementation upon the status of citizenship and the Nation State, they fail to protect the stateless, the refugees, and more generally those who don't belong to a legal entity that can enforce these rights. Stonebridge describes Arendt's use of Kafka as a »thought experiment« that contrasts past rightlessness with what Stonebridge calls »a different kind of political and ethical community, a possible future« (Stonebridge 2018, 30).

Stonebridge's insight into Arendt's use of Kafka to *diagnose* the ills of Human Rights is illuminating. But her affirmation of Arendt's view that Kafka's fiction provides a *cure* for these tribulations is less plausible. Arendt does indeed depict Kafka's protagonists, particularly the land surveyor K. in *The Castle*, as ultimate strangers, as embodiments of the vulnerability experienced by those who belong nowhere, are not recognized by anyone, and are in Kafka's words »nobod[ies]« and »nothing[s].«[1] These human »non-entities« serve as a literary adumbration of Arendt's portrayal of the stateless, those who are left defenseless in the face of rising nationalism and its exclusionary and homogenizing politics.

1 Franz Kafka, »Description of a Fight« (1908/9), quoted in: Arendt 1978, 289.

Arendt's analysis of the plight of Kafka's protagonists is compelling, but her suggestion that he also delivers *solutions*—visions of a new social order that would guarantee such rights—is questionable. This is not to say that Kafka's figures have no potential impact on their world at all. Arendt formulates this potential succinctly in her reading of *The Castle* as a minimal, yet crucial act of resistance. Arendt portrays K.'s distinguishing feature as a refusal to submit to the castle's authority. She can give only scant evidence for this feature of Kafka's protagonist; indeed, the novel offers barely more than hints to his resistance: he mainly thrives to gain access to the Castle, and to confront its authorities. In a later reference to Kafka (in the preface to the revised 1968 edition of *Between Past and Future*), Arendt intuits that she must go »a step further« than Kafka to align him with her own vision of the possibilities for political intervention (see Liska 2003). Surprisingly, however, Arendt and Kafka find common ground in their references to the Biblical figure of Abraham. Both Arendt and Kafka invoke Abraham's confrontations with divine authority, and both derive from his attitude the indispensable starting point to conceive of Human Rights: that no one is a »nobody.« By virtue of being somebody, everybody—even the lowliest of human beings—can contest the reigning authority and thereby intervene in the world.

Arendt Reads Kafka

Even a perfunctory reading of Arendt's »The Jew as Pariah« reveals its vicinity to her early writings about Human Rights, a term she repeatedly mentions in her essay. The introduction to this essay assesses the pariah as »a human type« who is »refused admission to the ranks of humanity« (Arendt 1978, 100).

In the final section of the essay, Arendt portrays the land surveyor K. as the »man of goodwill« who wants nothing else but the right to live a decent life and to be admitted into a society that persists in excluding him. In the village dominated by the opaque powers of the castle, K. remains a powerless outsider. Alone in his hopeless efforts, he ultimately ends up exhausted. For Arendt, Kafka's novel points to the hopelessness of the exiled, the homeless, and the displaced as well as to all those who believe that »playing along« or blending into the established society can solve their plight. Arendt writes of the protagonist of *The Castle*:

> K. finally comes to understand that the realization of his designs, the achievement of basic human rights—the right to work, to be useful, the right to found a home and become a member of society—are in no way dependent on complete assimilation to one's milieu, on being »indistinguishable« (ibid., 118).

In Arendt's view, K.'s exhaustion results from the failures of a system that did not protect him and a community that did not grant him access. Yet Arendt suggests that his presence in the village did bring about a significant change: he left the villagers with the sense that confrontation is possible. K. pointed out the bankruptcy of the world of the Castle as a bureaucratic society that demands subordination and assimilation:

> The very fight he had put up to obtain the few basic things which society owes to men, had opened the eyes of the villagers, or at least of some of them. His story, his behavior, had taught them both that human rights are worth fighting for and that the rule of the castle is not divine law and, consequently, can be attacked.

In the allusion to the »basic things which society owes to men,« the Benjaminian insistence resonates that it is not mere life, but a life worth living, that is sacred. If we think of Arendt's cryptotheological, *Marrano* imagination, we can build a bridge here to Agata Bielik-Robson's argument about birth as the factor that transforms mere life into an unnatural, human one: »if she often comes across as hostile to the notion of sheer survival, (...) it is only for the sake of supporting a life articulated and maintained by the tradition of life.«[2] It seems to be such an articulation of the meaning of a life, which is more than just natural being and which society, in Kafka's Castle, denies to man. Arendt distinguishes between the rule of the castle and divine law and implicitly suggests that »divine law« is beyond contestation. This distinction contrasts with Arendt's reference to a Biblical passage, in which the individual is empowered to intervene in God's ways.

Arendt's Abraham

In *The Human Condition* (1958), Arendt reflects on the mutual covenantal promise God gave to Abraham:

---

2 In this volume.

> We may trace [the binding status of the promise] back to the Roman legal system, the inviolability of agreements and treaties (*pacta sunt servanda*); or we may see its discoverer in Abraham, the man from Ur, whose whole story, as the Bible tells it, shows such a passionate drive toward making covenants that it is as though he departed from his country for no other reason than to try out the power of mutual promise in the wilderness of the world, until eventually God himself agreed to make a Covenant with him (Arendt 1958, 243—244).

Kierkegaard, whose works influenced Arendt in her youth, regarded Abraham as the embodiment of submission and a »knight of faith.« In contrast, Arendt stages Abraham as a daring challenger of God. In her version, Abraham sets out into the wilderness without guarantee that God will keep his word to give him progeny and provide his descendants with a homeland. Leaving his place of birth and venturing into the desert, he subjects himself and his progeny to the risk of becoming »a stranger in a land that is not theirs« (Gen. 15:13). Abraham compels God to keep his side of the promise, and thereby becomes the forefather of those who hold authority—even ultimate authority—to account. To quote Bielik-Robson once again, Arendt's conception of faith comes close to its »Hebrew meaning of *emunah*: trust in the reliability of the covenant, in this case—solid relation with the world as the arena of a good finite life.« Authority is, one could add, accountable to provide the conditions of a good life. In the words of one critic, Arendt's portrayal of Abraham as the one who challenged God into making a covenant turns him into the initiator »of law as politically binding« (Barrett 2019). More importantly, Abraham thereby becomes an active agent who forces God into keeping his side of the promise. As a result, Abraham becomes the forefather of those who hold the authority accountable and who act upon this right, even in the face of the ultimate power.

Arendt's reading might somewhat overstate Abraham's action upon God's designs, but it undeniably captures a fundamental insight: through the figure of Abraham, the Bible suggests a mutual covenant freely engaged in by man and affirms the ineluctable participation of human action in shaping the world. In this sense, Abraham is also a (somewhat more successful) precursor of Kafka's K. as seen by Arendt, a figure she calls a »*fabricator mundi*,« a »world builder, who can get rid of misconstructions and reconstruct the world.« It can seem overly optimistic to call Kafka's K. an »architect of the world.« A more modest version of this claim would be that the Bible affords man the right to stand up for himself and expect accountability of the powers that be. This claim represents in its own right a significant step towards the preconditions of Human Rights.

Kafka's Abraham

»I can imagine another Abraham« (Kafka 1977, 285). This is the first sentence of a text Kafka included in a letter to Robert Klopstock in June 1921.[3] Kafka's remark, even more directly than Arendt's, responds to Kierkegaard's praise of Abraham's submissiveness. Kafka imagines another Abraham, one who, unlike the Biblical one, would not ascend Mount Moriah to sacrifice his beloved son. Like the biblical patriarch, Kafka's »other Abraham« is a pious man who would be ready to execute the command to sacrifice Isaac »with the promptness of a waiter« (Kafka 1977, 285). Kafka's Abraham, however, »would still never be able to perform the sacrifice« (ibid., 285). In an imaginary reply to God, his Abraham argues that »he cannot get away from home, he is indispensable; the household needs him, there is always something that must be attended to, the house isn't finished« (ibid., 285). Later, Kafka elaborates on Abraham's excuses for procrastinating rather than obeying God's command. His »other Abraham« now stands in the plural; he has become a type, or better yet, an existential attitude. The other »Abrahams: they stand on their building sites and suddenly are supposed to go to Mount Moriah« (ibid., 285). These Abrahams, as imagined by Kafka, are called by God while attending to their home, their world-building. As much as Kafka's »other Abrahams« would otherwise have been willing to oblige, they declare themselves too immersed in the care of their house to heed the divine summons.

Kafka speculates about the motivations of this refusal: »All we can do is suspect that these men are *deliberately not finishing their houses* ... so as not to have to lift their eyes and see the mountain that stands in the distance« (ibid., 285; emphasis mine). Rather than staring at the awesome mountain of sacrifice, these Abrahams turn this house, the world, into an infinite, and infinitely improvable building site. The immaterial foundations of this house manifest themselves in the story as a politely irreverent refusal of the sacrificial logic Abraham is summoned to obey—a logic that the Bible itself, in halting Abraham's knife, ultimately rejects. As in Arendt's depiction of Abraham's action, Kafka's »other Abraham« affirms the Bible's own foundation in human freedom to act upon the world.

3 For a pioneer analysis of this text see Alter 1991, 73—74.

A Biblical Reading of Human Rights

However far Arendt and Kafka's portrayals of Abraham deviate from the Biblical text, they are not arbitrary distortions. Abraham's negotiations with God are already laid out in the Bible itself. The patriarch's haggling with God—as in the context of the divine plan to destroy Sodom—prefigures other biblical figures wrestling with divine authority, foremost among them Moses, as well as several prophets and, most hauntingly, the suffering Job. In attributing the right to contest the existing legal, moral, or political authority to Abraham, the model of righteousness, the Bible grants man the right to speak up for himself and protest in the face of injustice. This freedom is not only a foundation of Human Rights but also a potential inherent in—and central to—literature: another locus of the immigration of theological contents into the profane realm. Human Rights are not rendered obsolete by their weaknesses, such as their powerlessness to be enforced, dependence on extraneous legal entities, vulnerability to abuse, and their inevitably biased implementation. These constitutive weaknesses—still with us today—are manifestations of the necessarily utopian nature of the entire Human Rights endeavor and symptoms of the impossibility to conclusively rectify the world, that is, to finish Abraham's house. The contributions that Human Rights make to improve it are indisputable, but they remain a precarious and perennial construction site. Kafka suggests that his Abrahams have good reasons to deliberately build houses that cannot be finished. In focusing on improving the worldly building site, Kafka's Abraham doesn't deny that the mountain is there in the distance: he asserts the primacy of his world-building *in a dialogue with God*. It is true that he averts his eyes from the fear and trembling inspired by the mountain and the way it might be a sacrificial site. Approaching his gesture too narrowly, however, may prevent us from seeing this site as the place where, early on—along with the law and the commandments—the right to stand up for oneself and hold authority accountable, which is a precondition for Human Rights, was *also* accorded. This Abraham continues to toil on his building site, but Arendt, like Kafka, went further and defiantly included the mountain within their vision of the world.

Works Cited

Alter, Robert (1991). *Necessary Angels: Tradition and Modernity in Kafka, Benjamin, and Scholem*. Cambridge, Mass./ Cincinnati: Harvard University Press/Hebrew Union College Press.

Arendt, Hannah (1958). *The Human Condition*. Chicago: University of Chicago Press.

Arendt, Hannah (1978). *The Jew as Pariah: Jewish Identity and Politics in the Modern Age*. Ed. and introduction Ron H. Feldman. New York: Grove Press.

Arendt, Hannah (1994). Franz Kafka: A Revaluation. In Hannah Arendt. *Essays in Understanding, 1930—1954*. Ed. Jerome Kohn. New York: Harcourt, Brace & Co.

Arendt, Hannah (2004). *Origins of Totalitarianism*. Introduction Samantha Power. New York: Schocken Books.

Barrett, Henry (2019). Abraham and the Politicality of the Promise. *Macrina Magazine* 2. 12.07.2021 https://macrinamagazine.com/theology/henry-barret/2019/12/21/abraham-and-the-politicality-of-the-promise/#footnote_3_1184

Kafka, Franz (1977). Letter to Robert Klopstock, Matliary, June 1921. In Franz Kafka. *Letters to Friends, Family and Editors*, 284—286. Transl. Richard Winston and Clara Winston. New York: Schocken Books.

Liska, Vivian (2003). The Gap Between Hannah Arendt and Franz Kafka. Special issue: *Cultural History: Straddling Borders*, 329—334. Ed. Mieke Bal and Jan van Luxemburg. *Arcadia* 38(2). Berlin/New York: de Gruyter.

Stonebridge, Lyndsey (2018). *Placeless People: Writing, Rights, and Refugees*. Oxford: Oxford University Press.

Biographical Notes

Roger Berkowitz is Founder and Academic Director of the Hannah Arendt Center for Politics and Humanities and Professor of Politics, Philosophy, and Human Rights at Bard College. He authored *The Gift of Science: Leibniz and the Modern Legal Tradition* (2005). Berkowitz is the editor of *The Perils of Invention: Lying, Technology, and the Human Condition* (2021) and co-editor of *Thinking in Dark Times: Hannah Arendt on Ethics and Politics* (2009), *The Intellectual Origins of the Global Financial Crisis* (2012) and *Artifacts of Thinking: Reading Hannah Arendt's Denktagebuch* (2017). His writing has appeared in *The New York Times, The American Interest, Bookforum, The Forward, The Paris Review Online, Democracy: A Journal of Ideas*, and many other publications. Berkowitz edits »HA: The Journal of the Hannah Arendt Center« and the weekly newsletter »Amor Mundi.« He is the winner of the 2019 Hannah Arendt Prize for Political Thought given by the Heinrich Böll Foundation in Bremen, Germany.

Agata Bielik-Robson is a Professor of Jewish Studies at the University of Nottingham and a Professor of Philosophy at the Polish Academy of Sciences. She has published articles in Polish, English, German, French and Russian on philosophical aspects of psychoanalysis, romantic subjectivity, and the philosophy of religion (especially Judaism and its crossovers with modern philosophical thought). Her publications include books: *The Saving Lie: Harold Bloom and Deconstruction* (Northwestern University Press 2011), *Judaism in Contemporary Thought: Traces and Influence* (coedited with Adam Lipszyc, Routledge 2014), *Philosophical Marranos: Jewish Cryptotheologies of Late Modernity* (Routledge 2014) and *Another Finitude: Messianic Vitalism and Philosophy* (Bloomsbury 2019).

Mark Farrier holds an MA from the European Graduate School (EGS) where he is currently a PhD candidate. He has been a copy-editor for the book *Windrose* by Elisa Santucci-Nitis and *What is Education: An Anthology* (including essays by Wendy Brown, Elie During, Siegfried Zielinski, Mladen Dolar and others) as well as assisting with the English translation of an upcoming volume of *The Complete Works of Rosa Luxemburg*.

Ludger Hagedorn is a Permanent Fellow at the Institute for Human Sciences (IWM) in Vienna. He studied Philosophy, Slavic Languages, and Mathematics at both the Free University of Berlin and the Technical University of Berlin where he received a PhD in 2002. For many years he has been actively involved in Research at the IWM and is the head of its Patočka and Michalski archives. From 2005 to 2009, Hagedorn was holder of the Purkyne-Fellowship, awarded by the Czech Academy of Sciences. As a lecturer, he has worked at Gutenberg University Mainz, at Charles University Prague, Södertörns Högskola (Stockholm) and at NYU Berlin.

Milan Hanyš is an assistant professor at the Faculty of Humanities, Charles University in Prague and a research fellow at the Department of Modern Intellectual and Political History at the Masaryk Institute and Archives of the Czech Academy of Sciences. He studied at the Universities of Prague, Dresden and Bayreuth. In the course of 2018 to 2019, he was a visiting scholar at the Institute for Human Sciences in Vienna. His main research interests are the history of political philosophy and Central European intellectual history of the 19th and 20th centuries.

Jim Josefson is Professor of Political Science at Bridgewater College in Virginia, USA. He is the author of *Political Philosophy in the Moment: Narratives of Freedom from Plato to Arendt* (2019) and *Hannah Arendt's Aesthetic Politics: Freedom and the Beautiful* (2020).

Aishwary Kumar is Senior Fellow in Philosophy, History, and Government in the Stanford Global Studies Division at Stanford University. An intellectual historian and political theorist specializing in South Asian, European, and American political thought, his work spans issues of moral and political philosophy; constitutional theory and political justice; liberalism, inequality, and religion; and the history of freedom and rights in the Atlantic and Global South. Kumar has taught for over a decade in the Department of History at Stanford University and in the Department of History of Consciousness at the University of California, Santa Cruz. He is the author of *Radical Equality:*

Ambedkar, Gandhi, and the Risk of Democracy (Stanford 2015) and *The Sovereign Void: Ambedkar's Critique of Violence* (forthcoming).

Martine Leibovici is a lecturer emerita at the Université de Paris (ex Paris Diderot) and a member of the Laboratoire de Changement Social et Politique. She has published four books about Hannah Arendt: *Hannah Arendt, une Juive: Expérience, politique et histoire* (Paris, Desclée de Brouwer 1998), *Hannah Arendt, la passion de comprendre* (Paris, Desclée de Brouwer 2000), *Hannah Arendt et la tradition juive: Le judaïsme à l'épreuve de la sécularisation* (Labor et Fides 2003) and with Anne-Marie Roviello, *Le pervertissement totalitaire: La banalité du mal selon Hannah Arendt* (Paris, Kimé 2017), with Aurore Mréjen, she has also edited the *Cahier Arendt* (Éditions de l'Herne 2021).

Vivian Liska is Professor of German literature and Director of the Institute of Jewish Studies at the University of Antwerp, Belgium. She is also Distinguished Visiting Professor in the Faculty of the Humanities at The Hebrew University of Jerusalem. She has published extensively on literary theory, German modernism, and German-Jewish authors and thinkers. She is the editor of the book series »Perspectives on Jewish Texts and Contexts« (De Gruyter, Berlin). In 2012, she received the Cross of Honor for Sciences and the Arts from the Republic of Austria. Her book publications as author include *Die Nacht der Hymnen* (On Paul Celan's early poetry); *Die Dichterin und das schelmische Erhabene* (On Else Lasker-Schüler); *»Die Moderne—ein Weib«* (On turn of the century women novelists); *Giorgio Agambens leerer Messianismus* (2008); *When Kafka Says We: Uncommon Communities in German-Jewish Literature* (2009); *Fremde Gemeinschaft: Deutsch-jüdische Literatur der Moderne* (2011); *German-Jewish Thought and its Afterlife: A Tenuous Legacy* (2017).

Christina Schües is Professor for Philosophy at the Institute for the History of Medicine and Science Studies at the University of Lübeck and she is Titular Professor for Philosophy at the Institute for Philosophy and Art Sciences, Leuphana University of Lüneburg. Her field of research concerns the *conditio humana* and social relationships, questions of temporality, and the interrelation of anthropology, epistemology, and political philosophy. Related publications: *Philosophie des Geborenseins* (Freiburg 2016, 2nd ed.); »Hannah Arendt—Philosophie der Praxis als Welteröffnung,« in: Thomas Bedorf, Selin Gerlek (ed.), *Philosophien der Praxis—Ein Handbuch* (Stuttgart 2019); »Phenomenology and the Political—Injustice and Prejudges«, in: Sara

Cohen Shabot, Christinia Landry (ed.), *Rethinking Feminist Phenomenology* (London/New York 2018); »Penser et agir,« avec P. Delhom, in: *Cités* (Paris 2016).

Sigrid Weigel is the former director of the Center for Literary and Cultural Research (ZfL Berlin); former professor at Hamburg, Zürich, and TU Berlin; Visiting Professor at Princeton; and director of the Einstein Forum. Her numerous books include: *Body-and Image-Space: Re-Reading Walter Benjamin* (1996); *Genea-Logik* (2006); *»Escape to Life«: German Intellectuals in New York: A Compendium on Exile after 1933* (Ed. 2013); *Walter Benjamin: Images, the Creaturely, and the Holy* (2013); *Grundordnungen: Geographie, Religion, Gesetz* (Ed. 2013); *Testimony/Bearing Witness: Epistemology, Ethics, History, and Culture* (Ed. 2017); *Grammatologie der Bilder* (2015, eng. transl. forthcoming), and editions of the works of Aby Warburg, Susan Taubes, Stéphane Mosès, and Gershom Scholem.

Rafael Zawisza obtained his PhD degree at the Faculty of Artes Liberales at the University of Warsaw with his dissertation *Cryptotheological Defence of the Secular: Hannah Arendt's Anthropology and the Secularisation Thesis* (2019). The dissertation was distinguished in the Majer Bałaban Contest (2020), organized by the Emanuel Ringelblum Jewish Historical Institute in Warsaw. He received fellowships from the Institute for Human Sciences in Vienna and the Karl Jaspers Society in Oldenburg. From 2016 to 2018, he received a research grant from the National Science Centre (NCN, Poland). He was a visiting scholar at the University of Chicago (2017—2018).

INDEX